SO
WHEN
ARE YOU
HAVING
KIDS?

SO WHEN ARE YOU HAVING KIDS?

The Definitive Guide for Those Who
Aren't Sure If, When, or How They
Want to Become Parents

Jordan Davidson

sounds true
BOULDER, COLORADO

Sounds True
Boulder, CO 80306

This book is not intended as a substitute for the medical recommendations of physicians, mental
health professionals, or other health-care providers. Rather, it is intended to offer information to
help the reader cooperate with physicians, mental health professionals, and health-care providers
in a mutual quest for optimal well-being. We advise readers to carefully review and understand the
ideas presented and to seek the advice of a qualified professional before attempting to use them.

Published 2022

Book design by Meredith Jarrett
Illustrations © 2022 Merlin Evans

Printed in Canada

BK06394

Library of Congress Cataloging-in-Publication Data

Names: Davidson, Jordan (Health journalist), author.
Title: So when are you having kids? : the definitive guide for those who aren't
    sure if, when, or how they want to become parents / Jordan Davidson.
Description: Boulder, CO : Sounds True, 2022. | Includes bibliographical references and index.
Identifiers: LCCN 2022006885 (print) | LCCN 2022006886 (ebook) | ISBN
    9781683649250 (hardcover) | ISBN 9781683649267 (ebook)
Subjects: LCSH: Parenthood. | Parents--Psychology. | Family planning.
Classification: LCC HQ755.8 .D3725 2022 (print) | LCC HQ755.8 (ebook) |
    DDC 306.874--dc23/eng/20220224
LC record available at https://lccn.loc.gov/2022006885
LC ebook record available at https://lccn.loc.gov/2022006886

10 9 8 7 6 5 4 3 2 1

FSC
www.fsc.org
MIX
Paper from
responsible sources
FSC® C016245

To Zack

A NOTE ABOUT LANGUAGE

This book uses gender-inclusive language whenever possible, as well as the preferred terms and spellings that best represent the identities of those featured within these pages. Moving away from gendered parenting language is crucial when it comes to creating equity for all within the parenting space. The gender divide only serves to promote antiquated notions about parenthood and uphold the imbalance in regard to who performs what caregiving actions. Unfortunately, since surveys, studies, and other forms of data collection tend to rely on the gender binary, gendered language cannot be entirely avoided, as making everything gender neutral would change the meaning of quotes or research findings. As such, some language has been preserved in its original form.

CONTENTS

INTRODUCTION

AT SOME POINT IN your life, you've probably entertained the question of whether or not you want kids. In the back of your mind, you might have picked out a name you liked or imagined what a child would look like with your eyes and your partner's nose. Or maybe it's the other way around: you love other people's children but can't imagine having kids of your own. You might be thinking, *How can I have a baby when there is a mountain of dirty laundry that's practically festering in the corner of my room?* Or perhaps you're wondering how you can afford childcare on top of your student loans. And is your biological clock really ticking as loud as all of the egg-freezing ads popping up on your Facebook feed seem to suggest?

The truth is, you have more time to start a family than you probably think you do. Exactly how much time depends on a whole host of factors; the first, of course, being fertility. But even within the confines of fertility, there's still a lot of variability. Contrary to your aunt's snide comments at every family gathering, it's possible to become a parent later in life. There are fertility treatments, of course, but there are also adoption and fostering, which are not as age sensitive as your own biology.

Deciding to become a parent is one of the biggest decisions you'll ever make, if not the biggest. Despite the huge responsibility of having a child, the only how-tos you'll find on the subject are how to get pregnant and how to raise a child once you have one. There's very little information out there for people who are unsure if, when, or how they want to become a parent.

Think about the decisions you've made that have altered the course of your life. If you went to college, you probably researched schools, looked into scholarships, and calculated how long it would take to pay off your student loans. When you began applying for jobs, you likely researched the company and the benefits it provided. Or maybe you bought a house—good for you!—chances are you did a lot of research before deciding on a home and a mortgage.

Most of us don't actively plan for parenthood because we assume it will happen one day. You go to school, you get a job, you get married, you buy a house, and then you have kids. Sometimes the order is switched around a bit, but that's the gist of life, or so we're told.

In the past, deciding to have kids wasn't as difficult because it was practically mandated that you settle down with a partner of the opposite sex and procreate. As society's views progressed, parenthood began to look a lot different. Women don't have to be "homemakers" anymore. Today, the average age of a first-time mom is 26.3, five years older than it was in the 1970s.[1] For women with a college degree, it's even higher—30.3.[2]

Of course, it's not just cisgender men and women having kids. Same-sex couples, people who aren't partnered, and transgender folks can use assistive reproductive technologies to have biological children or children conceived using donor conception and/or surrogates. And with same-sex marriage now a federally protected right, queer couples can legally adopt children in all 50 states.

With so many options available, how do you choose and settle on a timeline that doesn't give you a panic attack? The answer is something we'll work through in this book. And when I say we, I mean we. You, the person reading this, and me, the person writing it.

I've always known I wanted kids, but wanting kids isn't the same as being ready for them. When I was 24, I was diagnosed with diminished ovarian reserve. If you want kids, you should have them now, my doctor told me. As if it was that easy. Sure, in some hypothetical universe where I was older, more established in my career, and a homeowner, I was ready. But in reality, at 24, in my fifth-floor walk-up, with tens of thousands of dollars in student loans, having kids felt irresponsible.

The depression that followed my infertility diagnosis was all-encompassing. I was consumed by a deep desire to get pregnant. Desperate, I tried giving up gluten, sugar, alcohol, and caffeine. I even debated signing up for a clinical trial that would dice up my ovaries, marinate them in a "growing medium," and reimplant them in my body in the hopes of producing more eggs. I wanted—needed—to know my body could do it. Even if it killed me.

Fortunately, I was able to realize that being cool with dying in childbirth just to one-up my body was a sign that I was very much not okay.

I started seeing a therapist, who, by some cosmic coincidence, happened to be involuntarily childless. And because time was of the essence, I made an appointment to see a fertility specialist. When I told him I wasn't ready to have kids and couldn't really afford egg freezing but still wanted to explore my options, his advice to me was to start having unprotected sex because "you never know, miracles happen."

Disappointed by his lackluster medical advice, I sought out a second specialist known for helping young cancer patients preserve their fertility. I don't remember much of the appointment because my brain stopped processing the conversation after he told my partner of two years that he was "a good man for being with someone like me."

Modern medicine, at that time, felt like a dead-end. It didn't seem worth spending money I didn't have on egg freezing, since there was no guarantee of success. Plus, I still wasn't ready to get pregnant. Instead, I decided to take a break from doctors and save some money so that when I was ready to do in vitro fertilization (IVF), I could afford it.

My break wasn't without anxiety. I knew I had to create a timeline. My ovaries were in bad shape, likely due to the five endometriosis surgeries I had as a teen, but I was back to menstruating and ovulating every month—a good sign. How do you know when you're ready to have kids? I asked everyone I could—friends, family, strangers at bars—only to receive a sea of *I don't knows* or arbitrary checkpoints that relied on a privilege I didn't have: time.

As alone as I felt, the deeper I dug, the more I realized my apprehension was fairly common. There were plenty of other 20- to 30-somethings, with and without fertility issues, asking difficult questions about modern parenthood. Questions like *How can I afford to have a baby in a gig economy?* or *Does it even make sense to have kids given the effect of global warming on the planet?* Fed up by the lack of answers, I began doing my own research. Research that ultimately helped me feel confident enough to begin fertility treatments.

I hope that this book can do something similar for you. This is your book. Write in it, highlight sections, dog-ear pages you want to come back to, take a photo of a page from the chapter about managing external expectations and send it to your mom when she starts talking about grandkids. You can even scream at it if the idea of family planning all feels like too much. I won't be offended.

This book contains four sections designed to help you determine if, when, and how you'd like to become a parent. I recommend reading the book cover to cover. (And no, I'm not just saying that because I wrote it.) Part of the reason you should read the book in its entirety is because it's written inclusively. There is no section dedicated to the LGBTQIA+ community because queer experiences show up throughout the book instead of being limited to just one chapter. If you're interested in adoption, you may think only the main adoption section applies to you, but adoption comes up frequently throughout the book as it relates to different scenarios, and you'd be missing out by not reading them. But there's another reason why you should read the whole book: you might be inspired to change course. I know I was.

Hearing stories from people who pursued different routes to parenthood made me realize there are other ways to build a family. I'm no longer willing to risk my life to get pregnant, because I want to live to be a mom. I want to watch my child grow, show them the beauty of the world (even when it's hard to find), and help them finish their class project the night before it's due because procrastination runs in the family, genetics be damned.

Learning about all of the different ways to become a parent might make you feel differently too. Alternatively, you may finish this book and decide parenthood really isn't for you. And that's great too. This is a judgment-free place for you to explore your options and figure out a decision-making timeline that works for you. I can't tell you what to do, but I can provide you with research, expert opinions, and personal stories from people who've been where you are so that you can make an informed decision about what's best for you. This way, the next time someone asks when you're having kids you'll know the answer—not that it's any of their business.

PART I

DO YOU

WANT KIDS?

1

THE WAITING GAME

WHEN SHE WAS 30, Amanda Smith told herself, and her mom, that 35 was the perfect age to have kids. She had a plan, and a nearly perfect one at that. Amanda would get a five-year intrauterine device (IUD) to prevent pregnancy, and by the time it was scheduled to come out, she'd be in a relationship and ready to have kids. If she didn't have a partner, she'd do it alone. But surely she would meet someone who was ready to settle down by then.

While 35 might have seemed like the age where "one does those things" to 30-year-old Amanda, a now 36-year-old single Amanda would have to disagree. "I'm angry," she says. "This isn't where I thought my life would be. It's unfair and it's shitty. I'm watching my friends have kids, and the prospect of doing it on my own with what adulthood looks like now is so difficult."

Amanda isn't alone in feeling unprepared for parenthood. Birth rates for cisgender women 30 and older have been on the rise since 1990. Today, more children are born to those between the ages of 30 and 34 than any other age group. And birthing parents over the age of 35 have a higher birth rate than teens, which was not the case decades ago.[1]

It makes sense that so many of us are waiting. The average US student loan debt is $36,510 per borrower for federal student loans and $54,921 for private loans, the median home price $374,900, and a year of daycare more than $17,000.[2] However, while waiting for the "perfect time" might seem like it increases the odds of being socially, financially, and emotionally ready, sociologist Lauren Jade Martin, PhD, argues that this relatively new societal pressure problematically reinforces the idea that there are certain conditions you must meet before having kids. This gives those who are relatively privileged freedom to reproduce while others struggle to meet the same bar of preparedness.[3]

Delaying childbearing is more common among those who are highly educated or middle-class.[4] Research suggests this is due to the way different socioeconomic groups view having children. Middle-class and highly educated young people tend to be more risk-averse, whereas those in lower socioeconomic groups view children as a way of finding meaning in a world that limits their options for upward mobility.[5]

Setting conditions might seem like a foolproof way to assess your readiness for parenthood, but meeting your goals doesn't guarantee you'll feel ready to have kids. Martin studied 72 childless women in the US between the ages of 25 and 40 and divided them into three groups according to their fertility intentions: delayers, people who would like to have children; debaters, people who could go either way; and decliners, those who didn't want kids. When she interviewed them again, four years later, only some of the people in the delayer and debater groups had children, and none of the people in the decliner group had. Some people ended up having children after achieving their goals. However, others continued to remain childless even after meeting their initial conditions. Those who still didn't feel comfortable having kids continued to move their goalposts, leading Martin to believe the group's decision to put off parenthood had more to do with personal choice than external factors.[6]

This isn't to say that delaying kids is bad. Research suggests waiting to have kids has its benefits. Older parents are more likely to experience an increase in life satisfaction following childbirth.[7] And those who delay having children tend to feel more in control of their lives and experience less depression than those who have children before turning 23. However, while cisgender men tend to benefit the longer they delay parenthood, cisgender women start to lose those benefits after they turn 30.[8]

Rather than make a decision now, Amanda took out an insurance policy: she froze her eggs. It wasn't an easy choice. Amanda, a writer living in Los Angeles, questioned spending over $10,000 on the egg-freezing process when she wasn't even 100 percent sure she wanted kids. But in the end, she decided that removing the burden of choice was worth the price tag. She didn't want to look back in five years and wish she had done something, so she bought herself more time.

"I will probably reassess at 40," she says. "I don't think that I would want to have a kid much older than that. I can't imagine having the energy and bandwidth for a baby at 45. I definitely feel like I could change my mind again when I hit 40, but freezing my eggs removes the burden of needing to make that decision."

Making a decision is hard. It's not just finances or societal pressures; it's a whole slew of factors that vary from person to person and can change over time. If you want to understand how you feel, it's worth looking outward, at all the ways society and our upbringing shape our understanding of parenthood, and then inward, at what you want from your life, and whether the benefits and stresses of parenthood align with those goals, which we'll begin to do over the next few chapters.

I always wanted to be a mom, but I'm not sure I'd call it a "decision." For me, it was just what you do: go to college, find a job, get married, have kids. I don't think I ever considered the alternative. I was 29 when I got married and was desperate to start trying. I went off birth control and thought it would be easy. A few months later, I started paying attention to things like ovulation cycles and cervical mucus. We tried like this for a year, because all the doctors said we had to try for at least a year on our own, and then started seeing a fertility specialist. All of our tests came back fine; they called it unexplained infertility. It took three rounds of intrauterine insemination, but then we were finally pregnant. I was 32 when I had my son.

For the most part, I do not enjoy parenthood, which is surprising given how much I wanted to be a mom. I wish I had known the depths of self-sacrifice required. I wish I could go back to my 25-year-old self and tell her to enjoy the life she's living, to really think about all that would change upon becoming a parent, to give her all the information I have now so she can then decide if and when she's actually ready to be a mom. Maybe I would have made the same choice, but I really wish I had known.

I am the primary parent. I think it can be summed up into the fact that the two of us are living completely different lives. He works full-time and I work part-time, manage the house, look after the kids, manage their care, manage their calendars, read parenting books, and research how to parent our kids at specific ages. The list goes on. The mental load I carry is heavy and it seems as if such a load doesn't exist for him. We've done some work to better divide the house chores, but it's just scratched the surface. I feel alone a lot of the time and that somehow our values don't align, which I never thought before kids. We're interviewing couples therapists, but at this point, I'd rather be happy and separated than try to muddle through more of this.

Kathleen, 37, California, she/her, accountant, cisgender, straight, married

WHY DO PEOPLE HAVE KIDS?

Ethicist Christine Overall writes, "In contemporary Western culture, it ironically appears that one needs to have reasons not to have children, but no reasons are required to have them. . . . No one says to a newly pregnant woman or the proud father of a newborn, 'Why did you choose to have that child? What are your reasons?'"[9]

When asked why they decided to have kids, an overwhelming majority of parents surveyed by the Pew Research Center, 87 percent, answered, "The joy of having children." However, nearly half of those same parents also said, "There wasn't a reason; it just happened."[10] These almost contradictory answers illustrate what we're taught to think of parenthood and what little thought, historically, goes into decision-making.

Deciding to become a parent is complicated, which is why some people opt not to decide and leave it up to fate. Though on the decline, unplanned pregnancies make up nearly half of US births each year.[11] Children provide what researchers call "uncertainty reduction."[12] Humans are naturally inclined to want to reduce uncertainty. We do this in one of two ways: we collect information so that we can make decisions with as little risk as possible, or we pick courses of action that have a predictable, set path. This book is the first strategy in action. You're learning about parenthood and its alternatives so that you can make the best decision for yourself and reduce the risk that you'll regret your future choices. Deciding to have children, without any research, is the second form of uncertainty reduction. Children put us on a set path because they are a long-term obligation. When you have children, it is assumed you will care for them for at least the next 18 years. So while you might not know what your future holds, you at least know that raising a child will be part of it.

A fear of the future is a pretty powerful thing. When I asked people who were *almost* certain they didn't want kids what the holdout was, the overwhelming answer was concern over who would take care of them as they age. Of course, having kids doesn't ensure you'll have someone who will care for you when you get old, but the thought of having a family to help you navigate aging is less anxiety-provoking than the idea of being alone or in a nursing home.

However, research shows parents are more likely to give aid to their adult children than receive it.[13] It sounds bleak, but there is no guarantee your children will take care of you. You could end up estranged from your children, they could die before you, or they could put you in a nursing home because they can't manage your care. If end-of-life care is the only reason you're thinking about becoming a parent, you'd probably be better off taking the hundreds of thousands of dollars you'd spend over your child's lifetime and putting it in a retirement fund. Raising a child costs the average middle-class family about $16,000 per year.[14] If you were to take the $16,000 you'd spend on kids and invest it each year with a 4 percent return rate, you'd earn over $120,000 in addition to the nearly $300,000 you save over 18 years. It's not enough to retire on, sure, but it's $400,000 more than you'd have otherwise.

The idea that our children can support us in old age is an outdated notion. Adult children and their parents tend to live linked lives in that adult children's problems often negatively affect their parents' mental health and overall well-being. Because we teach parents that certain types of parenting produce successful children, when adult children "fail" by society's standards, parents internalize it as their failure too.[15] So if you're only entertaining the thought of having kids because you think you'll be better off later in life, know that's not always the case.

The growing economic insecurity of young people affects their parents, too. Parents who feel their adult children need more support than others their age tend to report poorer life satisfaction.[16] Today's parents raise their kids for longer and provide more economic support over their children's life spans.[17] Parents spend about a third of what it costs to raise a child from birth to age 18 on their adult children.[18] So if, like in the example above, you spend about $300,000 on your child in their first 18 years of life, expect to spend an additional $100,000 supporting them in adulthood.

I haven't decided whether I want kids. I'm not sure if I want children or if I want to meet society's expectations of having children, especially my mom's expectations. She sends me pictures of baby items and talks about being so excited for grandchildren. I feel like it would be such a disappointment if I didn't have children. I struggle to differentiate between what she wants and what I actually want. I'm afraid to tell her that I don't really want children. I want to be able to travel when I want and live my life without interference. I got a dog last year and it's been a rough adjustment. I have to take him outside when he wants to go outside, even when it's cold or raining. I have gotten frustrated by his interference with my life. My god, if I feel that way with a dog, how would I feel about a child?

All of the reasons I want to have children just feel so wrong: I want someone to care for me when I get old, I want to please my mom, it's what I'm supposed to do. Kids can be cute but also awful. Maybe I'm not undecided. Maybe I'm just not at the point where I can let myself be true to what I want and just accept that I don't want children.

Megan, 29, Wisconsin, she/her, attorney, white, cisgender, pansexual, single

While some people default to letting unprotected sex decide whether they become parents, not everyone can or wants to let biology choose. Researcher Julia Moore, PhD, argues that the pathways to childbearing are not always linear but rather defined by twists and turns. Our feelings evolve over time and change depending on our environment and circumstances.

Moore interviewed 32 women who became mothers after being vocal about not wanting children as part of a study published in the *Journal of Marriage and Family* and found three mechanisms behind their change in parenthood status: accidental conception, ambiguous desire, and purposeful decision.[19] Those who conceived accidentally were all unmarried at the time of their pregnancies. Most were taking hormonal birth control that failed, while others didn't use protection because of diagnoses that led them to believe they couldn't have kids, or because they hadn't used protection in the past and had never experienced a pregnancy. Pregnancy for these women wasn't some epiphany that revealed they were lying to themselves and others about their intention to have kids. When they found out they were pregnant, there was no joy or relief. Most were angry and felt their lives were over, and many considered getting an abortion but ultimately decided against it.

A second group shifted from not wanting kids to uncertainty after entering committed relationships, in some of which their partners desired children. Many of the women in this group stopped using birth control and let nature decide the outcome of their ambiguity. Even though this group entertained parenthood later in life, most felt indifferent when they learned they were pregnant, and some considered, but ultimately decided against, abortions.

The last group of women studied switched from definitively no to decidedly yes. Those who set out to get pregnant cited feeling unfulfilled despite accomplishing the things they set out to achieve, conversations with their partner, and deaths in the family as the impetus behind the change.

Deciding to have children requires a lot more intention when you're queer. Research suggests gay and lesbian folks desire parenthood less than their heterosexual peers due to the pervasiveness of heteronormative parenthood ideals (the idea that children need a mother and father), the internalization of negative stigma, and barriers to parenthood such as discrimination when it comes to fertility treatments, adoption, and surrogacy.[20]

But this is changing in part due to marriage equality, improved acceptance of the queer community, and increased access to alternative paths to parenthood. Today, more queerspawn (children of queer adults) are born to parents who are out, whereas, in the past, being queer was associated with childlessness, and most queer parents were closeted. And while barriers to parenthood are lessening, equal access to parenthood is still limited for queer folks of color, who face increased discrimination, and queer families who cannot afford the steep cost of fertility services or adoption.[21]

The road to parenthood is even steeper for those who are transgender. About 25–50 percent of trans folks are parents; however, the majority of trans parents have children before coming out as trans.[22] Among out trans folks who aren't parents, trans women are more likely to want to adopt whereas half of trans men say they want to get pregnant.[23] Although trans and nonbinary folks tend to have parenting desires similar to their cisgender peers, very few seek out fertility preservation before utilizing hormone or surgical-based gender-affirming care. The expense of and often long journey to gender-affirming care can make fertility preservation too expensive or not worth postponing for both trans and nonbinary folks.[24] And although trans folks who undergo fertility preservation tend to feel largely positive about their decision, freezing sperm or eggs can add to feelings of gender dysphoria—not to mention the gender dysphoria that may pop up for pregnant trans men, a.k.a. seahorse dads, who are named after one of the only species in which the male gets pregnant and gives birth.

> I had my first kid at 23 because I got my girlfriend of one month pregnant and felt guilted away from any kind of abortive services because of my upbringing. I felt a lot of pressure from my family to "do the right thing." I was trying to figure myself out gender-wise and serve my time in the military.
>
> We had the first, then we got married a year and a half later, then we had another and another, and then a divorce. I love being a parent, but I don't get much time with my kids. They live on the West Coast, and I live on the East Coast. Every minute I get to spend with them, even just talking on video calls, is precious to me.
>
> I love my children, but if I could do things differently, I would not have had them. There are a multitude of reasons behind this, but largely that I never really wanted kids in the first place, much less three kids. I would gladly have been the aunt that swoops in and brings presents or lots of excitement and weirdness, but I never wanted to actually be a parent.
>
> **Matilda,** 34, she/they, white,
> genderqueer, queer, divorced

Straight and queer people tend to want to have children for the same reasons. Among the top reasons people cite are emotional fulfillment, pleasing a partner, satisfying a biological urge, and furthering their family's legacy. A biological connection to children, although important to some, tends to be less important for queer, nonbinary, and trans folks.

When looking at why people decide to have children, researchers use a slightly updated framework for the "value of children," which was originally developed in the 1970s.[25] People decide to have children because they think it will bring the following:[26]

- Adult status and social identity
- Expansion of the self, ties to a larger entity, immortality
- Morality: religion, altruism, good of the group; norms regarding sexuality, acting on impulse, and virtue
- Psychological benefits: affection and emotional stimulation through interactions with children
- Stimulation, novelty, fun
- Achievement, competence, creativity
- Power, influence, effectiveness
- Social comparison, competition
- Economic utility: financial contributions, household help, and old-age insurance

People do not have children because they dream of the unpaid, underappreciated labor of childcare—even though that's more aligned with the reality of having kids. For Ian, 22, the desire to have kids aligns with his desire to continue the family name. "Everyone dies, but your descendants are a stamp saying, 'We were here,'" he says. "I know kids can be annoying and hard to deal with from time to time, but it's ultimately a rewarding thing. I like interacting with my younger cousins, and I think that kids can be funny."

And just as there are many reasons to have kids, there are also many reasons why people decide not to procreate. This includes negative models of parenthood (i.e., your parents weren't great), negative feelings about children, concerns about population growth, personality, preferring an adult-oriented lifestyle, lack of parenting skills, ambitious career goals, demanding jobs, and prioritizing partnership, health, and education.[27]

When researchers study people's childbearing intentions, they often use a model called the Theory of Planned Behavior. Essentially, deciding to have kids comes down to your perceptions of the benefits and costs of having children; social influences like pressure from partners, family, friends, or society; and whether you think you'd be able to parent successfully. Your personality, values, past behavior, education, age, gender, income, religion, race, culture, knowledge, and the media also influence these factors.[28]

But this model isn't perfect. After all, how can scientists predict fertility intentions if half of US pregnancies are unintentional? Intentions don't always predict behavior, and critiques of the theory suggest that childbearing might be more of an unconscious process. Our brains understand information through schemas, which are patterns of thought or behaviors used to categorize and process the world. For example, if someone invites you to a birthday party, they don't need to tell you what the party entails for you to understand what that event might look like. Your schemas allow you to quickly process that there will likely be cake and off-key singing. These schemas paired with social context—circumstances, norms, and other people—affect our intentions and behavior. An example of this process would be someone who gets pregnant accidentally but does not get an abortion because their family would disapprove.[29]

Intentional or unintentional, becoming a parent comes down to how you both consciously and unconsciously view the world. That's why pros and cons lists fall short time and time again; they don't consider all of the factors at play but rather a highlight reel of the positives and negatives you anticipate. Making a decision that you feel good about requires a deep understanding of not only yourself but also the societal norms and external factors shaping your thought processes as well as what it means to be a parent. So let's dive in.

I became pregnant with my son when I was 27 while married and taking birth control pills. My daughter appeared three years later while I had an intrauterine device (IUD) and was divorced but in a committed relationship with a man 10 years my junior. I did not plan on having children. I had no desire. I figured if I got pregnant through two different forms of birth control, there was a reason and so I just went with it. I never resented or regretted having my kids, and now that both my kids are out on their own, I am extremely lonely and really miss being "mommy." It's very weird to miss parenting as much as I do. I always thought I would enjoy the freedom of middle age with adult children and I really don't. My kids live across the country, and I wish we were all physically closer.

M., 51, California, they/them, white, disabled, nonbinary, pansexual, divorced

2

WHERE DO PARENTING DESIRES COME FROM?

CHANCES ARE YOU'VE HEARD someone say they knew they wanted kids because they felt it in their gut. While knowing you want kids can make your decision-making a lot easier, the idea that everyone has this biological urge to reproduce often leaves those who don't feel a tug at their heartstrings every time they pass a stroller wondering what's wrong with them. So what are gut feelings? And why doesn't everyone have them?

Humans, like other beings, are considered "survival machines."[1] At an evolutionary level, we exist to propel our genes into the next generation, but our genes do not explicitly tell us to reproduce. "People don't selfishly spread their genes; genes selfishly spread themselves. They do it by the way they build our brains," psychologist Steven Pinker writes in "Against Nature." "By making us enjoy life, health, sex, friends, and children, the genes buy a lottery ticket for representation in the next generation, with odds that were favorable in the environment in which we evolved because healthy, long-lived, loving parents did tend, on average, to send more genes into the next generation."[2]

Behavioral geneticists believe we have genetically determined predispositions. In other words, our genes give us the capacity to act in certain ways.

These are not biological destinies but rather the start of a complex process influenced not only by our DNA but by our upbringing and environment.[3] A good example of this is language. Most of us are born with the capacity to learn and understand language. If you grow up deprived of language, you may learn other ways to communicate based on your environment, but you won't magically start speaking a recognizable language. Your environment teaches you language; your genes give you the ability to learn it.

One genetic factor that may predispose us to having children is our sex drive. Genes play a role in determining our libidos but are not the only factor. Before the advent of contraception, desiring sex and thus having more of it increased your odds of having kids. That doesn't mean a high sex drive endears you to children. It means you're more likely to have sex, which, without protection, increases your odds of having children.[4]

A second potential genetic factor is altruism. Altruism toward kin is how humans and other mammals who have few children survive. Species that produce dozens or hundreds of offspring don't invest time or energy into their young; they don't need to. Natural selection ensures that the strongest survive, and their genes enter the next generation. But when you only have one child at a time, their survival depends on long-term care. Our ancestors were those capable and willing to provide the intense care children need. Those genes got passed down, creating a genetic predisposition to support our offspring. Of course, having a predisposition toward caring for children doesn't mean you'll have that innate desire to have kids you hear other people talking about. The expression of that predisposition requires a favorable environment like witnessing rewarding parent-child interactions, either vicariously or in your relationships with your parents.[5]

But most importantly, our brains did not evolve to a point where they are naturally equipped to handle all of the options available to us in this day and age. "For 99 percent of human existence, people lived as foragers in small nomadic bands. Our brains are adapted to that long-vanished way of life, not to brand-new agricultural and industrial civilizations," Pinker writes. "There is no need to strain for adaptive explanations for everything we do. . . . Before there was effective contraception, children were difficult to postpone, and status and wealth could be converted into more children and healthier ones."

My biological clock made me obsessive about procreation. I had a high sex drive and could not stop thinking about making a baby with my partner. Even though we were early-career professionals and timing was less than ideal, we decided to "see what happens" after getting married. I was knocked up within three months, ironically around the same time I was reconsidering and thinking, *Hey, it might be good to be childfree a little bit longer.* I was 27 years old when my kiddo was born.

I knew I wanted kids because it was important to me to leave a legacy, to leave the world better than I found it. And what better legacy than children equipped and empowered to facilitate change? I always thought I would have more than one child, but after barely surviving (not an exaggeration) the past five years, I just cannot. My body physically cannot handle it again. For my mental health, I cannot subject myself to that again. I cannot pause my career again, and, honestly, that pause was the beginning of the end of my career in academia. We cannot afford another child or a larger home. And the Earth is already so overpopulated that we would feel like we are contributing to the problem with more offspring.

I don't really enjoy parenthood. It is hard, thankless work. It is exhausting. That being said, I absolutely love and adore my child. I am so glad to know them, especially now that they are autonomous. I am absolutely, 100 percent, committed to doing my best for them, providing for them, and continuing to sacrifice for them so that they can be safe, grow up in a secure and loving household, and become a self-reliant, kind adult.

Leslie, 32, Florida, she/they, corporate trainer, Puerto Rican, androgynous, pansexual, married

IF NOT NATURE, THEN NURTURE?

We all make parenting decisions regardless of whether or not we ultimately have children. We start planning for parenthood well before marriage or pregnancy. Researchers call these parenthood-related thoughts "buds of parenting." These buds are reflections of caregiving motivational systems; essentially we mirror the caregiving we receive as children.

Our motivation to have children is thought to tie into psychologists John Bowlby and Mary Ainsworth's attachment theory. Our experience of being cared for early in life influences our beliefs and expectations about everything from how lovable we are to the safety of our relationships and our ability to care for others. While we all are born with the capacity to care for others, having this potential doesn't mean it's cultivated in all of us. Genetics play a role, but it's our early relationships with parents and caregivers that design the blueprint for our desire and ability to be caregivers ourselves.

Children largely identify with their parents and internalize their parents' caregiving behaviors. Feeling consistently cared for promotes secure attachment and teaches us that we have the ability to care for others. Insensitive, unreliable, or rejecting caregiving promotes insecure attachment, which can lead to fear of abandonment or discomfort when others depend on you. If you want to better understand where your thoughts on parenthood might come from, examining the relationship you had with your parents growing up can be a good place to start. Research suggests our childhood attachment styles extend into adulthood and influence future parent-child relationships as well as friendships and romantic relationships.[6]

The following is a four-measure questionnaire developed by psychologists to help adults determine their current attachment style.[7] Out of the four options below, pick the one that most relates to how you feel in romantic relationships. (Note: intimacy and closeness relate to emotions, not sex.)

1. It is easy for me to become emotionally close to others. I am comfortable depending on them and having them depend on me. I don't worry about being alone or having others not accept me.

2. I am uncomfortable getting close to others. I want emotionally close relationships, but I find it difficult to trust others completely

or to depend on them. I worry that I will be hurt if I allow myself to become too close to others.

3. I want to be completely emotionally intimate with others, but I often find that others are reluctant to get as close as I would like. I am uncomfortable being without close relationships, but I sometimes worry that others don't value me as much as I value them.

4. I am comfortable without close emotional relationships. It is very important to me to feel independent and self-sufficient, and I prefer not to depend on others or have others depend on me.

If you selected option 1, you have a secure attachment style. Generally speaking, you don't worry about abandonment and feel comfortable developing close relationships with others. The rest of the option choices represent insecure attachments. If you picked option 2, you have a fearful-avoidant or disorganized attachment style. You want close relationships but find it hard to open up and get close to others. Option 3 represents a preoccupied or anxious attachment style; you prefer to be in relationships but have a strong fear of abandonment. And option 4 means you have a dismissing or avoidant attachment style; you don't like to depend on others or have others depend on you and aren't the best at expressing your emotions.

Those who had secure attachments as children experience more of a desire to become parents themselves, whereas those with insecure attachments tend to feel less inclined toward parenthood. Insecure attachments can also lead people to believe they won't be good parents.

While early interactions with caregivers set up attachment styles, other experiences throughout your life, like discrimination and oppression, can change them. Negative reactions from peers and loved ones when coming out as LGBTQIA+, for example, can lead to the adoption of a more avoidant world perspective as a protective measure.[8] Research suggests avoidant attachment styles may serve as a way to cope with oppression because they let people maintain positive views of themselves despite discrimination.[9]

About 36 percent of the adult population has an insecure attachment style.[10] So if you have an insecure attachment style, don't feel bad.

Attachment styles are malleable. Insecure attachment styles can become secure with community resources, therapy, or a supportive partner. Secure attachments can also face disruption, which happens typically due to the loss of an attachment figure like a parent or partner. I included this questionnaire as a tool to help you understand how early life experiences can affect parenting desires since we're unpacking how we think about parenthood. But having an insecure attachment style doesn't doom you or your relationships.

Witnessing your parents' divorce can also affect your desire to have children. A study of childbearing intentions among Dutch adults found that those whose parents divorced during childhood were more likely to have fewer children or not want kids. However, this negative trend was less influential for those who grew to have positive relationships with their parents in adulthood.[11]

Manuel, 28, cites his parents' divorce when he was 7 as part of the reason he doesn't want to have kids. "Being the product of a broken home, a broken family, for most of my childhood has heavily skewed what the parental experience looks like to me," Manuel says. "My dad had some pretty bad drinking problems during the divorce, and he and I never really clicked. He was kind of abusive verbally and emotionally to my mom and I, and that put a really bad taste in my mouth. I often get told by people, I'm the polar opposite of him and that I'm going to be a great dad. I can see that and I can know that logically, but internally and emotionally, it's really hard to grapple with." Still, despite his upbringing and concerns he might somehow mirror his dad, Manuel thinks he'll end up having kids since it's important to his wife.

Other studies of parenting buds found that young people with avoidant attachment styles were less interested in having kids and anticipated less satisfaction caring for young children.[12] Avoidance and anxiety also made it harder for younger adults to imagine what their relationship with their child would look like. Many thought they would be less warm, strict, or easily irritated by their kids—if they had them.[13] And while queer folks are more likely to have avoidant attachment styles and less likely to desire kids, research suggests queer avoidant attachment styles do not factor into parenting desires. When comparing the parenthood desires of heterosexual and queer folks, avoidant attachment styles only decreased the desire to have kids for heterosexual women.[14]

> I never wanted kids. My parents fought a lot when I was younger, and it was very clear to me that they wouldn't be together if they didn't have kids. I hate the way women lose their identity when they have kids. I spent 33 years becoming me and I didn't want to lose all the things I accomplished to becoming "so-and-so's mom." I think having kids should be a calling, something you are deeply sure of, and I never had that. I have endometriosis and recently had a hysterectomy so this is all very settled for me. My husband is supportive as he was ambivalent about having them.
>
> **Kelly,** 33, Illinois, she/her, white, cisgender, straight, married

THE ROLE OF SOCIETY

Boiling down our desire, or lack thereof, to become parents as an issue of nature or nurture ignores many of the external factors that affect whether we have kids. A study of childless women in the UK found that women's decisions around childbearing were most influenced by social norms. Age-related declines in fertility were not often factored into decision-making.[15]

There are conscious and unconscious reasons people choose to have children. Social pressures and "compulsory motherhood," the idea that cisgender women are designed to have children, tend to factor into the inexplicable pull some people feel toward having kids.[16] This societal force, what's known as pronatalism, promotes parenthood as the normal way of being. Pronatalism basically says, if you don't want kids, there must be something wrong with you.

Research shows our first interactions with pronatalism start at home. Consciously or unconsciously, parents teach their children that parenthood is a stage of life. Mothers especially tend to pass down gendered messages about the importance of mothering.[17] Since we inherit at least some of our views of parenthood from our parents, it's worth looking at the social influences that shaped their views and their parents' views, too.

For most of humankind's time on earth, having children wasn't a choice. Whether people in ancient times knew to use the pullout method is a discussion for another day. (Hippocrates thought babies came from the mixing of semen and menstrual blood.[18]) But choice only really became an option in the 1960s and '70s thanks to the advent of birth control and legalization of abortion.

Over the past century, adulthood has more or less been defined as leaving home, completing school, entering the workforce, getting married, and having kids. However, the timetable for reaching those milestones changes with every generation. To understand how this trend came to be, let's look back 100 years when children weren't the protected class they are today. In the early 1900s, most people in their late teens either left home to work or remained home to help out on the family farm. Like today, most young people waited until they could become economically self-sufficient enough to establish their own households. But this independence effort slowed significantly in the decade following the Great Depression of the late 1920s and early 1930s, delaying both marriage and parenthood.[19]

Between 1900 and 1940, the idea of who should have children mirrored the burgeoning eugenics movement. White women with socially desirable traits were not only encouraged to reproduce but to have large families too. Women of color and women considered "feebleminded" were dissuaded from reproducing, told to have fewer children, or encouraged to undergo sterilization procedures. Many states enacted mandatory sterilizations for those deemed unfit to reproduce under the guises of disease prevention and the "best interests" of society. By 1947, 30 states had sterilization laws and nearly 44,000 people were sterilized.[20]

Much of the pronatalist messaging at the time was based on the principles of eugenics. Women's media endorsed the idea that it was cisgender women's moral responsibility to reproduce, equating patriotism to motherhood. By having children, women were putting the needs of the human race above their own needs, a self-sacrifice meant to "build character." Women who chose not to reproduce were told they were flawed, infantile, selfish, aimless, and self-indulgent. Books and magazines geared toward women deemed fit for reproduction emphasized the importance of family and duty. Other women, those less fit to reproduce, were told their children would likely be disabled or criminals, and that sterilization was a less expensive alternative than caring for those children.

These views were not of a fringe few. Eugenicists permeated academia, popular media, and even American politics. US President Theodore Roosevelt, an attendee of the First International Eugenics Congress in London in 1912, regularly penned letters railing against birth control and feminism, letters that were published in women's magazines. One letter he wrote in 1905, during his presidency, read:

> The man or woman who deliberately avoids marriage and
> has a heart so cold as to know no passion and a brain
> so shallow and selfish as to dislike having children, is in
> effect a criminal against the race, and should be an object
> of contemptuous abhorrence by all healthy people.[21]

The declining fertility rates after the Great Depression were blamed not on circumstance or choice but on presumed infertility. The idea that "socially fit" people would choose not to have children was seen as so preposterous it was easier to believe those who didn't have children physically couldn't.

The eugenics movement lost its momentum by the end of World War II in 1945. By that time, marriage and childbirth immediately followed the end of one's schooling. The economic prosperity that followed the war led to a baby boom and cemented a shift that made starting a family synonymous with adulthood.

With the mid-20th century came the rise of the nuclear family: a husband who worked and a wife who stayed home and cared for the kids. Between 1950 and 1970, most women were married by the time they were 21 and had at least one child by the age of 23.[22] A survey conducted in 1962 found that 85 percent of moms believed married couples had an obligation to have kids.[23] This period also brought new opportunities for women in the workforce and higher education, but a college education wasn't necessary for either sex. A high school degree was enough to guarantee a decent living. All socioeconomic classes flourished. Between 1949 and 1970, the incomes of those in the lower and middle brackets grew 110 percent or more, while the top income brackets rose at least 85 percent.[24] It's these two decades of postwar prosperity, 70 to 50 years ago, that created the model of adulthood so many of us feel pressured to conform to today.

Pronatalism isn't always easily recognizable. In the 1960s, sociologist Judith Blake argued that gender differences in the workplace serve a pronatalist agenda.[25] Limiting women's employment options and denying them the salaries enjoyed by men ultimately pushed women toward marriage and childbearing.

Although workplace gender differences are not as pronounced as they were in the 1960s, women are still less likely to hold C-suite positions, and they earn less than men, about 82 cents on the dollar.[26] However, having one parent leave the workplace to raise children is no longer economically feasible for most families. In 1970, nearly half of families with children under 18 followed the nuclear family model of the 1950s and '60s where the dad worked and the mom stayed home. By 2016, that number shrank by nearly half. Only 27 percent of families had a dad who works and a mom that stays home. Both parents work in about 46 percent of households with a mother and father, up from 31 percent in 1970, and mothers are the primary breadwinners in 40 percent of US families.[27] Ironically, the workplace now serves as a force for antinatalism. Without paid parental leave, flexible workplaces, and other incentives for parents, choosing to have children often comes down to what you're willing to sacrifice: economic stability, your future career path, or having kids.

The period of prosperity that led to the rise of the nuclear family ended in the 1970s. Wages stagnated, inflation grew, and the job market dwindled, especially for the working class. With fewer industrial-type jobs, pursuing higher education became the ticket to the middle class. These new economic and employment challenges combined with the introduction of reproductive choice, again shifted the timeline for parenthood.

Though many media reports make the declining birth rate seem like a new problem, the truth is it's dropped over decades. This trend started in the US in the 1970s following the Food and Drug Administration's (FDA) approval of oral contraceptives in 1960 and the Supreme Court's legalization of abortion in 1973 and has continued downward, with occasional spikes, ever since. Even before the 1970s, the birth rate fluctuated. Unsurprisingly, people don't want to have children during times of crises, especially financial ones. The birth rate dropped 26 percent over the decade following the Great Depression and dropped again after the recession in 2008. Birth rates also fell during the COVID-19 pandemic. A little more than 3.2 million children were born in the US in 2020, the lowest number since 1979, although the figures are not exactly comparable since the total number of people living in the US in 2020 was 47 percent higher than what it was in 1979.[28]

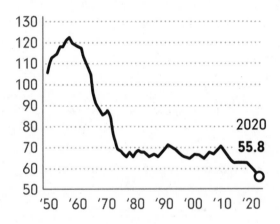

General Fertility Rate
1950–2020
BIRTHS PER 1,000 WOMEN
AGES 15-44

(Includes data from Gretchen Livingston, "Is U.S. Fertility at an All-Time Low? Two of Three Measures Point to Yes." Pew Research Center [website]. May 22, 2019.)

Researchers use three measures when assessing population fertility: general fertility rate (GFR), the number of children born that year; completed fertility, the total number of children born to one person; and total fertility rate (TFR), the average number of children a hypothetical childbearing person is expected to have based on fertility patterns. Societies typically want a TFR of about 2.1 kids per childbearing person, what's known as the replacement rate. (The 0.1 accounts for replacing those who die before adulthood.) If every person capable of giving birth has two living children, the population stays roughly the same. While reducing the birth rate might seem like a good thing, since it controls population growth and decreases natural resource consumption, some economists argue the opposite. The burden of taking care of aging populations often falls on the younger ones. Because preceding generations were so large, more economic resources are needed to take care of them. But with every generation shrinking, older generations are depleting resources faster than the younger generations can contribute.

While reproducing for the sake of the economy might seem like a gross capitalistic ask, the underlying fear of *Who's going to take care of me when I get older?* is a real one. There are more millennials alive now than there are baby boomers. This is great for boomers because the money young people pay into government-funded programs for seniors can take care of them, but it's not necessarily great for younger generations. Could we, as a society, decide to create better caregiving systems for aging adults? Yes. *Will we?* is an entirely different question.

When I was much younger, I pictured my life following a similar path to my mother and most other adult women I knew at that point: marriage by your early 20s, followed by kids a few years after. At some point, probably in my mid-20s, I started to realize that assumption had very little to do with what I actually wanted. I felt no excitement or pull toward being pregnant, giving birth, or raising small children. It's less of a feeling of "not wanting," and more a simple lack of wanting. For a long time, my mom and others believed that when I met the "right person," I would want to have kids with them. While I can't predict the future, in my gut I really don't believe that will happen.

I am currently single and have been by choice for about three years. I do have some fear of falling for someone and then learning that the kids issue is going to be a deal-breaker. I don't know if I worry about regret, exactly, but I do wonder, maybe a bit morbidly, what the later years of my life will look like without children and grandchildren around me. I don't have many models of what it looks like to age and reach the end of your life as a childfree person, so there's some fear there.

People tend to assume that I dislike kids or am not a nurturing person simply because I don't want kids of my own. In reality, I love children and I really value having them in my life. At times, it also feels as though society sees me as less mature or less of a legitimate adult than other women in my same age bracket who have kids, especially since I am also unmarried and don't own a home. It feels as though I am lacking many of the outward markers of adulthood.

Blair, 30, Massachusetts, she/her, director, white, cisgender, straight, single

Another significant change from our parents' and grandparents' generations is the decoupling of marriage and childbearing. Marriage has typically been a key step on the road to adulthood, with children born out of wedlock historically stigmatized. Given the high cost of living, many people now choose to cohabitate before getting married. Since couples are already living together, marriage is more of an achievement and event than it is a stepping-stone to children. Between 1960 and 1980, the average age of marriage rose from 20 to 23.[29] Today, average newlyweds are in their late 20s.[30] A Pew survey of millennials shows today's childbearing generations prioritize parenthood over marriage. About 52 percent of respondents said being a good parent was one of their most important goals in life, whereas only 30 percent felt that way about a successful marriage.

Given the amount of control we have over pregnancy nowadays, the rise of births outside of marriage suggests a conscious choice to have kids. About 40 percent of children are born outside of marriage, up from 28 percent in 1990.[31]

The majority of these births, 62 percent, are to cohabitating couples, and many are planned as opposed to accidental. If we can change the way we think of marriage as a necessary stepping-stone to both adult- and parenthood, then, surely, we can reevaluate the seemingly mandatory nature of parenthood.

I'm an only child and the last in my family line. My parents never insisted I have kids. They were always supportive of whatever I wanted. I wanted to have children but didn't want to be too old when they were in their prime. I found an awesome partner that I wanted to start a family with. I was 30 when we had our first and 32 for our second.

After having our kids, I realized I was in over my head. We had a rough birth and dealt with postpartum depression, among other things. I don't enjoy parenting right now, but I love my kids. I know I'll enjoy it more when they're older. Another dad told me he felt the same way when his kids were younger, which made me feel like much less of a monster than when I kept those thoughts to myself. Watching my kids learn more skills is such a trip. I can't wait to go hiking with them, play video games, and teach them how to drive.

The main thing I wish I could change is sleep. Neither kid slept through the night for years, and my wife was not down for crying it out. I gained about 60 pounds over five years, and walk into walls every week because of how tired I am. I know that sounds kind of bleak, but I'm in it for the long haul and I'm confident it will all pay off.

I don't regret having kids, but I do regret how I've managed my time with them. I took on the "breadwinner" role, but we don't traditionally split the housework as they did "back in the day." My wife definitely does more when it comes to nights and driving the kids to daycare, but I'm right next to her with the diaper changes and kid time. She works nontraditional hours throughout the week, so there was a big stretch where I would work during the day and solo the kids at night while she worked. It was brutal.

You're going to sacrifice a lot of your independence, depending on your lifestyle before kids, once the kids come. In my opinion, you live for your kids, so realize that you need to not be a selfish person afterward.

Carl, 35, New Jersey, he/him,
cisgender, straight, married

3

MANAGING EXTERNAL EXPECTATIONS

ANUPRIYA KNOWS WHAT IT'S like to have to reinvent yourself. Anupriya's parents emigrated from India to the US in 1979 as part of an influx of Asian immigrants who came to the country based on policies promoted by the US government. The plan wasn't to stay; her dad would complete his medical residency, and then they would return to India. But when do things ever go according to plan?

Anupriya grew up in a "strict" Asian household. Her mother, a psychologist with a master's degree from India, couldn't practice in the US, and so she stayed home and focused her attention on her children. As the oldest of three children and the only daughter, Anupriya resented the pressure she felt to both succeed and conform to traditional gender roles.

As she got older, Anupriya decided she didn't want to have children. She feared becoming her mother and shunned the idea that she should settle down and have a traditional life. At the same time, she was eager to get married. "In my mind, getting married was a way of getting out of being sucked into this family dynamic where you protect the girl, and you don't let her do a ton of things other than go to school and come back. I figured that when I got married, my parents would sort of release some of that control," she says.

Anupriya wasn't really in tune with herself, and starting medical school in her mid-20s didn't give her much time or energy to look inward. In her 30s, she met someone and got engaged, but she found the life she worked so hard to build quickly unraveling toward the end of her residency. She was constantly tired and growing progressively weaker, symptoms she attributed to the rigor of her program. Her symptoms got worse after a mission trip providing medical aid abroad. When she returned home, blood tests revealed she had leukemia.

Neither her parents nor her partner had the emotional resources to deal with her diagnosis or each other, often leaving Anupriya responsible for diffusing the tension. There was no time to freeze eggs, she was too sick, and the treatment she needed would render her infertile. This brought up mixed feelings for Anupriya, who, almost instantly, lost something she never thought she wanted, and devastated her mother. And then, in the middle of wedding planning, chemotherapy, radiation, and a bone marrow transplant, she and her fiancé broke up.

Eighteen months after her diagnosis, a cancer-free Anupriya moved from Philadelphia to Boston to start over, just her and her dog. Once in Boston, she began a fellowship program and online dating, the second of which proved harder. "I kind of resigned myself that I would probably not meet somebody who would be okay with my inability to have kids," Anupriya says. "When I was initially dating, there were people who ghosted me or who told me this wasn't something they were interested in engaging in." Harsh responses followed no matter how she disclosed her infertility. She tried putting it in her dating profile, telling people up front, sharing it a few dates in—nothing worked. And then she met Nathan. He didn't flinch or say anything bad; he just accepted her for who she was—and that's when Anupriya realized she might want kids after all.

"I think a lot of my desire to have children came out of my own negative experiences growing up with immigrant parents and all the things that I felt like I needed, emotionally, but never had," she says. "I wanted to feel I would be wholly accepted for who I was versus the very strict sort of rules around studying and the grades and success and a lot of things that I found to be really unhealthy; things I felt I didn't see happening for my non-Asian friends."

It makes sense that Anupriya would feel this way. Parenting in a foreign country comes with its own unique challenges, and those pressures can trickle down within the family. Immigrant parents are more likely to experience parenting stress due to the cultural and economic challenges that come with adjusting to a foreign country's way of life. But this assimilation-related stress doesn't just affect immigrant parents; it can seep into the next generation too. Research shows the more conflict second-generation parents face around assimilating, the less confident they feel as parents.[1] But the answer isn't as simple as adapting to a new culture, especially if you feel pressure to maintain a multigenerational household or uphold family traditions. And that can make it difficult to decide what's best for you.

I knew around the age of 16 that I wanted kids but didn't feel a need to be partnered or for my kids to be biological. I had my first kid when I was 24 and in grad school. I knew I wanted to get my doctorate but didn't want to wait to have kids until I was done with my education. Having a chronic illness, I knew there was no assurance of future good health.

I feel there is a lot of pressure on moms in particular and I could do without the gendered pressure to perform. My oldest thinks I don't like parenting because I don't want to police their behavior. I try to separate out that not enjoying societal expectations is not the same as not being appreciative of being a parent. My husband does a lot of the tasks, but the emotional aspects and behavioral management fall to me. We need to do more to support folks socialized as male to help them deal with their emotions and coach others in nurturing ways.

Sabrina, 40, Massachusetts, she/her, works in public health, biracial/Black, cisgender, straight, married

RACIALLY BIASED MESSAGES
OF FERTILITY AND FAMILY

Regina Townsend, 37, and her husband decided they wanted to wait to have kids. They got married at 23 and felt they were too young and not established enough to have children. When she was 25, Regina came off her birth control pills. She expected to get pregnant soon after but didn't.

"Black women have been told so much about what we need to do to overcome our stereotype about not being able to go to college, being a teenage mother. It takes a lot for us to take that mindset and put it to the side and actually admit that we want to be parents. It takes time to get it in your head that you can want that," Regina says.

Levels of childlessness are similar for Black and white communities and are both largely influenced by education level. Although pregnancy outside of wedlock is less stigmatized in the Black community, Black women often feel pressure to choose against single or nonmarital childbearing due to the stigmas associated with being a single Black mother.[2]

"Sometimes, by the time we've come to the conclusion we want kids, we've been so focused on making sure that we're not the stereotype, making sure that we've got the good job and the right house now that we're 35. Now that we're 40," Regina says. "Sometimes it's that we've been waiting so long, because we were trying to make sure we had everything in a row, that when we finally say we do want to have kids, we're fighting against that stigma of *Am I going to be judged for wanting something that isn't seen as progressive for my community?*"

Without health insurance, Regina's medical care was limited to trips to the emergency room. There were no answers to be found there, just unhelpful suggestions from doctors to lose weight or use birth control to regulate her erratic periods, despite the fact she was trying to get pregnant. Infertility isn't something frequently discussed in the Black community, even less so 15 years ago. Stereotypes of Black women being hyperfertile and infertility being a career-driven white woman's problem underlie society's notions of who can and can't get pregnant. Though research suggests Black women may have higher rates of infertility, Black women are underrepresented among IVF recipients.[3]

A study from the University of Michigan found that 26 percent of Black women believed their encounters with infertility-related care were influenced by race or class discrimination. Women surveyed said doctors assumed they were promiscuous or would be unable to pay for childcare.[4] In part because of these stereotypes, Black women endure infertility for longer before seeking care than white women. They also require more ovarian stimulation, which can affect the IVF success rate, lead to more expensive cycles, and create a lower likelihood of achieving live births compared to white women.[5] "I didn't think infertility affected us because everything that I had always heard was that we don't have a problem in that area," she says.

A librarian, Regina started researching what the problem might be on her own. In an effort to find answers, Regina began discussing infertility online. "I went on Facebook and said, 'You know that aunt that always had all the kids with them, always did all the sleepovers and everything but never had kids? Did you ever think that maybe they couldn't have any?' And I started to get people responding and sending me messages saying, 'Thank you for saying that because nobody's ever mentioned it,'" she says.

Regina began hosting fertility programs at the library to help others learn something she was trying to understand herself. Along the way, she learned she had polycystic ovarian syndrome, a hormonal disorder known to cause irregular menstrual cycles, and blocked fallopian tubes. Then her husband learned he had unresolvable male factor infertility resulting from a hernia he had when he was an infant. There was no way for them to get pregnant naturally.

"I found that there was so much shame and stigma among Black people about so many things. I started to research where that stigma comes from, and a lot of it comes from a place of fear whether anything was wrong with you or perceived as wrong with you. Back during slavery, that was dangerous for you. If you were someone who couldn't get pregnant or had a lot of experience with miscarriage, that made you more expendable. You could get sold away or separated. It was more than just a health issue; it was a livelihood issue," Regina says. "As we've moved on from generation to generation, we've learned to be more private if there's something wrong, whether it's a mental issue or a physical issue or any kind of issue because it is safer for us to keep those things in-house and figure it out ourselves. Don't ask questions.

Don't make problems. Don't draw attention to yourself. But without that context, it just looks like we just choose not to go to the doctor."

Through the programming at the library, Regina found a doctor who would ultimately become the one to treat their infertility. Still, it was hard to see IVF as something accessible to them. "My husband said it's like private school: you need to be able to afford it before you even ask about it," Regina recalls. "If you need to ask, you can't afford it kind of thing." Regina got pregnant following her first IVF cycle. They retrieved 20 eggs, 13 of which were mature. Nine eggs that fertilized and 7 that became embryos. Regina transferred one of those embryos, which developed into her now 5-year-old son. Six embryos remain, one of which she hopes to use soon.

"When I was pregnant, I was anxious. I didn't know why I was anxious, because this is supposed to be what you want, what you waited for. You feel like you're not supposed to be upset, you're not supposed to be uncomfortable, so then you're kind of isolated in that," Regina says. "When he was born, I was very anxious. I couldn't drive. I couldn't connect what was wrong because I thought, *Well, you should be happy now because that's what you wanted.* I realized I was suffering and went to a therapist and was diagnosed with postpartum anxiety and depression. It was difficult because that part, that infertility is a trauma, doesn't get included in the conversation. You don't just turn that off when you get pregnant or when you have the baby. He's 5 now and I still struggle with sometimes not really feeling like a 'real mom' or that I don't fit in with other people. People start asking, 'Well, when are you going to have another one?' or 'Don't you think he's lonely?' But giving him a sibling entails a lot more for me than it might for somebody else."

Black parents face unique stressors, especially when it comes to the safety of their children. Black parenting requires hypervigilance; parents must teach their children how to navigate the racist systems that permeate society, including how to interact with police and authority figures at school.[6] Even mother blame looks different for Black moms. While kin and community care are more accepted forms of childcare in the Black community, Black moms report feeling solely responsible for monitoring their children and protecting them from anything that might get them into trouble. Black moms are also more likely to blame themselves for any hardships their children face.[7]

While it might be fair to say that motherhood is a policed concept, in the sense that society enforces a rigid code by which mothers must abide, for mothers of color, Black mothers especially, policing exists in both the societal and literal sense of the word. The child welfare system is rife with racial disparities. Black families are overrepresented in reports of suspected maltreatment and face more child protective services investigations than other families. Black and indigenous children are also more likely to be placed in out-of-home care than other children. Black children make up about 14 percent of the US child population but account for 23 percent of the children in foster care, while indigenous children make up 2 percent of the foster care population and only 1 percent of the US child population.[8]

Cora, 47, once had the cops called on her just because she doesn't look like her son. Cora is biracial, her husband is white, and their son is white-passing. People constantly ask if her son is adopted or, "Where is his mom?" One time, when Cora was breastfeeding, someone called the police thinking she was a nanny doing something inappropriate rather than a mother feeding her child.

"Being biracial has its own stresses and concerns. Growing up, I never felt like I fit in anywhere. I was always too white for the Black people and too Black for the white people," Cora says. "I always thought I would have a brown kid, but I didn't. I had a very white kid. For me, the hardest part is when people say stuff in front of him, even innocent things like, 'He looks nothing like you,' I can see him get sad. There's an immediate change in how he carries himself and the expression on his face. He's a momma's boy and he loves the hell out of me. I have conversations about why that's hurtful in front of him, and then we can go home and I have those conversations with him. Now that he's 9, he just snaps back and says, 'Actually, I look just like her. You just can't tell because you're not looking past color.' He gets all proud of himself for saying it. But for a while, before he felt like he could speak up for himself, it was really hard when that happened."

BE FRUITFUL AND MULTIPLY?

In an alternate reality, Margaret Bienert is a stay-at-home mom with a house, a dog, two kids, and a breadwinning husband all before the age of 30—and she's happy. At least the Margaret in this timeline thinks the alternate version of her *could* be happy.

Present-day Margaret is also happy. She's got the house, the dog, the husband—all she's missing are the kids. Well, she's not exactly missing them. Margaret has spent the past decade undoing what purity culture and growing up in a religious household in the Midwest taught her: that the greatest thing she could do with her life is reproduce.

"When I was growing up, our religion classes taught that women are made to have children. That is our goal in life. That is what God intended us to do," Margaret says. "If I believed in what I was raised to believe, then having kids was just part of the package deal. I'd never heard or seen a woman who directly disobeyed by deciding not to do what she was 'born to do.'"

One of the best predictors of childbearing comes down to religion. People of faith are more likely to have children than those with secular beliefs. The differing birth rates between those who are and aren't religious is significant enough that it could reverse secularization in some countries. Those religiously affiliated have one child more, on average, than those with secular views. Given the differences in fertility rate, births to religious parents globally more than make up for any attrition, which researchers predict will cause a substantial decline in the secular population by 2050.[9]

Religion affects childbearing both directly and indirectly: it promotes "traditional" family values and sets norms that keep people on prescribed paths. Those who are religious are more likely to get married, and marry young, and are less likely to use contraception.[10] Religion also provides a sense of community, which lessens the perceived costs and burdens of raising children for its most active members.

Margaret, 31, and her husband Corey, 33, both come from large families. Margaret is one of six children and Corey, one of seven. The pair met as undergrads at a religion-affiliated university in the Midwest. Following their engagement, Margaret's family gave her books about natural family planning. "There were chapters about how even condoms were bad," she says. "But my sister told me, 'Just so you know, we don't believe the condom part; you can use condoms.'"

Getting pregnant was Margaret's worst fear. She began tracking her cycle like every other 20-year-old she knew, except they were doing it to get pregnant whereas she was not. There were no major discussions about having kids. It was something they both assumed would happen, an unspoken part of marriage. Everyone at church had children; having kids was just what you did. But what if they didn't?

"One of the huge things that changed my perspective was money. I came from a family where the man provides and the woman has kids. It was never something you had to talk about. That was that," Margaret says. "So when I got married, I didn't even realize I was expecting that. Everything changed literally overnight when suddenly I had to go to work. I was like, 'I'm sorry, are you expecting me to also have a baby?'"

The other factor that helped Margaret build an identity for herself that wasn't "mother" was Corey. Rather than live the life her parents envisioned for her, Corey encouraged Margaret to discover what she wanted. What if they moved to Los Angeles and tried being artists? They could forge new identities, ones that fit who they actually were. "I feel like that shift probably only happened because I married Corey, someone who, for lack of better words, disappointed people enough," she says. "Disappointing people was my biggest fear. When I finally said, 'What if I don't want kids anymore?' It felt like a huge deal. To him, it was just, 'Then don't do it, done.'"

Nearly a decade later, Margaret has yet to perfect the art of not caring what her parents think. As much as Margaret and Corey have forged their own identities—they live in Los Angeles, they bought a house in the Midwest, they have their own production company and tour the country cataloging America's fantasy hotel suites—her parents still inhabit the world she left behind. Every time Margaret calls with big news, there is still hope, at least on their end, that she might be pregnant. Little do they know that Corey got a vasectomy years ago. It took years of discussion before Margaret was even comfortable with Corey getting the procedure. She didn't want their families to be mad. And that fear was not unfounded. Margaret fielded the questions, a year later, when Corey told his family. Namely, why did she let him do it?

"I think part of why our families have such a hard time relating to us is we're finding meaning outside of children," Margaret says. "They're kind of shocked we're doing what we're doing, but I've had to slowly work out that just because they raised me and gave me a life doesn't mean I owe them the rest of my life. I've had to change my beliefs pretty drastically to figure out who I actually am, years of unpacking what I actually think, and there are still days that I feel guilty."

Whether religion factors into your decision-making depends on the strength of your beliefs. The less religious you are and the more committed you are to those secular views, the less likely you are to have kids. That's why atheists are the least likely to have children.[11] The link between religion and childbearing isn't specific to one denomination, though some religions value family size more than others. In Islam, there's a lot of emphasis on getting married, for example. "They say that when you get married, you complete half of your *deen*, half of your religion," says Azmia Magane, 36. "It's rarer for people to talk about family as including just you and your spouse. A mother has an elevated status. The Prophet Mohammed emphasized honoring women, but there is a special emphasis placed on mothers; paradise lies under the feet of your mother. Having children that can pray for you and doing good deeds, those also contribute to your worship."

Azmia met her husband, who is originally from Morocco, through a mutual friend when she was 30. They planned on having kids fairly early in their relationship, but Azmia's health had other ideas. "One of the reasons a man may choose to seek a separate second wife is if his first wife is not able to bear children," Azmia says. "It can create a lot of hardship for everyone involved, but certainly more so for women."

Though Azmia wears the hijab and feels strongly about her faith, religion isn't what fuels her desire to have children—it's childhood trauma and wanting to do better than her parents did. She's not close with her biological family, but her husband's family supports their journey no matter where it leads them. If it ends up that they can't have biological children, Azmia, who is a social worker with experience working in the child welfare system, would like to adopt.

"I spent so much time on this false narrative about myself that maybe I couldn't be nurturing or that maybe I couldn't be a good mom. I feel like I wasted so many years of my life, in my younger days, internalizing stuff I picked up from other people about myself," Azmia says. "It makes me regretful that I didn't get married sooner and that I didn't start trying sooner."

PART II

SHOULD

YOU HAVE

KIDS?

4

MOVING
FROM DESIRE
TO INTENTION

HAVE YOU EVER SEEN a child throw a full-blown temper tantrum in public and wondered to yourself, *Do I even want kids?* The ability to ask ourselves that question is in many ways a privilege. While we've made a lot of strides over the past century, deciding not to have children is still culturally devalued compared to becoming a parent. Because society expects most people to both want and have children, it can be hard to separate societal pressure from our own desires. And since parenthood is often tied to adulthood, forgoing kids can feel like missing a major life milestone. Of course, kids are not without sacrifice, a loss of personal freedom that becomes more apparent the longer you delay having them.

The first part of this book discussed parenting desires: where they come from, what influences them, and why people make the choices they do. Parsing your desires requires a lot of self-reflection. The early chapters of this book are meant to help you examine the different messages you've consciously and unconsciously received about parenthood and how they shape the way you think about kids. But what if you look inward and still don't have a personal preference or feel too bogged down by all of the external factors to make a decision? Actively deciding to have children requires a shift from desire to intention to plan. That's what part two of this book is for: exploring the factors that give us pause—the loss of personal freedom, the labor involved in parenting, our relationships, the environment, money, genes, pregnancy, and childbirth. Is parenthood really worth all the sacrifices?

The thing about intentions is they're not stable. The longer the interval between setting an intention and choosing an action, the higher the likelihood of unforeseen events changing your intentions. For example, you might say you want to have kids by the time you're 35, but you end up breaking up with the person you planned to have kids with, throwing your plan for a loop. As much as you can set an intention now, it's best to approach these things with a spirit of openness to the fact that circumstances may change your decision-making.

Growing up, E. Miranda Hernandez, 40, never wanted children. She began opening up to the idea in her late teens and decided that she would settle down and have kids by the time she was 30. While that idea sounded nice, Miranda began to worry around the age of 25 that she wasn't going to meet her timeline, which is when she started to think about what it would be like to have kids on her own. Like Miranda, many people's childbearing intentions shift with time and circumstance. Finding a partner who wants children might push you from indifference into planning mode. Financial security might make you realize your ambivalence was really a fear of living beyond your means. There's no right or wrong answer here, but it's worth exploring why you feel the way you do, while acknowledging that how you feel today could change in the future (maybe even by the end of this book).

After ending a serious relationship in her late 20s, Miranda realized she wasn't going to meet her goal of having kids by 30. She needed to change the goalposts, and so she started planning for single parenthood. She wasn't in a rush, but she also knew she didn't want to have children in her 40s. Miranda wanted to pay off her debt and be better situated in her job. By the time she was in a place where she felt ready, she was 34. Soon after, she began looking for someone who could donate sperm as a known sperm donor. She had her first child through artificial insemination when she was 35 and her second, also through artificial insemination, when she was 38.

Age frequently creates a time crunch that pressures people into making a decision, often within a short period. Some people cope with this pressure by making an active plan to have children regardless of circumstances, whereas others begin to disengage from their desire to have children to cushion the blow of "running out of time." Which strategy a person picks may relate to their personality and problem-solving style.[1] In other words: Do you like to tackle things head-on or do you prefer to avoid problems or change expectations?

Research suggests how you handle this time crunch often shifts with age. Compared to younger single, heterosexual, cisgender women without children, single, childless women in their mid-30s were more likely to have polarized childbearing intentions. They either had short-term plans to have children soon or had decided not to have them at all, whereas the younger group was markedly less decided. When looking at men in the same age groups, the most common answer among men in their mid-30s was that they planned to have children in the future, which was also the most common answer for younger single and childless men. Only 19 percent of women in their mid-30s planned to further postpone having kids, compared to 42 percent of men their age. Most women in the group— 48 percent—said they had no intention of having children, compared to 33 percent of men.[2]

Ultimately, kicking your decision down the road has to have an endpoint. If you don't want time to be the deciding factor, it's worth determining, like Miranda, what you would need to have happen to feel comfortable having children—if you think you might want to have them at all. One thing that might help you decide is having realistic expectations of parenthood and a good understanding of how much time you have to choose, i.e., how long you will remain fertile, but we'll get to that second part later.

> All these years of dating online and offline and I've just never found the right person to do kids with, and our society makes it near impossible to do kids alone. I always thought I would meet the right person, and it's hard to believe I haven't. I envy my two younger sisters and their new babies. I also can't believe how inflexible my sisters'

lives are now, how much money they'll be funneling into my niece and nephew, and how these babies might be living in a climate-ravaged world by the time they're my age. Maybe one day I'll be grateful for my circumstances, but right now it's hard.

Kirsten, 38, Oregon, she/her, white,
cisgender, straight, single

5

THE DEMANDS AND REWARDS OF PARENTHOOD

TAKE A MINUTE AND think about what you have going on this week. Now add caring for a child to your schedule. Chances are your plans and childcare don't fit seamlessly together. Unless you have tons of money, it's impossible to maintain every aspect of your childfree life once you have children. Even if you have the financial cushion, there are only so many hours in the day. If you're not sure what caring for a newborn entails, below is a feeding schedule shared by a new mom who is currently nursing. Note, "nap" refers to the baby napping, not the mom.

7:00 a.m.: Feed	5:30 p.m.: Nap
8:00 a.m.: Nap	6:30 p.m.: Play
10:00 a.m.: Feed	7:00 p.m.: Bath
11:00 a.m.: Nap	7:30 p.m.: Feed
1:00 p.m.: Feed	8:00 p.m.: Bed
2:00 p.m.: Nap	2:00 a.m.: Feed
4:00 p.m.: Feed	And repeat

If you spend any time watching parenting influencers on social media, you'll leave with the impression that your kids will fall behind their peers if you don't buy them Montessori toys, make healthy lunches molded into the shape of cute animals, and set strict limits on screen time. The amount of financial, emotional, and physical resources expected from parents today can make the prospect of parenting feel not only terrifying but impossible. But parenthood didn't always look like this. Think about your childhood, your parent's childhood, their parent's childhood. Heck, US child labor laws are only as old as some of our grandparents. Kids weren't being chauffeured to 900 extracurriculars, they were leaving school early to earn a wage and help support their families. Even in our parents' generation, kids were largely left to their own devices.

What makes a good parent has shifted over time. Today, intensive parenting is considered the standard for good parenting. This shift began shortly after World War II and gained momentum in the 1980s and '90s. Intensive parenting typically focuses on cisgender women as the primary caregiver and requires that parents provide extensive time and financial resources as well as emotional and labor-intensive child-centered care. The start of this shift in the 1950s and '60s promoted the separation of mothering from paid work.[1] Then in the 1980s and '90s, when one parent staying home was no longer economically feasible, the shift expanded to pit working moms against stay-at-home moms.

These generational shifts explain why most of our childhoods looked different from our parents', and why our children's childhoods will likely look different from ours. Economic anxieties following the financial crash in 2008 further cemented "parental determinism," the idea that parents determine their children's educational and developmental outcomes when they cultivate their children's skills and abilities.[2]

Increasing financial insecurity has also led parents to emphasize the importance of developing their kids' work ethic in childhood. While upper- and middle-class parents clamor to make sure their children at least maintain the social status familiar to their parents, lower-income parents struggle to provide the carefully curated extracurriculars and financial resources required by intensive parenting. The more sacred and protected childhood becomes, the more pressure parents face to make sure they parent perfectly. Society expects parents, especially mothers, to give children their all. And that pressure to be both perfect and fully self-sacrificing can make parenthood seem a lot less enticing. If you can't do it perfectly, why do it at all?

Researchers Jenna Abetz, PhD, and Julia Moore, PhD, argue that the way we view parenting now sets the majority of US mothers up to fail. They write, "The danger of constructing complete child centeredness as natural and instinctual rests largely in the valorization of a sacrificial and essentialized view of women who fulfill their highest calling through becoming mothers. . . . Each of these practices is unrealistic for working mothers and single mothers, making it an unattainable ideal for the majority of mothers in the United States."[3]

> I don't have a good relationship with my parents and am an only child. I felt very lonely growing up and always craved the connection of a close-knit family. I imagined the joys of parenthood and the sense of fulfillment it would bring. I did not realize how hard it was, nor did I have open conversations about not having kids, and I wish there was more space for that. Being a parent is a full-time job, and I take care of people for a living as a therapist. Coming home and taking care of more people is hard. Yes, I still feel joy and fulfillment, but I wish there were more spaces and conversations about the anger and resentment that comes with being a parent.
>
> **Claire,** 35, Virginia, she/her, therapist, white, cisgender, straight, married

We're taught to believe intense parenting results in more successful children, but children have worse developmental outcomes when parents experience parental strain, difficulties with the demands and conflicts associated with parenthood, and poor parental well-being.[4] And studies show that mothers who believe in or practice intensive parenting are more likely to feel guilty, anxious, stressed, and depressed. Perfectionist parents are also more likely to experience increased anxiety, exhibit overprotective behaviors, and have harsher interactions with their kids. The problem is you can't opt out of intensive parenting. Research suggests that even those who don't subscribe to intensive parenting ideologies face increased stress, anxiety, and guilt due to the pervasiveness of "the perfect mom" stereotype. Mothers who feel pressure to be perfect report higher levels of stress and lower self-efficacy. And moms who feel guilty when they don't conform to these standards, whether they believe in them or not, experience greater stress, lower self-efficacy, and more anxiety.[5]

The pressure to be perfect leads to seemingly inescapable guilt and shame, making motherhood all the more a thankless job. Mothers are often disproportionately blamed for their kids' actions, behaviors, and well-being even as their kids become adults. This "mother blame" only serves to deepen feelings of inadequacy and guilt. Whether you work part-time or full-time, or you stay at home, the perfectionist model is unwinnable.

Fathers also feel pressure to meet society's high expectations of parents. Stress for fathers typically results from financial strain. Dads feel pressured to be breadwinners and feel less confident in their parenting abilities than moms. A Pew survey found that only 39 percent of dads felt they were doing a "very good job" raising their kids compared to 51 percent of mothers.[6] While dads might be less confident in their abilities compared to moms, they're just as likely to say parenting is important to their identity and nearly just as likely to say they find parenting rewarding and enjoyable.[7]

While you can work to challenge these belief systems in your own life, real widespread change can only come from the societal level. Shifting your thoughts and beliefs about parenting can help loosen the bonds of intensive motherhood, but the pressure to be perfect can influence you well before you decide to have kids. Even if you don't know where you stand on having kids, it's worth challenging the intensive model of parenthood early as first-time moms who believe in perfectionistic models of parenting tend to experience more anxiety during the transition to parenthood.[8]

I think a lot of my thoughts around having kids have been informed by the pressure that's put on people because of their gender—or perceived gender—and how that changes the question from, Do you want children? to How do you feel about this social responsibility to your family and your friends to be normal? I would love to be a parent. I have a lot of feelings about what being a mother means to me and what gender means to me . . . but the desire to have children is not necessarily the same as the desire to be a "normal woman," whatever that means.

I think when you talk about what womanhood is, everyone has a different answer. But one of the things that people talk about a lot is the idea of womanhood like an inheritance. I receive womanhood from my mother, and I become a mother and give it to my daughter. This cycle is how we teach generations to be, and there's a part of that that's really meaningful and powerful and good. I know that my relationship with my mother is really good, and the idea that I can be like her, as good a mother as she is, is emotionally resonant. The idea that when she talks about her mother, she's also talking about herself in me. There's also the reality that those responsibilities are there because being a dad is often not as much of a responsibility. It makes me sad because it doesn't have to be entirely focused on how women are the people who deal with babies, even if it's a good and powerful thing. It's not fair.

Assimilation is something we talk about online in the trans community. There's sort of a dichotomy there that asks, Do you want to be a heterosexual-like trans woman or do you want to be a queer person living in a queer life with queer people? Part of the reason I want to have biological children and be a parent by 30 and settle down in the suburbs is because I want to, to some extent, be normal and assimilate. Not totally, I'm still a socialist, but there is some part of me that wants that. There is this good energy in the trans community that says *you don't have to be normal. You don't have to do what straight people do; it's not actually that great.* But there's also a conflict in me, and I think in a lot of trans people, where it would be nice to be a soccer mom, at least a little bit.

Tess, 23, Maine, she/her, illustrator,
white, transgender, single

THE "MIXED BAG" OF PARENTHOOD

Parenthood has positive effects on life satisfaction, but those effects tend to be offset by the financial and time strains associated with parenthood. Pros and cons lists may not do you any good when trying to decide if kids are worth the stress because the good and the bad tend to cancel each other out. Social scientists have a name for this. It's called the demand-reward perspective. Essentially, parenting is a "mixed bag with joyful, meaningful, and rewarding experiences interwoven with frustrating challenges and exhausting workloads of care."[9]

Parenthood tends to satisfy emotional needs. You've likely heard the spiel before: "I didn't know the true meaning of love until I had children." Children provide excitement and mental stimulation. Leslie, 33, says she had kids because she just started wanting them. "I looked for a lot of logical reasons to have them, but at the heart of it was that I thought I would be a good mom and would enjoy them. There was no greater, better reason than that," Leslie says. That tug that she felt worked out for her, and she's happy with her choice.

Kids also provide social capital. In pronatalist societies, having children serves as a status symbol. Children increase their parents' participation in the local community, and through their activities, help their parents make friends (with other parents).[10] Parenthood creates a new identity. That doesn't mean the person you were before children goes away; it just becomes secondary to your child's needs. You can still have friends, hobbies, and vacations—they're just going to look different. If you like the way your life is right now and don't want it to change, it might be a sign you don't want kids or at least, don't want them right now.

You don't have to, and won't, love every bit of the parenting role. A survey study that looked at how people spend their time, found that parents ranked taking care of their children one of the least enjoyable activities of their day. Childcare ranked just above working, housework, and commuting.[11] Although parents don't enjoy caring for their children, they do enjoy spending time with them. Parents who spend more time doing enjoyable activities, like reading and playing, with their young children report experiencing less parenting strain, and for dads, the added benefit of less depression.[12]

The other benefit frequently cited by the parents interviewed for this book was an increased sense of meaning and purpose. Having children is the closest you get to immortality. Parents get to experience life again through the eyes of their children. You get to share your joys and passions and watch as your child hopefully learns to love them too. The satisfaction you feel as a parent also shifts as your child ages. Parents of children under the age of 5 report higher levels of self-esteem, self-efficacy, and satisfaction as well as less depression than parents of older children.[13] Though parenting young children comes with sleep deprivation and higher levels of parenting overload, parents tend to find caring for young children the most meaningful. Moms report the least satisfaction when their children are in middle school, the time that coincides with everyone's favorite milestone—puberty.[14] And parents of teenagers tend to report less happiness than parents with younger kids.[15] Adult children, on the other hand, tend to have a positive effect on their parents' well-being, except when they themselves are not doing well.[16] In general, parents of adult children report similar levels of well-being as those who are childfree.[17]

The stress process model offers some insights when it comes to understanding how and why parenting stressors affect some people and not others. Essentially, stress is a process made up of three main components: stressors, resources, and stress outcomes. Stressors are typically either major life events or chronic issues such as parenting, work, relationships, financial pressures, or time strains. There are four types of parenting strain: parenting role overload, parent-child relationship conflict, parenting role captivity, and interrole conflict. Parenting role overload occurs when parents feel overwhelmed by the demands of parenting, whereas parent-child relationship conflict happens when you have a negative relationship with your child, which is known to negatively affect mental health. The remaining two, parenting role captivity and interrole conflict, occur when parents feel stuck due to their responsibilities and when roles like parenting and work conflict with one another.

Balancing out these stressors are resources. Put simply, resources help us cope. These can include personal resources like self-efficacy, community, or government aid; social support from family and friends; assistance from your workplace; and other beneficial programs. Stress outcomes are things like physical health and mental well-being. Whether parenting stressors affect your well-being depends on the extent to which your parenting-related stress bleeds into other aspects of your life. In other words, parenting itself can be stressful, but you tend to feel those effects more when those stressors make other problems worse, like increasing financial woes, or create new problems, such as fights with your partner. The other important part of this model is the influence of social factors. Your race, ethnicity, gender, sexuality, social class, and immigration status all affect your stressors, resources, and stress outcomes.[18]

Ultimately, there are a lot of factors that determine whether or not you find parenthood satisfying, and you can't predict them all ahead of time. What you can do is try to create realistic expectations of what parenthood is. Yes, having a child furthers your family's legacy another generation, but it's also a lot of hard work. Are the two equal? Does one make the other worth it? That's something only you can decide.

> I was 31 when I decided, or rather we decided, to have children. I consistently said I was not interested in having children. After being married for about seven years and working for about two after finishing school, we finally had enough

money to travel and have some fun, but in all honesty, I felt like something was missing. In hindsight, I wasn't happy in my marriage. When my husband suggested maybe it was time to have children, I thought perhaps that was what was missing.

I don't regret having children. I just wish I had more resources, more time, or more help. I specifically remember bringing my baby home and thinking I made a huge mistake. I felt like my life was over; I had to accept it wasn't about me anymore. As the kids got older, the challenges changed and the time investment and expenses increased. I wish I'd been more introspective and taken the time to look at my life and goals objectively. It is not that I regret having children, not at all. I love them. But society should not make you feel like you need to have children to be successful and complete.

Amy, 50, Virginia, she/her, attorney,
white, bisexual, polyamorous

6

FAMILY PLANNING AND RELATIONSHIPS

VERONICA NEVER DREAMED OF having kids. For most of her teens and 20s, children were just something to think about later. Growing up, Veronica didn't see portrayals of families that looked like hers. The perfect American TV family—straight, white, middle to upper class with two kids—didn't represent her experience growing up as a biracial Vietnamese-American. It did, however, match the childhood her partner experienced.

Whereas Veronica was fairly certain she didn't want kids, her partner, Connor, was fairly sure he did—not for any particular reason other than that's what he was taught to believe was normal. Early on in their relationship, Connor spoke with ease about having two kids, because he just assumed it would happen. It was almost similar to how Veronica would kick her decision-making down the road—assuming one day fate would decide. And then they adopted a dog.

When they first discussed getting a puppy, Veronica was adamant they split the caregiving responsibilities. It was the only way she would agree to getting a dog. Connor's mom was a stay-at-home mom, who did most of the caregiving, and Veronica didn't want to follow that model. If they were going to get a dog, they would each have to do half of the work—that was the deal.

Five sleep-deprived days spent trying to crate train an 8-week-old puppy was all it took to change Connor's mind about kids. He looked at Veronica a week later and told her he didn't want kids. He couldn't do it. His previous perceptions of parenthood had been broken. While it was doable, such intense caregiving was not fun.

Most of the research looking at childbearing intentions doesn't make international news, but in 2014, a study from the UK that found that couples only had one discussion before deciding not to have kids spawned headlines around the globe.[1] The media ran wild, calling such "short" decision-making irresponsible and rash, but the truth is most people determine their preference for having kids individually before discussing it with their partner. And in cases where both partners don't want children, decision-making tends to be quick and painless.

Although we determine our childbearing desires at an individual level first, sometimes our intentions don't gel with our partner's. Differing desires don't always lead to conflict. Intentions change with time and circumstance, and for many, partnership is that circumstance. Research shows people revise their plans to account for their partner's childbearing intentions. People with partners who want more children tend to revise their plans upward, while those whose partners want fewer children revise their plans downward.[2] Communication scholars Wesley Durham and Dawn Braithwaite studied childfree couples and developed the following four planning trajectories based on each spouse's individual childbearing preference and the level of satisfaction it leads to.[3]

People in the accelerated-consensus trajectory typically didn't have many discussions with their partner about kids because they were on the same page relatively early on. For people in this group, being childfree is typically a core part of their identity, and so they pick a partner who also doesn't want kids. Meanwhile, couples who weren't sure where they stood on kids, the mutual-negotiation trajectory, approached the conversation by discussing the pros and cons of parenthood versus being childfree as well as their goals in life. Discussing the way they hoped to live their lives helped some couples realize they didn't want kids.

Satisfaction Levels of Childfree Couples

Planning Trajectory	Definition	Satisfaction Level
Accelerated-consensus trajectory	Both partners don't want children	High level of satisfaction
Mutual-negotiation trajectory	Neither partner is certain about their family planning preference	Variable levels of satisfaction
Unilateral-persuasion trajectory	One partner persuades the other to not have children	Variable levels of satisfaction
Bilateral-persuasion trajectory	One partner wants children and the other does not	Low levels of satisfaction

The undecided couples studied were more likely to find the decision-making process stressful. Mutually undecided couples took more time to come to a conclusion and checked in with their partner periodically at different points throughout the relationship. Although the decision process often felt stressful, once decided, partners typically felt a sense of relief and found they enjoyed being childfree. When it came to the unilateral-persuasion camp, the partner that didn't want to have kids typically had more sway compared to the indecisive partner. In heterosexual couples where the woman didn't want children and the male partner was unsure, the man would often try to "wait it out," assuming some maternal urge would kick in and change the woman's mind. People in this group tended to have a lot more conflict when it came to family planning discussions, leading to guilt, ultimatums, and passive-aggressive behavior. Similar to Veronica and Connor, here's how one couple included in the Durham and Braithwaite study negotiated during their decision-making:

We did actually sit down one day. I said, "You know, you're the one who wants kids more than I would. And if we had a child would you be willing to take care of this child 50 percent of the time? I'm not asking for more than 50 percent," . . . and I think he finally said, "30 percent." He could firmly commit himself to taking care of a child 30 percent of the time. And I said, "Don't you think there's something wrong with this picture that if you're the one that wants the child more than I do, but yet you're expecting me to take care of the child at least 70 percent of the time?" Something's wrong with that picture. We did have fewer chats about family planning following that.

Problems can arise when one partner convinces the other. It may feel frustrating if you feel strongly and your partner wavers, especially if you have always been open about your desire to have kids, or lack thereof, early on. If you convince your partner to align with your decision, you may feel guilty, like you decided their future for them. Your partner may also harbor some resentment if they feel like their desires weren't fairly considered. When partners disagree, there tend to be varied levels of satisfaction; however, Durham and Braithwaite found that in childfree couples, those who convince their undecided partner not to have kids tend to be happy with the outcome.

The most conflict occurs when partners vehemently disagree with one another. One wants kids, the other doesn't. In Durham and Braithwaite's study, ultimatums were commonly used to bring one partner over to the other side, namely the childfree-advocating partner declaring, "It's me or kids." In these scenarios, the partner who wanted children often felt as though their feelings weren't considered and that there was little opportunity to have a discussion, resulting in very low levels of family planning satisfaction.

When I was a young girl, I didn't think I wanted kids. As I got older and began working in the reproductive rights world, I realized what I really didn't want was to be pregnant and give birth, and that the choice to parent was actually different from pregnancy. I don't think our American culture acknowledges that these are two different choices. The choice not to parent has been one that I've reconsidered many times in my adult life, and I told both of my spouses, my ex-husband when we were married and my wife now, that if they decided they wanted to parent that I would entertain a conversation about it. Neither has taken me up on that. I brought my thoughts about parenthood up very early on when dating. When I met my wife, she assumed she would be with a partner who would get pregnant and have children because she also didn't want to ever be pregnant. As our relationship has grown over the years, she is as certain as I am about not parenting. The only way we would likely ever end up with kids is if something happened to one of my siblings and we took on their children.

People in my life always assume I will regret not having kids, but I believe I've given more thought to not parenting than most parents give to deciding to have children. I couldn't be more sure.

Heidi, 44, Texas, she/they, nonprofit CEO,
white, cisgender, bisexual, married

So what can we learn from this research? Simply put, it's better to be honest. If you know, without a doubt, where you stand, you should let your partner know early on. How early depends on your goals for the relationship, your age, and how far into the future you see yourself having kids. If you know you want to start trying within the next two years, it's worth disclosing your intentions before things start getting serious. It doesn't have to be the first date, but you don't want to wait a year only to find out your partner doesn't want kids and assumed, because you didn't bring it up, that you didn't either.

Of course, not everyone knows where they stand before getting into a relationship. For some folks, relationships bring a sense of clarity or make them think about parenthood in different ways. This seems to be especially true for people who had significantly different upbringings from their partner. A common response that came up during interviews for this book was, "I didn't want children until I met my partner." Some people can't "see" themselves as parents, but over time, their partner's enthusiasm for kids helped them envision what parenthood could look like. Take Anne, for example, who at 24 wasn't sure she wanted kids until she started dating her current partner. Anne's boyfriend always knew he wanted kids and hoped to have them early. "Just seeing how excited he was about the idea of having a family and how that vision could be fully realized really made it exciting for me in a different way," Anne says. "We just have really aligned values and goals, and I think we'll be really great parents."

Of those I spoke to who changed their mind, most said it was something they knew their partner wanted, and so they thought about it, typically on their own, and gradually warmed up to the idea. Others knew it was important to their partner, and because their partner was important to them, decided to "go for it." In that scenario, the partner who wanted kids felt more strongly about having kids than the other partner felt about being childfree. In other words, couples typically landed on the side of the partner who felt the strongest. Those who felt comfortable with their ultimate decision said they never felt manipulated or forced into deciding, whereas those who expressed some level of regret or dissatisfaction with parenthood felt rushed or coerced.

Negotiation exists among queer couples as well. When one partner has a strong desire to have children, the other partner will often rethink their decision-making.[4] In these cases, the persuaded partner became equally committed to parenting.[5] Queer parents who have a strong desire to have children typically stay on paths that lead them to parenthood, even if that means ending their relationship. A study of gay men who wanted to have children found that they were more likely to end their relationships if their partner was not fully willing to become a parent.[6] For lesbian couples, the parenting desires of one partner did not change the other's intention to parent or remain childless.[7]

Heterosexual couples tend to have differing opinions of parenthood because of gendered role expectations. A study of men between the ages of

28 and 45 found that men chose parenthood after becoming disillusioned with their careers. Their jobs met many of their external goals but did not provide the internal satisfaction they were looking for, making fatherhood seem more appealing.[8] For women, the decision-making was nowhere near as simple. Women are more likely to factor in social factors, the opinions of their partners and families, and what they stand to gain and lose. For example, wage trajectories tend to shift dramatically for highly skilled female workers after they have children. A working paper from the National Bureau of Economic Research found that people lose 21 to 33 percent of their lifetime earnings after having a child. Delaying children helps lessen these losses. Those with a bachelor's degree who waited until they were 30 to have children earned $125,000 more over their lifetimes than those who had children in their early 20s.[9]

I got pregnant when I was 29 and wasn't totally sure I was ready. I thought I could be a cooler, more cosmopolitan version of myself, but I think I figured I would get bored of that and then it would be a little too late to try. My mom died when I was 26 and I thought I couldn't have kids without her. But kids were also really important to my husband, who is a little older and was a little more ready before I was. I don't know what made me decide. It wasn't a deep thought process; it was just like, "Welp, let's do it."

I mostly love being a parent. I definitely do more work in parenting. I'd say it's 80 percent me and 20 percent him. I'm touched out, tired, and just get "the ick" really easily. My youngest is 7 months, so I'm hoping, like after my first, I will get back to my preferred normal, but my husband and I are still happy together. Also, if I'm feeling resentful that I'm doing more, I communicate that and he gets it and steps up.

Kathryn, 33, Rhode Island, she/her, works part-time at a nonprofit, white, cisgender, straight, married

It makes sense that some partners may not be enthusiastic about parent-hood if they suspect they'll be the ones doing most of the work. One of the greatest predictors of parental well-being is the division of labor. Women who are ambivalent about their marriages and perceive less support from their husbands are more likely to experience depressive symptoms during the transition to parenthood.[10] Whereas new moms who feel supported by their partners are less likely to experience an increase in depression.[11] Even though the gender divide in childcare and household tasks has improved over time, moms continue to do much of the unpaid labor in heterosexual relationships. This imbalance helps to explain why mothers experience more stress, more fatigue, and less happiness than fathers.

Dads report spending eight hours per week on childcare, about triple the amount of time they spent on childcare in 1965, and spend 10 hours per week on housework compared to only four hours in 1965. Moms, on the other hand, say they spend about 14 hours per week on childcare and 18 hours per week on housework. These uneven divisions persist even when you factor in one parent staying home. Stay-at-home moms spend an average of 26 hours per week on housework and 20 hours per week on childcare, more than triple the amount of time their working partners spend on the same tasks. When the roles are switched, stay-at-home dads spend 18 hours per week on housework and 11 hours on childcare, about eight hours more than their working partners spend on the same unpaid tasks. How-ever, stay-at-home dads tend to have nearly double the amount of leisure time as working moms, whereas stay-at-home moms get less than four hours more of leisure time than working dads. The division of labor is split more evenly when both parents work; however, moms still tend to do more of the unpaid labor.[12]

When it comes to paid labor, more than half of working parents in the US say they find it difficult to balance caring for their kids and working. Among those with kids under 18, nearly 40 percent of working parents say they always feel rushed, and 33 percent say they do not spend enough time with their kids.[13] A study of Canadian parents came to a similar finding. Half of employed parents said they felt as though they didn't spend enough time with their kids. When parents felt this way, they were more likely to also experience sleep issues, anger, and distress.[14]

Even though managing work and parenting is often stressful, employed parents of children under the age of 18 tend to report less parenting strain than unemployed parents. Parents fare even better, unsurprisingly, when there are resources in the workplace. Schedule control is one of the most crucial factors. Parents who have more control over their schedules report less parenting strain, better well-being, and more time spent with their children.[15] Blurred work boundaries, emails, Slack, and all of the other notifications you get on your phone can also make it hard for parents to find separation between home and work life.

I have always wanted kids, and as someone who was raised by effectively a single mother, I never saw an issue with being one myself. In my ideal world, I wanted to adopt and started this process but realized that the cost of adoption was so prohibitively high that I couldn't afford it as a single woman on a social worker's salary. I thought about fostering but had to be honest with myself about whether I'd have the emotional capacity to start to raise a child and then have the child reunited with their birth family. I simply did not think I'd be able to handle that, despite knowing it may be in the child's best interest.

During the pandemic, I began dating someone who was a good friend. She knew I wanted to have children and went back and forth on whether it was something she was open to. Ultimately, it wasn't and we broke up because it isn't something I'm willing to compromise on. The hardest part of this was that for the first time really, I realized how lovely it would be to do this with a partner, but starting to date as you're doing artificial insemination is so challenging. I'm still trying to figure out how and when to tell people. I'm also very clear that I don't expect whoever I start dating at this point to rush into parenthood with me, but that's also a really tricky line to walk.

Fortunately, all of this has really brought my mom and me much closer together. She moved across the country to be present for me through this. We've started talking tons about the values I want to instill in my child, about my dating life (I was able to come out to my mom as bi), about the ways in which she wants to help out and the things that I need not just in her relationship with my child but in my relationship with her. That has been such a gift.

Claire, 32, Massachusetts, she/her, social worker, cisgender, queer, single

Since the division of labor fuels most arguments among new parents,[16] it makes sense to include who does what as part of family planning discussions. Greater perceived inequalities in the division of labor lead to worse outcomes for all couples regardless of sexuality. Partners who want a more equitable division of labor or experience the majority of unpaid labor-related stressors tend to report worse well-being. Much of the imbalances in the division of unpaid labor come down to gender roles, which is why same-sex, trans, and nonbinary couples tend to take more equal approaches when dividing tasks.[17]

Like with Veronica and Connor, building a mutual understanding of expectations can help the decision-making process. In Veronica's case, fairness was splitting the unpaid labor 50–50. But fairness doesn't have to mean equal. Satisfaction occurs when both partners are happy with the arrangement, whether that's 50–50, 60–40, or 70–30, the ratio doesn't matter so long as both partners feel it is fair. One partner staying home and doing more unpaid labor while the other partner works can be fair if both partners willingly agree to it.

Since our parents pass down gender norms and parenting behaviors, the best way to challenge these beliefs is to take a critical look at the way your parents raised you. What are some things you liked about your childhood? What are some things your parents did that you would want to do differently? How did your parents divide labor? How do you feel about that division?

Is it something you'd want to replicate, why or why not? Ask your partner these same questions. What are their expectations? Do they expect you to do all the childcare-related tasks just because their mom did? These can be thorny topics, so if you feel uncomfortable, you can bring these discussions to a neutral space, like couple's counseling.

If you can't make a decision, stop trying to decide and pretend like it's happening. It's easier to envision a childfree life because that's the life you're living. Not much would change if you don't have children. But everything changes when you have kids. Sure, it's fun to think about baby names, but that won't ease your apprehension. Go beyond who's doing what percentage-wise and get granular. Say there is a baby in the house, would you breastfeed, pump, formula feed? Who is doing nighttime feedings? What about diaper changes? What about food for the adults? Who is cooking and cleaning? Then there is childcare. Who is watching the baby? Can you afford childcare, or does it make sense for one parent to stay home? Answer the questions independently and see how your responses compare to each other. Think about ideological differences. Will you raise your child with a certain religion? How would you respond to difficult parenting situations? How would you discipline a child? It's easy to say I don't know to a lot of these questions, but these are decisions you will have to make at one point, so why not now? If you find yourself dreading these types of conversations, it might be a sign that you aren't ready or don't want kids. Alternatively, planning might help you envision what parenthood could look like for you.

Pay attention to how you and your partner feel during these conversations. Go into baby mode. Follow parenting accounts on social media, check out the baby section of a store and marvel over all the different types and price points of strollers, make a baby registry, take a parenting class. It might feel silly at first, but stick with it. Spend a few weeks engaging, together and separately, in parenting spaces. Pay attention to how you feel. Do you find yourself skipping over parenting posts in your feeds, or have you kind of gotten into it? There are no right or wrong answers; there's only what works best for you.

And if you want to do a dry run and test out some of the responsibilities of parenthood, but with less commitment, take a page out of Veronica and Connor's book. A lot of people recommend babysitting as a test of parenthood, but the problem with that is you get to go home at the end of the day. A pet is a big commitment, so you don't have to adopt a dog, like Veronica and Connor did, instead you can try your hand at fostering. Call up your nearby animal shelter or look for local rescue groups and see if they are looking for fosters. Fostering a puppy is not the same as raising a child, of course, but it can give you an idea of how well you and your partner work together when the dog has to poop at 5:00 a.m.

I was 29 and my girlfriend was 34 when we had our son. We had already bought a house and had careers, and she wanted to start a family before she was 35. We decided to stop trying not to have kids, and she was pregnant two weeks later.

Even as a kid, I always wanted to be a "grown-up." I thought a house, a dog, and a kid were part of that. I honestly don't enjoy being a parent. I feel like I was hoodwinked by the overwhelming messaging from relatives and society that "everything changes, and it's wonderful." Five years of sleep deprivation wasn't wonderful. Figuring out schools and work schedules isn't wonderful. Always having a part of my brain occupied for kid stuff isn't wonderful. The truth is that my partner was satisfied with those things, but they never really clicked for me.

I don't regret having children, but if I could go back and tell myself to change my life's path to one where I was the "fun uncle" instead of "somewhat detached part-time dad," I would. I think we're doing a disservice to folks by implying that fulfillment through parenting is a sure bet. People who really want kids should have them. People who aren't sure should tune out relatives and friends pressuring them to and consider the opportunity costs and risks. I love my son, but I'm happy hanging out with him one or two days a week. In retrospect, I should have followed my heart instead of traditional social and romantic templates. Now we split custody, and I'm married to someone who wants less traditional things, and it's far more rewarding.

Marc, 39, he/him, works in IT,
cisgender, bisexual, married

7

KIDS,
IN THIS CLIMATE?

WHEN STEPHEN THINKS ABOUT all the waste humankind makes, he can't help but remember childhood trips to the local recycling center near where he grew up in Virginia. His parents would save their trash until they had bales of cardboard and big bags full of cans to recycle. When the bins and bundles began to pile up, they would schlep them into the car and drive to a place where they could properly dispose of them. They didn't have to do it, but they did. The trip took 25 minutes. Stephen remembers it as a "huge pain in the butt."

Regardless of whether or not his parents recycled to instill environmental values, it worked. Stephen, 30, now investigates the effectiveness of programs meant to mitigate the effects of climate change. To say he cares deeply about the environment would be an understatement.

But caring is a complicated emotion when it comes to the environment. How do you care about a problem much larger than yourself? For Stephen, it presents as a sort of factual numbness. "I have a lot of grim predictions that people get bummed out about when I talk about them," he says. "Because I'm so used to thinking about this, I kind of forget that it's supposed to bum you out."

Stephen is one of a growing number of young people deciding to forgo kids due to climate change. Approximately 38 percent of Americans ages 18 to 29 believe that couples should think about climate change when deciding to have kids, and about 33 percent of those between the ages of 20 to 45 cited climate change as a reason to have fewer children.[1] But not having children for the sake of the environment is not a new idea. The zero population growth movement in the late 1960s was the first to promote limiting reproduction to preserve Earth's resources.[2]

To Stephen, global warming is not an environmental issue; it's a social issue. "The change of the climate in and of itself is not good or bad; it just is. It's the fact that the society and civilization we built is so dependent on climate being the way it was when we started. That's where the problem comes from," he says. "Suddenly we have to change, and we can't even abolish the freaking penny or daylight savings time. Now we have to say, 'Sorry, no more gas cars or we're all going to starve.'"

Adapting to an uncertain world feels daunting enough to Stephen without kids; with kids it's almost unimaginable, and that doesn't even factor in the sadness that comes with passing on a world so different than the one he grew up in. "I was at the Vancouver Aquarium, where I worked during grad school, and there was this tiny little toddler just totting around barely cognizant of anything. He wanted these stickers with shiny whales and dolphins on them, and my stupid brain was like, *What are you going to tell your kid if those go extinct and they see those stickers somewhere? 'There used to be animals called whales?'* Imagine having to explain that to a kid. It makes me so sad."

I want kids but through adoption. As an environmental scientist, the thought of condemning my potential future children to a failing planet is overtly distressing. That feeling, intense protective love for children who have not yet come into being, overwhelms my desire to bring them into this world. My disabling chronic conditions would also make pregnancy and childbirth dangerous, and I want to be as active a parent as possible.

Lebanese poet Khalil Gibran tells us that children come through us, but are not ours—they belong to life itself.

I cling to that. I would be blessed to experience parent-hood through adoption, provided I had a good partnership and community support. I have to bring up my desire to adopt when dating because the thought of not having biological kids or adopting is too much for some people, especially in the context of building a life with someone with chronic disabling health issues. It's best for everyone if I'm honest from the beginning. We both deserve to know the waters before diving in.

There are so many ways to be a parent and so many ways to enrich the lives of kids in our communities. I won't sacrifice my long-term health at the altar of pregnancy. Adoption is the way for me. If my future life partner also has a uterus, we'd need to discuss their feelings on the situation. I feel very uneasy about using artificial means to achieve pregnancy, at least in the face of climate disaster, and there are so many children waiting for a stable and loving home in the US already.

Monica, 25, Idaho, she/her, climate scientist, white, cisgender, queer, disabled

OUR CHANGING WORLD, OUR CHANGING BODIES

Like humans, Earth has a temperature. Our average temperature is 97.9°F, while the average temperature for the planet is 59°F. Just like we function optimally at our average temperature, so does Earth. Earth's temperature naturally fluctuates, but thanks to increased carbon dioxide emissions, temperatures are rising faster than ever. Today, Earth is about 1.8°F warmer than it was before the Industrial Revolution thanks to increasing levels of carbon dioxide in the atmosphere. Over the past 60 years, we added 100 times the rate of naturally occurring carbon dioxide to the atmosphere, which makes up about two-thirds of the total energy imbalance responsible for rising temperature.[3]

"There's a certain amount of carbon that we married ourselves to 100 years ago because the life span of carbon dioxide in the atmosphere is so long that the carbon emissions from 100 years ago are in the atmosphere now," civil engineer and executive director of Climatepedia Kimberly Duong, PhD, says. "And so the carbon emissions we're emitting now are going to impact those future generations in the next 50 to 100 years, and we can't take that back."

Our way of living isn't just destroying the environment, it's harming our bodies, too. Changing weather patterns, decreased food and water resources, air pollution, and rising sea levels strain both our physical and mental health.

As temperatures increase, so does the risk of pollution, allergens, and diseases.[4] Extreme temperatures also intensify the pollutants released by cars and factories. This increase in pollution leads to more hospitalizations due to asthma and cardiovascular disease. Pollution also causes higher levels of pollen and a longer allergy season.[5]

Rising sea surface temperatures have already started to cause an increase in marine life and human disease.[6] Estimates suggest sea levels will increase anywhere from 8 inches to 6.6 feet by 2100 due to warmer temperatures, increasing the likelihood of floods, which carry disease risks of their own.[7] Floodwater introduces toxic materials into our water supply, making it easier for water-borne and vector-borne illnesses to thrive. Water damage to homes can also cause post-flood mold, worsening allergy or asthma symptoms.[8]

Environmental change has insidious ways of trickling down to affect human health. Changing weather patterns influence the migration patterns of animals and bugs, leading to an increase in vector-borne illnesses like Lyme disease and Zika virus.[9] And altered seasons change our food supply, lowering crop yields and nutritional quality.[10]

Children are some of the most vulnerable to these health impacts. Pollution, toxins, and other stressors can all take a toll on a child's physical and emotional well-being, causing issues that can follow them into adulthood.[11] Climate-driven physical stress can cause adverse birth outcomes and affect fetal development.[12] Fortunately, children are also resilient. Studies on air quality show that children's lung function improves following reductions in air pollution.[13]

When it comes to mental health, the stress of extreme weather events can lead to increases in trauma, shock, post-traumatic stress disorder (PTSD), stress, anxiety, depression, and substance abuse. After Hurricane Katrina, suicide and suicidal ideation nearly doubled for people living in the path of the storm. One in six meets the criteria for PTSD, and nearly half of those living in areas affected by the storm developed a mood or anxiety disorder.[14] High levels of stress also affect our physical health, causing lowered immune system responses, sleep disorders, digestion issues, and memory loss.[15]

Episodes of violence and aggression also rise when temperatures soar. The average American will experience four to eight times more days above 95°F each year between now and the end of the century.[16] In places like Arizona, this would add nearly 100 more 95°F-plus days per year by 2099.[17] Heat has a negative effect on cognitive functioning, increasing aggression while decreasing attention and self-regulation.[18] A study from the Harvard Kennedy School at Harvard University estimates that climate change will cause an additional 30,000 murders, 200,000 rapes, and 3.2 million burglaries due to increased average temperatures between 2010 and 2099.[19] Domestic abuse, including child abuse, also increases following natural disasters.[20] And this violence will only grow as resource depletion and climate-induced mass migration become major issues.

The increase in violence is one of the many things Stephen finds troublesome about the social aspects of climate change. "I'm more worried about the way people will treat one another in the context of a very visible decline in quality of life than I am about the actual decline in quality of life itself. I think everyone's going to be looking for somebody to blame, and it's going to get just ugly and violent," he says. "Whatever happens in the next century or so, we're not going to go extinct. I don't think there's going to be some dark age that's so bad that every living memory of the past will be gone, but there will be more turbulence than people alive right now are accustomed to. I think wisdom will prevail. I just don't know how long it will take for it to do so."

I'm entirely too undisciplined to have kids. I want other things out of life that I'd have to give up to have kids. I'm also solo poly, so I'd end up raising children alone. In addition to all this, as the world rushes headlong into a climate crisis of our own making, having more kids seems extremely shitty. I don't want to bring someone into a world where they're going to have to struggle for resources, live through increasingly common wars, and maybe be around for the extinction of the human race.

Evan, 33, California, they/them, queer, polyamorous

WILL NOT HAVING KIDS REALLY SAVE THE PLANET?

Unless you are the chief executive of an oil company or hold a high-level government position, having fewer kids is by far the most effective thing you can do to lessen your carbon footprint. A study published in *Environmental Research Letters* found that having one less child was the highest impact action a person could take to lower their carbon footprint.[21] It's a hard truth to sit with, especially if you think you might want kids, but when you think about the role humans play in pushing forward climate change, it's not surprising that having fewer of us here would be better for the planet. So now that you're past the shock of hearing that having fewer children is by far the best thing you can do for the environment, let's discuss what exactly that means.

Population growth is one of the main drivers of carbon emissions. A study published in the *Proceedings of the National Academy of Sciences* found that slowing population growth by 0.5 births per woman globally could provide 16 to 29 percent of the emissions reductions needed by 2050 to avoid dangerous climate change.[22] Of course, not all population growth is the same. The lifestyles of high-carbon individuals, those from industrialized nations, produce more than 50 percent of all emissions. Meanwhile the poorest half of the world's population, those most at risk of suffering the negative effects of climate change, produce only 7 percent of global carbon emissions.[23]

In order to limit the increase in global warming to less than 2°C by 2100, we need to get to a place where people stay within a budget of 2.1 tons of carbon dioxide per year by 2050.[24] To put this into perspective, the average American produces 15.2 tons of carbon dioxide emissions per year. Just eating meat and taking one transatlantic flight per year is enough to exhaust your yearly 2.1-ton carbon budget.[25]

Naturally, this poses quite a few challenges for environmentally minded folks who want to have kids and also want to lower their carbon footprint. Is there an ethical way to have kids, or should we all just abstain from procreating?

A simple way to look at this is to look at the rate of replacement. If every person has one child, two per couple, the population more or less stays the same. If a couple has one child, the population decreases. If having kids is important to you, you can choose to have fewer kids than you originally intended. But it's not really the number of children that's the problem; it's our lifestyles. Niger has the highest total fertility rate of any country with 6.91 children born per birthing person.[26] However, a child born in Niger doesn't consume as many resources as their American counterparts do. The average Nigerien produces only 0.1 tons of carbon dioxide emissions per year.[27]

At the heart of research around the environmental impacts of population growth is a message about consumption. It's not about the number of people; it's about the resources they consume. The studies talking about decreasing population growth don't say, "Have zero kids," they say, "Have fewer kids."

Denying our role or ability to promote change is an emotion-based strategy that leads to less environmentally protective behaviors. When we think of climate change as something that will affect faraway regions more than ours or occurs at a later date, or we see it as purely the responsibility of government, scientists, and corporations to solve, we create what's known as psychological distance between us and the problem.[28]

Emotion-focused coping typically doesn't help either. Fearmongering often leads people to deemphasize climate change or ignore it, making them less likely to engage in behaviors that help the environment.[29] A lot of times when we feel bad, we shift our focus from the problem to getting rid of our negative emotions associated with the problem. Instead of thinking, *What can I do to help the environment*, we think *What can I do* to get rid of the anxiety I feel when I think about global warming? And for many folks, the answer becomes, *Well, if I don't think about it, then I don't feel scared.* If you're someone who tends to avoid negative emotions, about climate change or any life issue, try focusing your attention on meaning. Spend some time in nature. Take a hike. Try your hand at gardening or foraging. Think about the parts of nature you love and look for people and conservation efforts fighting for change in those spheres. Promoting hope is half the battle; the other half involves not only learning how to sit with complicated emotions but finding ways to reframe the negatives and empower yourself to act.

I used to want a literal litter of kids. I really wanted kids and thought that I would be married with kids by the time I was 26 or 27. That changed as I got older and the world started changing. I'm a millennial. I'm of the age where the economy was totally tanked when I started trying to earn money and become an adult. I also have a huge student loan burden. But even beyond the financial stuff, the climate crisis is right in my face, and I'm watching these uprisings happen in cities across the country over police brutality. Any kids that I would have, either biologically or adopted, just as a personal decision, would be Black. So there're considerations there about my level of responsibility and culpability.

When my last relationship fell apart, I was not optimistic. I've been with my current partner for four years going on five now. It's a completely different space. It's definitely the relationship that I want to keep forever. We've talked about having kids, and decided that if we have kids, we'd adopt. I think probably two maximum, so not a litter. One right now would be a huge financial stretch, which is why we haven't started that process yet. We also want to get married first.

But I went from wanting biological kids to deciding that adopting was the way to go just because I didn't want the moral weight of procreating to be part of that process. I am not optimistic about the future. I think that's why I do the type of work that I do. I fight against that horrible future because I'm so afraid of it. The likelihood of it scares me and motivates me to change as much as I can possibly change and help other people to change anything they can possibly change to make things better.

Jordan, 35, Rhode Island, he/him, nonprofit director, Black, cisgender, queer, in a relationship

PARENTING IN THE AGE OF CLIMATE CHANGE

California-based environmental scientist Alan Talhelm, PhD, 39, strongly believes that optimism guides the decision to have a child. It's part of the reason he and his wife decided to have their son, who is now 1 ½.

"As somebody who works in the climate and environmental field, I am probably somewhat more optimistic than most people because I am aware of all the actions that are happening; the government programs, the people trying to provide leadership, the scientific advances related to carbon capture, and other climate mitigation measures we can take. I also see the resilience of life in a biological sense out there in the environment," Alan says. "That doesn't mean there's not catastrophe over the horizon, but it sort of gives me some sense of optimism."

The other part of Alan's optimism is a sentiment echoed by others interviewed for this book: a desire to leave this world better than they found it and a fear that if people with their values don't have children, those values won't get passed on. Parents shape the way their children understand the world. Trips to the recycling center as a kid taught Stephen there was no such thing as "away," that just because trash disappears from your sight doesn't mean it's gone.

If you want to have kids, one of the best things you can do is raise them with pro-environmental values. Research supports talking to your kids about global warming.[30] When you model pro-environmental behaviors, your kids learn from your example. Talking about climate change doesn't have to be scary. The best way to start the conversation is to teach your kids to love nature, so that they're naturally inclined to want to protect it, and then give them the tools to do so.

Moral and political philosopher Elizabeth Cripps, PhD, argues parents owe it to their children to protect them from climate change as part of their responsibility to meet their child's basic needs, prepare them for adulthood, and provide an environment that lets them continue to live a decent life. Cripps writes:

> If the child is starving and the parent could but does not prevent this continuing only to give hugs and bedtime stories, it would seem a mockery of caring for them. Equally, if the child will face starvation or serious disease in the future and the parent could but does not prevent this, the same can be said for her other efforts to prepare that child for adulthood.[31]

We know that the planet will get warmer and our way of life will devolve without intervention. Therefore, if a parent's job is to act in the best interests of their child, it's also their job to fight against climate change. Parents, Cripps says, have a shared duty to fight for collective action on climate change mitigation and adaptation, something Alan feels deeply about: "Having a child has really made me think in a much more profound way about my impact on the environment and what I am doing to solve the climate change problem."

Your children don't just inherit your eyes or your sense of humor; they inherit the world you leave behind. What we do now affects generations—children whose lives we likely won't live long enough to see but for whom our climate-driven actions over the next few decades will definitely impact.

"It's given me a much greater sense of urgency in terms of the actions that I take," Alan says. "That's not to say that I wasn't motivated before, but there's something so deep and fundamental about having a child and knowing that they are going to be living in a world that's a product of your actions. The future is living with you in your house, and it's staring you in the face every day. I think it makes you value the future more than you otherwise would have, having a child who's going to be living in it."

8

GETTING
YOUR FINANCES
IN ORDER

JASMINE TILLERY'S TWO PREGNANCIES couldn't look more different. The first, her son, was an unplanned pregnancy when she was 19. Her second, twin daughters, were conceived nearly a decade later through IVF. While the two pregnancies, and the financial circumstances around them, fell on opposite ends of the parental preparedness spectrum, they both taught Jasmine, 30, the same thing: there is no amount of planning that can prepare you for parenthood.

Kids cost a lot of money. How much money? Well, it depends. No matter how your kid comes into the world, it is going to be expensive. Raising a child from birth until age 17 costs an average of $284,570 for a middle-income family, nearly $16,000 per year. According to the US Department of Agriculture, the branch of the US government that puts together these figures, it's housing, 29 percent; food, 18 percent; and childcare and education, 16 percent, that make up the bulk of money spent.[1] And it's not just the early years that are costly. Research shows that parents spend about one-third of the total cost of raising a child from birth to age 18 on their adult children in the form of college tuition, housing, and other types of monetary assistance.[2] If your first thought is, *Where am I getting that kind of money from?*

you're not alone. Around 42 percent of parents feel financially unprepared to have a child.[3]

Jasmine's first pregnancy came, unplanned, when she was in college. She had no money so she lived at home with her parents while the father of her son worked. Eventually the two moved in together, and Jasmine got a job after she graduated. And although they made good money for 21-year-olds, the couple lived paycheck to paycheck. When they split up a short while later, Jasmine found herself facing a new financial challenge: how to raise a 2-year-old on a single income. "It was a struggle," Jasmine says. "I didn't know how to manage money because I saw my parents being able to provide us everything. I didn't know how to prioritize money, how to budget."

The magnitude of Jasmine's financial woes hit with the monthly daycare bill when her son was 3 ½. Between paying her half for childcare, student loan payments for her master's degree, and financing a brand new car, Jasmine realized she had to make some changes. A quick Google search will pull up a dizzying number of budgeting apps and charts but what worked for Jasmine wasn't any formulaic plan. "I failed so many times before I got it right," she says.

What ultimately worked for her was a plan based on her needs. She didn't want to keep living paycheck to paycheck, so she improvised using the model of paying yourself first. She started by giving herself $10 a paycheck to save and worked her way up to $900 a month. It took a while for her to switch from a spender to saver mentality but she got there. Things clicked even further into place once she learned about the zero-based budget. She had to give every dollar a job; if it didn't have a job, she was just going to spend it. Jasmine also gave herself spending limits for each category. She had to be "responsible" and learn how to say no or cut down on things she enjoyed. When she was younger and raising her son alone, she had to cut back and reprioritize to make her budget work, but now she budgets for things like getting her hair and nails done.

"Nobody's ever really prepared," Jasmine, who now runs her own personal finance resource, Money and Momming, says. "Don't let societal pressures or money issues sway you either way. At the end of the day, it's your decision, but forget this idea of being ready. Nobody's ever ready."

I'm very undecided about having kids. If I had to make the decision today, the answer would be no. I think one of the biggest factors is the student loan debt I have. It's very concerning to me because if I were to stop working, I don't know how I would be able to pay my student loans and survive without needing a lot of help from loved ones. I have to focus on making money. I have to have a plan that'll get me to the end of that debt, even if that plan is 10, 15, 20 years away. I can't see the light at the end of the tunnel yet because I own a house-worth ($130,000) of private student loans.

Ashley, 26, Pennsylvania, she/her, producer, white, cisgender, partnered

THE FIRST COSTS

Before the costs of kids comes the expense of pregnancy. How much your pregnancy costs depends on a lot of factors. If you need to use fertility treatments, you'll likely spend thousands to tens of thousands of dollars just to get pregnant. A year after Jasmine and her husband got married in 2017, they learned they would need to use IVF to build their family. This presented them with a difficult choice: do they continue to prioritize their debt-free journey or do they prioritize family planning? Together they decided expanding their family was more important; their debt could wait. In the midst of saving for IVF, Jasmine changed engineering jobs, and her new employer's insurance fortunately paid for IVF, leaving her with just her deductible.

Once you're pregnant, the cost depends on your health insurance. In other countries, much of this cost will be subsidized by publicly funded health care. In the US the cost largely depends on the type of health insurance you have. When it comes to giving birth, vaginal births are less expensive than C-sections. With insurance coverage, the average out-of-pocket cost (the cost you pay) ranges from about $1,000 to $2,500 depending on the state you live in. When you add in the costs of pregnancy and postpartum care, the average total out-of-pocket cost is about $4,314 for vaginal deliveries and $5,161 for C-sections.

If you don't have insurance, the cost is going to be higher. Before insurance, the national average cost for an uncomplicated vaginal birth works out to about $15,000. But this fluctuates wildly depending on where you live. An uncomplicated vaginal birth will cost you $26,380 without insurance in California compared to $9,623 in Maine. Even within states, the rate can fluctuate with births in city hospitals costing more than those in more rural areas. And these are just the rates for uncomplicated vaginal births. The price increases if you have emergency complications, a preexisting condition, need a C-section, or if your child requires neonatal intensive care (which can cost hundreds of thousands of dollars)—scenarios that can't always be predicted or planned for ahead of time.

But what if you don't want to give birth in a hospital? Is giving birth at home cheaper? Not necessarily. Home births are largely births delivered by a midwife. Generally speaking, most midwives are out-of-network providers, meaning not covered by insurance unless you have out-of-network coverage. There is no database for midwife costs, but looking at midwife providers across the US, the average rate seems to be around $5,000. This does not include ultrasounds, bloodwork, or other testing you might need as well as a home birth kit, which costs around $30 to $80.

You may also want to have a doula attend your delivery. Doulas provide emotional and physical support to birthing people before, during, and after childbirth and have been shown to improve the birthing experience. Doulas can cost anywhere from $500 to $2,500 depending on where you live. Some insurance policies will cover part or all of a doula's fees as will some state Medicaid programs.

Unfortunately, it's nearly impossible to figure out how much you'll spend on health care until the bill arrives. If you have health insurance, reading over the details of your plan can provide at least a few clues. First, you'll want to determine your deductible (the amount you have to cover before your insurance kicks in). Let's say the hospital you plan to use charges $10,000 for its birthing services, and you have a $1,000 deductible. If you haven't met your deductible yet, you'll have to pay the first $1,000 of the bill before your health insurance kicks in. Once your deductible is paid, you should only be responsible for your co-pay and/or coinsurance, the percentage or amount not covered by insurance. Coinsurance rates can vary based on the service, so you'll want to look at how your insurance company breaks it down. If it's not clearly stated in your plan, call the insurance company and ask. Equally if not more important when it comes to avoiding surprise bills is making sure all of your health-care providers, including the hospital itself, are in-network with your provider. If your insurance doesn't have out-of-network benefits, you may wind up responsible for the entire bill.

While paying for health insurance can be expensive, the savings it affords when it comes to maternity care often make the costly premiums (the amount you pay each month for coverage) worth it. If you know you want to start trying within the next year or so, you're going to want to assess the plan you have or, if you don't have one, start looking for one. Both employer- and government-based health insurance plans have limited open enrollment periods, which means you can only sign up for health insurance within that short window. The open enrollment period for plans offered by the federal government is 45 days, though states can opt to keep this window open longer. Employer-based plans set their own enrollment periods, often a few weeks at the end of the year. If you are married and not on your partner's insurance, it may be worth comparing the coverage their employer offers to yours. If your employer offers multiple plans or different tiers, check out the other plans and consider upgrading. If you don't change or enroll in a plan during open enrollment, you may have to wait until the next year. While employer- and government-based health insurance plans offer special enroll-ment periods, pregnancy does not trigger special enrollment for government plans. Having a baby, however, does. So while you might not be able to get health insurance while pregnant, you can at least enroll your child once they are born. If you can't work full time, you may be able to find a company that offers health insurance to people who work a certain number of hours.

If you can't afford health insurance, you may qualify for coverage under your state's Medicaid or Children's Health Insurance Program (CHIP). State Medicaid programs are required to cover prenatal care, labor, and delivery. The requirements for Medicaid's pregnancy coverage are often dif-ferent from regular coverage, so if your income disqualified you in the past, you may qualify once you are pregnant. Guidelines vary by state and factors such as household income and size, age, and disability. Those who qualify for Medicaid are covered from pregnancy until 60 days after giving birth.

And unlike government-based health insurance plans, you can enroll in Medicaid and CHIP year-round. There is no shame in needing Medicaid or other government assistance. Medicaid covers approximately half of all US births.[4]

Unfortunately, try as you might, it's hard to prepare for everything ahead of time. Despite how financially prepared Jasmine was for her second pregnancy, she still faced a number of unexpected costs. Her twins were born at 25 weeks, necessitating a long newborn-intensive-care-unit stay. Then, six weeks after their birth, one of her daughters died, and Jasmine had to pay for a homegoing service while still grieving. "Even though we saved from the moment that I got pregnant and saved as much as we could to prepare for maternity leave, life keeps happening," Jasmine says. "There is no clear-cut answer of what you need to do to prepare for baby; no, *this is when you'll be ready*. You'll never be ready. The expenses keep coming."

> My ability to still be on my parents' health insurance was a huge factor because childbirth was 100 percent covered on my dad's work plan. I had my first daughter at 24 and will be having my second soon. I always assumed I would want kids. After I had my first daughter, I realized it was much more work financially and emotionally, which made two kids much more appealing than three.
>
> I enjoy parenthood, but I also enjoy time to myself. I am grateful to have my parents close by to come over to help me. I have responsibilities now that I never had before. I'm in a heterosexual marriage and as the mother, I feel like I do a lot more of the mental work. My husband works a lot to support us financially, so he is gone some evenings. It is a give-and-take type of setup, but it is what works for us right now. It definitely puts a strain on our relationship at times, especially when there are issues like teething, not sleeping, etc.
>
> **Hannah,** 26, Minnesota, she/her, lawyer,
> white, cisgender, straight, married

FIRST YEAR BABY EXPENSES

There are quite a few items you'll want to have on hand when your baby arrives. Below are the basic items your newborn needs. The prices listed reflect average costs for reputable brands and products (i.e., we're looking at the Toyotas of strollers, not the Teslas). We'll get to food, childcare, and other costs later.

Crib, crib mattress and protector, crib sheets: $360

Car-seat-compatible stroller: $230

Diapers and wipes: $60/month

Clothes: $60/month

First year total: $2,030

There are ways to lower the cost of all of the items on this list. If you have friends or family members with kids, ask for hand-me-downs. You can also find gently used baby essentials at places like GoodBuy Gear, eBay, Facebook Marketplace, and other secondhand stores. Some things, like car seats, you should not buy secondhand, especially if they are older than 10 years, as safety standards frequently change.

You can also cross some items off your list by creating a baby registry to send to family and friends. If you choose to have a registry, focus on things your child will need within the first three months. You can also have people contribute to a diaper fund or savings account.

How much you spend depends on your priorities. If you live in an urban area, you might want to spring for a lightweight stroller that is easier to carry on public transportation—and in that case, you might not need a car seat (though you will need one to take the baby home from the hospital).

There is even variability in the cost of diapers. A year of basic disposable diapers costs $600, while a premium diaper and wipe subscription service can set you back over $1,000. Reusable cloth diapers can be a less expensive option. Like disposable diapers, the cost depends on your preferences. Among the options are all-in-one cloth diapers ($18–$30 per diaper) and hybrid diapers ($12 for the cover and $8 for 100 flushable inserts). Of course, you have to factor in the cost of washing the diapers: trips to the laundromat or purchasing a washing machine if you don't have one, electricity to run the washing machine, detergent, and water. (Note: You can't just throw poop-soiled diapers into the wash. You'll need to scrape the poop into the toilet or use flushable liners. Technically, you're supposed to scrape the poop from disposable diapers into the toilet too.)

Want even more savings? You can skip diapers almost entirely and use elimination communication instead. Elimination communication, or EC, is a practice that essentially starts potty training from birth. You use cues from your baby, such as face scrunching or fussiness, during times in which they are most likely to pee or poop (like after feedings) and hold them over a bowl, sink, or baby potty so they can do their business. While this option may be the most affordable, it isn't free. You'll still want some spare diapers, wipes, and a newborn potty. It's also worth noting that if you send your child to daycare, the facility may have rules prohibiting cloth diapers or EC. The point is savings can be found everywhere. Sometimes it's a decision between convenience and cost. Yes, you can wipe almost the entire cost of diapers from your budget, but do you have the time to hold your child over a bowl every time they need to go to the bathroom for at least the first year of their life?

When we found out we were pregnant, we mostly just prepared by cutting back on all of our expenses, making note of things we didn't need. So even everyday things like haircuts, we cut back on that. My husband still cuts my hair to this day. We didn't spend money on clothes, we didn't eat out as much, and we were more purposeful with our meal planning. We cut out every category we could that wasn't essential, because we realized when we started looking at all of the baby products and necessities, we probably needed a lot more than what we were anticipating. We wanted to have children, so cutting back didn't really feel like much of a sacrifice.

I have a 3-year-old and an 8-month-old now. I breastfed our first child, so I didn't have to spend a lot of money on formula. But with our second, we chose to add in formula earlier on, and that expense has been a bit surprising. I never realized how costly formula is. We also didn't know that childcare costs so much money. We enrolled our first in childcare around 18 months, and that was expensive, about $1,400 a month. Fortunately, we found a local childcare subsidy that helped offset the cost. My best advice is to get as many things used as you can. We went to a yard sale and offered them $40 for 12 boxes of baby supplies, and the items were all good quality. I feel like a lot of times people just want to get rid of baby things, and babies don't really use things up to the point that they can't be used again.

Jacqueline, 38, Ontario, Canada, she/her, founder of Mom Money Map, Chinese-Indonesian-Canadian, cisgender, married

But what about all of the other baby supplies? Here are some additional items you'll likely want. Again, the prices represent average costs for reputable brands and products.

Baby carrier: $65

Baby monitor with camera: $130

Baby thermometer: $15

Bassinet: $120

Blankets: $25 for a set

Bouncy seat: $40

Burp cloths: $20 for a set

Changing table: $60

Diaper bag: $100

Diaper pail: $30

High chair: $80

Hooded towels: $15 for a set

Infant tub: $40

Mobile: $20

Nail clippers: $6

Nose aspirator: $16

Nursery glider: $200

Pacifiers: $5 for a set

Play mat: $70

Playpen: $60

Silicone bib: $12

Soap: $50 for the year

Toys and books: $360

Washcloths: $10 for a pack

Were you to buy everything on this list, you'd be spending an additional $1,549. This doesn't factor in needing multiples of the items above or the cost of designing a nursery and buying additional furniture. Fortunately, the American Academy of Pediatrics recommends having your baby sleep in your bedroom for at least the first six months of their life, preferably the first year, so if you don't have space or money to set up a nursery immediately, don't worry.

Now let's add on the cost of food and childcare. Your child will solely rely on breast milk or formula for at least the first six months of their life. After six months you can start introducing solids, but we'll get to that in a minute. A year of formula feeding costs, on average, $1,200 to $1,500.[5] Does that mean that nursing is free? Absolutely not. The Affordable Care Act requires that insurers cover the cost of a breast pump; however, your options through your insurer might be limited. A hands-free wearable breast pump will cost you $500, though less expensive versions are definitely available. Then there's the cost of bottles ($20 for a multipack), nipple cream ($10), and nursing bras ($30). If you can't breastfeed, and you can't afford formula, you may qualify for Women, Infants, and Children, or WIC, and/or the Supplemental Nutrition Assistance Program, or SNAP, two government programs that provide food and assistance to families.

Then, at around six months, you'll start introducing your baby to solids. Buying specialty baby food can cost anywhere from $50 to $120 a month, whereas baby-led weaning, which skips over purees, may be less expensive if your child mostly eats the same foods you do (just in handheld pieces). Or the prices might be comparable. One research study out of New Zealand found that baby-led weaning saved less than a dollar compared to traditional spoon-feeding.[6]

Childcare in the US is notoriously expensive. The US is one of only eight countries to have no mandated form of paid parental leave. The other seven countries are Papua New Guinea, Suriname, and five island nations in the Pacific Ocean—Micronesia, the Marshall Islands, Nauru, Palau, and Tonga.[7] A study of 22 countries found that happiness levels between parents and nonparents differ from country to country. Parents were less happy than their childfree counterparts in 14 of the 22 countries, with one country really standing out when it came to the gap in happiness. That country? The US, which had the largest gap due to the lack of policies that help parents balance work and life and virtually nonexistent public support for early education and childcare.[8]

You have three options, four if you're lucky, when it comes to childcare: one parent stays home, daycare, at-home childcare, or grandparents (or other retired family members). Having one parent stay at home likely isn't possible if you plan on being a single parent, unless you have a ton of money, which in that case, what are you doing reading this chapter? The best option is free childcare through a retired family member, but that only works if your relative lives nearby and is available.

Childcare is incredibly cost prohibitive. The US Department of Health and Human Services considers childcare affordable if it costs families no more than 7 percent of their household income.[9] However, a 2021 survey found that 85 percent of US parents spent 10 percent or more of their household income on childcare, and childcare costs nearly doubled in 2020.

Hiring a nanny is the most expensive childcare option. The average yearly cost for a nanny for one child is $31,824. Somewhat more feasible, at half the average price of a nanny, are childcare, or daycare, centers. A month of daycare for one child averages about $1,462, for a yearly cost of $17,680. If you have two young children, that cost balloons to $33,280.[10] Childcare costs also depend largely on where you live. These figures are the average costs for the US, but if you live in a rural area, it's likely cheaper, whereas if you live somewhere more urban, it's probably going to be more expensive.

Given the prohibitive cost of childcare, especially if you have multiple young children, it may make more economic sense for one parent to stay home. If one parent stays home, you lose the cost of childcare, but you also lose their salary. Unfortunately, salary losses often extend beyond the period in which you're unemployed. It can be hard to reenter the job market after taking years off. A study from 2014 found that if a 26-year-old woman earning the median salary for younger full-time workers took off five years to raise children, she would lose $467,000 over her career, reducing her lifetime earnings by 19 percent. A man in the same scenario would lose $596,000 over the course of his career, a 22 percent reduction in lifetime earnings.[11]

If you're thinking about having kids, take a look at how your workplace treats parents. Are there flexible policies in place? Work-from-home opportunities? You can also ask your coworkers about their experiences. If your workplace doesn't do a good job of accommodating parents, you can always consider switching employers if that's something you think would ultimately benefit you. Moms tend to feel less supported in the workplace when their children are young, so having a supportive workplace early on can help reduce parenting strain in those early years.[12]

You'll also want to figure out your company's parental leave policy. Queer families who feel supported by their workplaces experience decreased work-related stressors.[13] And the best outcomes occur when both parents can take a period of leave. For heterosexual couples, both parents are more satisfied when dads take paternity leave.[14] Sometimes companies only offer leave to parents who physically give birth or only offer less or unpaid leave to parents who build their families through adoption, surrogacy, or foster care. If you plan on building your family through adoption, foster care, or surrogacy, ask your company's human resources department what, if any, parental leave they offer.

If your company doesn't offer paid leave, you may qualify for 12 weeks of unpaid leave under the Family Medical Leave Act (FMLA). Unfortunately, small businesses do not fall under FMLA, and therefore, do not have to grant any sort of leave. If you work for a company with 50 or more employees in a 75-mile radius, and you worked at least 1,250 hours the previous year, the company must grant up to 12 weeks of unpaid leave. If your company offers a flexible savings account, or FSA, you can also save money in that fund pretax to help pay for any pregnancy-related medical costs.

Say you buy all of the first-year baby essentials listed above ($2,030), use basic diapers and wipes ($700), buy everything listed on the baby supply list above ($1,549), breastfeed using the pump provided by your insurance company ($150), and then at around six months start feeding your infant prepared baby foods ($500 in groceries for the remainder of the year), the cost of supplies and food for the first year would be about $4,929. Now let's add on the cost of childcare. Your workplace doesn't have a paid maternity leave, so you take 12 weeks of unpaid leave and then enroll your child in daycare, making the cost for the year (minus those 12 weeks) $13,600. That brings the cost of your child's first year of life to a whopping $18,529. (This is why people love baby showers and hand-me-downs!)

As much as you plan, you can't plan for everything. And it's not just the first year that's expensive, though the price of childcare tends to decrease significantly once kids start public school. However, the costs associated with kids shift as they grow, especially when it comes to the trends and tech kids learn to covet young.

Neither my husband nor I ever deeply wanted to have children. We always say things like "one day when we have kids," but we never set a time or age that we'd be ready to start trying. We're nowhere near ready to have kids financially or mentally but face a lot of pressure from family.

I grew up very poor. My dad would purposefully quit his job every few months so that my mom would have to work more and suffer. She worked two to three jobs to provide for me and my three siblings. We were on food stamps. I was 10 and knew how much money my parents would have to bring in for us to make rent. My mom would be stressed about finances and tell me, "I can't pay rent next month. I don't know what we're going to do. What if we end up on the street?" and then just walk out of my room. So I've always had this high-stress financial mentality. It's taken a really long time to trace it back and understand what it is. I'm scared of inflicting someone else with that kind of pain and trauma.

Hannah, 28, Canada, she/her, photographer, white, cisgender, married

FIGURING OUT YOUR FINANCES

It's understandable if you feel overwhelmed reading all of this. The good news is pregnancy, if all goes well, lasts nine months, which can buy you time to get in a more financially stable position. Before you start stressing over which kind of diapers to buy, you're going to want to assess where you are financially. If you plan on adopting, the adoption process can be just as lengthy, if not longer. And if you plan on adopting older kids, your costs will look entirely different.

First, do you have any money saved? Experts recommend having at least three months' worth of living expenses saved as an emergency fund. The more you can save, the better. But plenty of people make parenting work without having money saved, including Jasmine, who successfully parented her first child largely as a single mom for years. If you don't have money saved, look for ways to budget or cut back on expenses. While babies come with expenses, they also lead to cost cuts in other places. If you're someone who goes out for dinners and drinks with friends multiple times per month, once the baby comes, your mimosa fund becomes your diaper fund.

Once you have your child, you're going to want to add them to your health insurance or register them for their own health insurance. While pregnancy doesn't trigger a special enrollment period, childbirth does. You should also change your paycheck withholding to reflect that you have a dependent, which reduces the taxes taken from your paycheck. Depending on your household income and the policies for the year, you may be able to take advantage of two child tax credits to lower your tax bill. One of those credits, the child and dependent care tax credit, is meant to offset some of the costs of daycare, at-home childcare including babysitters, day and summer camps, before- and after-school programs, nursery school and pre-school, and services for disabled children.

Once your child arrives, you can help them save for college early or pay other educational expenses through a 529 plan, a tax-advantaged invest-ment account that grows and saves money for a variety of educational costs, including K–12 education, vocational school or apprenticeships, college, and graduate school. The account accrues earnings as it sits, growing the funds you add to it.

You should also consider getting life insurance. The cost of individual life insurance varies wildly by age, health, sex, and type of insurance (either term life, which covers you for a fixed amount of time, or permanent life, which covers you until you die). Some companies offer life insurance group policies for employees and subsidize much of the cost. If you aren't using an employer-subsidized plan, it might make sense to buy young since age and health factor into the cost. Term life plans tend to be less expensive because they expire. If your plan expires before you do, you don't get the money back, but these insurance policies can help you ensure some money is left to your children if you die before they reach adulthood.

As much as you may want to provide for your kids, giving them a "good life" is about so much more than the amount of money in your bank account. As Jasmine recalls, "My son asked, 'Mom, do you think we live a rich life?' And I said, 'Yeah.' 'Well, how much money?' he asked. And I said, 'No, I'm not talking about money. I have a healthy family, we have shelter, we have food—that's a rich life.'"

I cannot wait to have kids and be a mom. I'm engaged, and while we don't want to put pressure on ourselves to have a kid right away, we're definitely open to start trying or just start prepping after the wedding. As funny as it sounds, we've been financially planning for kids for years. I knew I wanted to pay off the $36,000 I had in debt before having kids. I stuck to that goal and paid it off. I then went on to create an emergency fund and save for different things. Although not directly related to having a kid, I knew that I wanted to be in a certain financial place to have a child and not be stressed about finances. We're being selfish now financially, hitting our own financial goals, so we can be ready for when we want to have kids. We want to have three to four kids in an ideal world, but we're also really open to adoption, which comes with its own price tag.

Chloe, 25, Missouri, she/her, founder of Deeper Than Money, white, cisgender, straight, engaged

9

IS PASSING ON YOUR GENES REALLY THE BEST THING?

"THIS IS THE GENETICS reveal for our baby," Rachel, 32, says, smiling proudly at the camera. Behind her and her husband, Greg, are giant letters, almost as tall as they are, that spell out the word "baby" and a balloon arch with white and green balloons intertwining.

"The colors you see are green and white," Rachel, who is seven months pregnant, explains. "Green is the color of dwarfism awareness . . . and there's actually no average height awareness or anything, so we're just choosing white."

Rachel and Greg are little people. Both were born with achondroplasia, the genetic condition most commonly associated with dwarfism. Growing up, Rachel, one of six, and Greg, one of two, were the only little people in their families. The two met in 2014, when they both were 26, at the Little People of America conference in San Diego. Greg was there to socialize. Rachel, on the other hand, was all business. She came to study the marital attitudes of little people for her college capstone course. Greg was more interested in chatting than taking a survey. But as fate, and irony, would have it, within a year the two were married.

Achondroplasia is caused by a mutation in the FGFR3 gene. In most cases it's spontaneous, arising from a new mutation as opposed to being inherited.

Approximately 80 percent of people with achondroplasia have average-sized parents. The other 20 percent have parents like Rachel and Greg.[1]

The condition follows an autosomal dominant pattern, which, as you may remember from your high school biology class, means you only need one copy of the altered gene to have the condition. Both Rachel and Greg carry one altered copy of the FGFR3 gene, which means there are three potential outcomes for their children: a 25 percent chance their child is average height with no copies of the altered gene, a 50 percent chance their child is a little person with one copy of the altered gene, and a 25 percent chance their child is a little person with two copies of the altered gene—a pattern of inheritance that is often fatal.

Rachel's first daughter is average-sized with zero copies of the mutated gene. As for Rachel's second daughter, that's what friends, family, and Rachel's social media followers were watching to find out.

As soon as Greg pulls the tab on the smoke cannon, Rachel's sister, the event's camerawoman, giggles in delight. Green smoke quickly envelops the beaming couple. "That's so cool," her sister squeals. "Congratulations, guys! Little baby!"

The news was not a surprise to Rachel, who knew her daughter would be born with achondroplasia well before the smoke and light-up signs. Around week 25 of pregnancy, her daughter's measurements began falling behind what doctors typically expect. The genetics reveal wasn't meant to be a surprise, it was designed to celebrate their daughter in a way often denied to people whose lives differ from the aspirational norm. And just as Rachel intended, there was no sadness that day.

AS LONG AS THEY'RE HEALTHY

What constitutes a life worth living? Ask five people that question and you'll likely get five different answers. South African philosopher David Benatar believes we'd all be better off if we were never born. In his book *Better Never to Have Been: The Harm of Coming into Existence*, Benatar argues, "While good people go to great lengths to spare their children from suffering, few of them seem to notice that the one (and only) guaranteed way to prevent all the suffering of their children is not to bring those children into existence in the first place."

Taken as a whole, the antinatalist belief that life is full of suffering and therefore, not worth living, might seem a bit extreme, but we know the underpinnings well. Most of society already subscribes to the belief that it's wrong to have kids if their lives would be worse than a "typical human life." We extend this belief largely to kids who would be born into poverty, "unsafe" homes, and disabled bodies. It's acceptable to refrain from having children if you know they'll experience hardship, but how do you define hardship?

If you ask someone like Benatar, life itself is hardship. Most humans have to work to survive, we get sick, we age—life is predominantly bad. "We infrequently contemplate the harms that await any new-born child—pain, disappointment, anxiety, grief, and death," Benatar writes. "For any given child we cannot predict what form these harms will take or how severe they will be, but we can be sure that at least some of them will occur. None of this befalls the nonexistent. Only existers suffer harm."[2]

But most people don't think of hardship in such broad terms. Instead, we define hardship by comparing our life experiences to those we view as less fortunate. By "counting our blessings," we're really just counting an absence of hardships.

Rachel knows an average-sized parent wouldn't be able to celebrate having a little child the way she did. They have to grieve the life they thought their child would have, a life without the perceived hardship of "being different." But as a little person who frequently fields questions from average-height parents with little children and hurtful comments from trolls, she feels a responsibility to share that lives like hers are worth living.

"People will say, 'How dare you pass on your genetics to another person?' And honestly, I don't see the world that way," Rachel says. "The term *normal* is relative to your life experience; there is no standard for normal. It's sad that people make the assumption my life isn't worth living. I haven't suffered: I lived in New York City, I graduated college with honors, I've had work published in national magazines, I'm married. I have a life worth living."

While it's natural to want to protect your child from hardship, only you can decide what counts as suffering. For example, if you grew up poor, you might wait for financial stability before having children because you want their childhoods to look different from yours. Other people want financial stability, not because they've been poor, but because they want their children's lives to look like what they know. And then there are folks who choose to have children without sufficient financial means. If they feel ready to become parents, are they selfish for choosing to raise children in a way that mirrors the life they know?

Like the financial example above, deciding whether or not to pass down a health condition depends not only on your experience but how you measure a life worth living.

> The US has a real shitty maternal mortality rate and I like the woman I married. We also have some minor hereditary issues that we don't want to pass on given the punitive cost of health care.
>
> **Jake,** 31, California, he/him, white, cisgender, straight, married

DETERMINING YOUR RISK OF PASSING DOWN HEALTH CONDITIONS

If you want to understand your risk of passing down a health condition, the best place to start is with a family tree. The more information you have about your family's medical history, the better, says genetic counselor Dena Goldberg, MS, LCGC.

When Dena counsels patients, she wants to know about everyone in their family, not just their parents. For each family member, you should know whether they are living or deceased, as well as any major or minor health issues, what age those problems started, and if anyone has a history of miscarriages or stillbirths. (For deceased family members, you'll also want to gather their age and cause of death.) Collecting all of this information can help you identify patterns that may be relevant to your health as well as the health of any potential children. And since your child inherits half their DNA from each parent, you'll want your partner's or donor's family history as well.

Of course, like Rachel and Greg's achondroplasia, not all conditions are inherited. Some arise from de novo, or new, mutations. These mutations play a role in a variety of disorders, from rare genetic conditions such as achondroplasia to more common complex disorders like autism and schizophrenia. Why these mutations occur is still somewhat of a mystery, but advanced parental age and environmental factors are thought to play a role.[3]

A genetic counselor, like Dena, can help you make sense of your risks based on your family tree. Thanks to telehealth, finding a genetic counselor these days is easy. It just requires a bit of googling or a referral from your doctor. Most insurance plans cover genetic counseling. Without insurance coverage, the price is typically less than several hundred dollars.

Although direct-to-consumer genetic testing may seem appealing, Dena advises avoiding services that provide health reports along with information about your ancestry. "The technology they use is really great for ancestry, but it's not sequencing," Dena says. "It's really only looking at very specific sites along very specific genes, and so it is in no way comprehensive for any condition."

A genetic counselor can help you find tests that screen for certain genes like the panels that assess breast cancer risk. You can also opt for carrier screening, which tests you and your partner for a variety of recessive diseases.

Recessive diseases follow a pattern of inheritance you may remember from the Punnett squares you made in biology class. Take cystic fibrosis, for example. You need a copy of the recessive cystic fibrosis gene from both parents to have the condition yourself. If you carry one copy of the gene, and your partner carries one copy of the gene, neither of you have cystic fibrosis, but you have a 25 percent chance of having a child with the condition. If you carry a copy of the gene but your partner does not, you have a close to 0 percent chance of having a child with cystic fibrosis.

Both partners don't always need to do carrier screening. If one partner undergoes testing and learns they are a carrier, the other partner should also be screened for that gene mutation to assess the risk of passing down the condition. Basic carrier screening tests for dozens of conditions, most of which are fatal. Expanded carrier screening tests for nearly 300 conditions, some of which do not affect life expectancy.

The first fertility clinic I went to required couples carrier screening before starting treatments, a fairly standard requirement for clinics. My test revealed that I carry the gene mutation for nonsyndromic hearing loss, a leading cause of deafness, and so my partner was tested as well. As it turns out, we both carry the gene mutation. There are no Deaf or hard of hearing people in our families, so we had no way of knowing our carrier status without the test. Together, we have a 25 percent chance of having a child with some form of hearing loss.

We decided we are okay with that risk. I spent five years learning sign language when I was younger. Part of learning any language is learning the history and the culture that comes with it. Deaf people have a rich culture; their lives are no less because they can't hear. To me, choosing not to have a Deaf child feels in line with eugenics. If we both carried gene mutations that ensured nothing except a horrible early death for our child, we would select embryos without that faulty gene. But we won't select an embryo based on its future ability to hear. That is our choice. It's also why we ultimately left that fertility clinic: because they wouldn't let us proceed with treatment unless we signed a form that said we were going against medical advice, and that wasn't the environment I wanted to conceive a child in.

If you and your partner carry one of the conditions detected by carrier screening, you can do IVF and test the embryos you create using preimplantation genetic testing for monogenic, or single-gene, disorders (PGT-M). PGT-M tells you which embryos have the condition you carry, allowing you to choose which embryos you want to transfer.

What you do with the results is up to you. Although the examples I highlight here focus on letting nature decide what happens, Samantha, 27, who is in the process of doing IVF with the intention of becoming a single mother by choice, chose a sperm donor *without* the gene for spinal muscular atrophy, or SMA, a condition she lives with, so she wouldn't pass it down to her child. And Victoria, who you'll meet in the surrogacy chapter, used PGT-M to select embryos that didn't have Marfan syndrome, a condition she herself has.

Making parenting decisions based on genetics isn't easy. Part of the reason Dena chose not to work in a prenatal setting was because her sister has a chromosomal abnormality, and counseling couples who might want to terminate a pregnancy with the same genetic disorder as her sister might have been difficult for her.

But carrier screening isn't just about avoiding passing down conditions. It's a tool you can use to better prepare for a child who may have health challenges. "Carrier screening isn't just for purposes of termination, but more for information in preparation of your child's birth," Dena says. "For example, learning that you may have a child with an inborn error of metabolism empowers you to start them on a certain enzyme or avoid certain chemicals early enough, which, in some cases, can be the difference between organ damage and living a healthy life."

There are also tests that can screen for chromosomal abnormalities such as Down syndrome, an intellectual disability caused by a third copy of chromosome 21, during pregnancy. Most of the conditions tested during pregnancy are the result of chromosomal errors in the egg or sperm as opposed to inherited conditions. You can also screen for chromosomal abnormalities in embryos using preimplantation genetic testing for aneuploidies, or PGT-A.

"No matter what anyone tells you, unfortunately, there's no way to guarantee having a completely healthy pregnancy or completely healthy baby," Dena says. "There are a lot of things that can come up, both genetic and nongenetic, but we can use these tools to try and mitigate that risk if possible. Most of the common diseases that people ask about, like mental illness, diabetes, heart disease, we just don't have enough information now to be able to predict."

GENES VS. ENVIRONMENT

Things get a bit tricky when it comes to passing down more common conditions like mental illness and heart disease—polygenic diseases that arise from multiple genes.

"If there's a condition and only one person in the family has it, we do a test for all the syndromes and if they're negative, we assume that it's probably caused by multiple genes and environment working together or something straight up environmental that we just haven't figured out yet," Dena says.

There's a lot we don't know about polygenic conditions, and there are some conditions we don't understand the genetics of at all. Not to mention, genes don't always equate to illness. A great example of this is mental illness.

Depression has a genetic component. Biological children of depressed parents have twice the risk for major depressive disorder and other mental illnesses compared to children whose parents don't have depression. The risk increases if you have both a depressed parent and grandparent.[4] But genetics only tell part of the story here. The other half depends on your environment.

Psychiatry and medical genetic counselor Jehannine Austin, PhD, CGC, explains this concept using what she calls a "mental illness jar." Essentially, you develop a mental illness when your jar is full. The contents of that jar are a combination of genetic and environmental factors. Everyone has some genetic vulnerability to mental illness. For the sake of this example, let's say genetic risk factors make it so that your jar is half full. Without environmental factors to fill up the rest of your jar, you can go your entire life without experiencing mental illness despite having the genetic risk factors. Of course, it's not always possible to avoid chronic stressors like financial woes or family problems. These environmental factors can add to your jar to the point where you develop depression or anxiety. There's good news though. You can modify your jar. Protective factors like a good social support system and rest can help prevent symptoms if your jar fills up.[5]

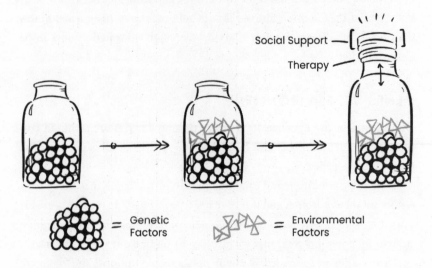

New tests claim they have the ability to assess an embryo's risk of certain polygenic conditions like schizophrenia and diabetes, but buyer beware. The research behind these tests is not even that accurate, Dena says. "We don't have enough information to give those scores, and the scores are only helpful for certain races." In the future, we'll likely be able to assess the risk of many more conditions including polygenic ones, but the science just isn't there yet.

Still, the complicated relationship between genes and the environment gives you much more control over both your and your child's health than you think. You may not be able to select their genes, but you can do your best to make sure they grow up in a loving and supportive environment so they have the protective factors to handle whatever comes their way. Ultimately, it's worth remembering you can't protect your child from everything. There is no genetic test that predicts the likelihood of being in a car accident or getting your heart broken, and maybe that's a good thing.

I haven't decided whether I want kids. I have an autoimmune disease that is very rare and not fully understood, and I worry about passing along a condition that could lower a child's quality of life. I am on medications that are known to cause birth defects, so I'm further concerned about the timelines required for the medication half-life before being able to safely carry a child, and I worry about whether I'll reach remission when I'm still of childbearing age.

I come from a very sentimental family. We are very interested in family history, and I think I could regret not feeling like I'm continuing our family legacy by continuing our family tree and creating new stories to cherish and share and continuing our existing family storytelling with the next generation. I also worry about missing out on what many say is the most rewarding life experience in the world. I am a very loving and empathetic person, and I could see myself wishing I had children in whom I could invest those caring instincts. My partner and I are also both creative people (he is a musician, and I'm an artist), and it would probably be sad to not be able to share those passions with children.

Hannah, 30, Massachusetts, she/her, graduate student, white, cisgender, straight

10

YOU'RE
CONCERNED
YOU MIGHT NOT BE
A GOOD PARENT

PARENTING ISN'T SOMETHING WE'RE explicitly taught, but it is something we learn—for better or worse—by virtue of watching our parents raise us. If you want to know what you'll be like as a parent, start by looking at your parents. Research shows that upbringing is one of the most powerful predictors of parenting behavior.[1] But if your parents weren't great, does that mean you're doomed to be a bad parent?

Azmia Magane, whom you met in chapter 3, grew up largely without her parents. If anyone raised her, it was her grandparents. Though Azmia remembers her grandparents fondly, the experience of being abandoned by her actual parents still leaves a scar. "For a long time, I didn't want kids because I was afraid that there was something wrong with me and that I would pass that down to my child or that if I had a child, I would screw them up," Azmia says. "It wasn't until my late 20s when I had really done a lot of healing work around my abandonment issue that I realized I was a child and not responsible for the relationship or the parental abandonment, but it took me many years, and it still really makes me angry."

You're not destined to repeat your parents' failings. The fact that you can recognize your parents' shortcomings as "things to avoid" suggests you'll be a better parent than you might think. It took Azmia years, and a lot of hard work, before she realized her parents' behavior didn't have to predict hers.

A number of factors may influence how parents respond to their children, including gender norms and characteristics of the parent. Several studies have shown that parents are more likely to put up with difficult sons than difficult daughters.[2] Meanwhile, a different study found mothers provided more maternal care to hard-to-soothe girls than they did boys.[3] And when you throw social supports, like help from family or public childcare assistance, into the mix, challenging situations tend to become a lot more manageable. The point is there are so many factors that go into parenting, it's impossible to predict what kind of parent you'll be. And while that might seem kind of scary, it's actually a good thing! It means your future isn't written in stone.

> I don't really know if I want kids. I come from a physically and sexually abusive background, and never had an example of family without abuse, so I don't know if I'm even cut out for it. I told my wife when we were engaged that I thought I was okay with having a child since that's all she wants, but it fucking terrifies me. After 10 years of sexual abuse, I kind of just want to live my life carefree in a way kids don't afford. It's selfish, and I'm sure I'll have a kid with my wife. I just don't want to resent her or the kid.
>
> **Patrick,** 32, New York, he/him,
> cisgender, straight, married

WHAT OUR PARENTS PASS DOWN

Parenting is in many ways inherited. This goes for both "positive" and "negative" models of parenting. There is a learned component—our parents act in ways that shape our experiences and perception of the world—and a genetic component—we inherit genes that influence the way we interact with our environment. Parents can pass down maladaptive parenting strategies both directly and indirectly. A study of Mexican-origin mothers in the US found that poor parenting strategies can pass through generations from grandparents to parents and down to their kids.[4] Moms who report more maltreatment in childhood also tend to be less sensitive with their infants and experience greater parenting stress.[5]

When we think of bad parenting, we often think of extreme examples of abuse or neglect, but bad parenting is not always easily distinguishable. Inconsistent, insensitive, and hostile parenting behaviors are enough to decrease childhood well-being, too. Our parents' actions within the first years of our lives set in motion our desire and capacity to care for others. The developing brains of young children are highly sensitive to the world around them, allowing for the rapid development of language, cognitive, and emotional skills. During childhood, we learn what it feels like to be cared for and internalize our parents' caregiving behaviors. Healthy parent-child relationships—ones where our parents are available and provide safety and support—teach us that we deserve love and promote secure attachment.

Your attachment style, which we discussed in chapter 2, can affect how you parent. Parents with insecure attachment styles tend to struggle more with the stresses of raising children and are less likely to exhibit sensitive, supportive, and responsive parenting behaviors. Parents with insecure attachments also tend to have a hard time regulating their emotions, which can make it harder to show empathy, compassion, and forgiveness. And mothers with avoidant or anxious attachment styles report feeling less emotional closeness with their children.[6] Insecure attachment styles can also predict how your children will interact with you. Insecurely attached parents tend to have insecure children, though this tends to come out later in childhood as opposed to the infant years, which can repeat the generational cycle.[7] And when attachment styles form within the context of trauma, it can have a lasting impact on relationships. A history of childhood trauma can impair your ability to accurately read and respond to your child's emotions.

While this all might sound like horrible news, with the right resources, you can arm yourself with the skills you need to parent effectively. Take Andrea, 32, for example. Andrea always knew she wanted to be a mom. Growing up in a conservative Christian family with a stay-at-home mom, Andrea never really considered any options other than motherhood. But there was one thing she knew she wanted to do differently from her parents: she didn't want to pass her trauma down. Even though she knew she wanted to have kids, it took years of therapy before she felt ready. "I was hoping for that parent-child relationship I didn't get as a kid, but you can't put pressure on your kid to do that healing for you; you have to do that for yourself," Andrea says. "It is a very rewarding relationship being a mom, but I still have to work on myself. In addition to parenting my child, I have to continue parenting myself to make up for the parents I didn't get as a kid. You can't go into it thinking kids will fix your problems. I went to therapy and found other people in my life, like my partner and my friends, to help me."

I decided I was ready to parent when I was 32. I was raised in an abusive family, so I never thought I would have children. I didn't feel like I was prepared to be a human, much less a parent. It was only when I established a nonfamilial community with good role models, as well as a doctor with whom I felt comfortable and safe, did I begin to feel the urge to become a parent. I will say that I felt jealous when others became parents.

I do enjoy parenthood. There is joy in seeing a person grow and mature with your help. I can't imagine my life at this point without my son. Becoming a parent changed my life in many ways. I became more staunchly feminist and aware of social issues. I felt so much more confident in myself, my body, and my abilities in the workplace. There are challenges that come with being a parent, of course. It's triggering for me when my son starts irrationally yelling at me. It brings up so much childhood trauma and makes it very hard for me to soothe myself.

Kelli, 41, Ohio, she/her, works part-time at a nonprofit, white, cisgender, straight

THE ROLE OF TRAUMA

Childhood trauma can affect every aspect of your life including your desire to become a parent. A study of more than 8,000 English families found that mothers who experienced sexual abuse early in their lives were less interested in becoming mothers. Those who ultimately became mothers had weaker parenting skills, less confidence, and struggled with emotional control in parenting situations.[8]

Between 1995 and 1997 the Centers for Disease Control and Prevention (CDC) and Kaiser Permanente conducted a study that changed the way we think about childhood trauma. Through surveys and physical examinations of over 17,000 people in California, researchers found that adverse events in childhood predicted negative health outcomes like heart disease, depression, and cancer. Those who experience four or more adverse events had 4 to 12 times the risk of alcoholism, drug abuse, depression, and suicide attempts, and were more likely to rate their health as poor.[9]

Adverse childhood experiences (ACEs) are common. More than half of adults have experienced at least one type of ACE, and nearly one in six report experiencing four or more types of ACEs. Women, racial and sexual minority groups, and people from low socioeconomic backgrounds are more likely to experience adverse events.[10] If you're curious what your ACE score might be, take a look at the list below. Adverse childhood events include experiencing any of the following before the age of 18:

Physical abuse	Mental illness in a household member
Emotional abuse	Witnessing your mother being abused
Sexual abuse	Substance abuse in a household member
Physical neglect	Having an incarcerated family member
Emotional neglect	Parents divorcing

Since the initial ACE study, thousands of researchers have used the ACE framework to build upon our understanding of the role childhood trauma plays throughout the life span. Children exposed to early adverse events that disrupt bonding and attachment have a higher risk of developing anxiety, depression, and other stress-induced illnesses throughout their lives.

They're also more likely to adopt parenting behaviors that continue the cycle of abuse. It's important to note that while experiencing abuse as a child can increase your risk of abusing your child, the vast majority of people who've been physically or sexually abused do *not* abuse their children.[11]

More recent research also ties ACE scores to parenting outcomes. The more ACEs experienced early in life, the greater a mother's current parenting stress is likely to be. Researchers believe this parenting stress might come from issues with the body's stress-response system as a result of traumatic experiences. The brain changes with childhood trauma, and it also changes during the transition to parenthood. And early brain changes may in turn affect later ones.[12] Parents with greater ACE scores are also more likely to have children with behavioral health problems.[13]

Ultimately, how we respond to adversity depends on a whole host of factors including our genes. In the previous chapter, we talked about the jar model of genetic expression. The same sort of principle applies here. The environment you grew up in plays a role, genes play a role, and interventions play a role. One of the best ways to reduce adversity early in life is through societal change and policies that help eradicate poverty and educational disparities. Though early interventions are the best way to reduce negative outcomes in childhood, social supports and counseling can also help later in life. Emotional regulation, impulse control, and stress management—skills that make for good parenting—are all teachable. Just because you didn't learn them as a child doesn't mean you can't learn them as an adult. And there are lots of protective factors you can put in place to help your kids. Children excel when they are in safe, stable, and nurturing environments and have positive relationships with peers, adult role models, and caregivers. Doing well in school is also a protective factor, as is having a parent who has a college degree or higher and steady employment.[14]

> Growing up, I always wanted children. However, I don't want my children to suffer the trauma of absent parenting or limited food that I did. My wife is deaf, and her parents and family did not learn sign language even

though that is how she exclusively communicates. We have talked about possibly adopting or fostering Deaf or hard of hearing children since we both know sign language and work in the Deaf education system. We know there is a need in this area, and many typical families pass on children with differing abilities. Many straight couples take for granted their ease in having children.

Danielle, 28, Minnesota, she/her, teacher, white, cisgender, pansexual, married

WHAT MAKES A GOOD PARENT?

There are so many parenting philosophies out there today, picking one can feel overwhelming. However, good parenting doesn't require any flashy tricks. What children need is a nurturing, safe, and consistent environment. But if you didn't grow up in an environment that made you feel safe and cared for, you may feel lost when it comes to cultivating that for your children.

For Andrea, the biggest parenting challenge has been dealing with emotions and learning how to respond when her child cries. "I struggle with letting myself feel emotions, because it was not allowed growing up. If I cried as a kid, I would be shamed for crying," she says. "I've had to learn how to give my daughter space to have her emotions without minimizing how she's feeling. I definitely catch myself sometimes minimizing her when she's crying because it's hard to hear your kid cry. You want to fix it, so you'll say something like 'you're fine.' I definitely don't go so far as my parents did when I was a kid, but I do see myself starting to go in that direction a little bit. And then I have to catch myself and think, *Maybe she is hurt or startled. I'm not in her head. I don't know how she's feeling.* And I remember just how awful it felt when my parents would minimize my feelings about something, and I don't want to do that to her."

Developmental psychologist Diana Baumrind, PhD, came up with a system that describes the ways parents attempt to control their children. Baumrind identified three different styles: permissive, authoritarian, and authoritative.[15] A fourth style, indifferent or neglectful, was later added by Eleanor Maccoby, PhD, and John Martin, PhD.[16] These parenting styles were then ranked by how demanding and responsive parents are. The main traits of each style are shown in the image below.

The Four Parenting Styles

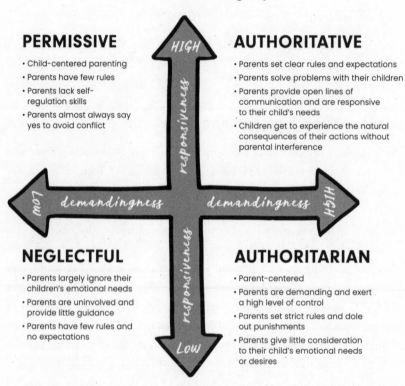

PERMISSIVE

- Child-centered parenting
- Parents have few rules
- Parents lack self-regulation skills
- Parents almost always say yes to avoid conflict

AUTHORITATIVE

- Parents set clear rules and expectations
- Parents solve problems with their children
- Parents provide open lines of communication and are responsive to their child's needs
- Children get to experience the natural consequences of their actions without parental interference

NEGLECTFUL

- Parents largely ignore their children's emotional needs
- Parents are uninvolved and provide little guidance
- Parents have few rules and no expectations

AUTHORITARIAN

- Parent-centered
- Parents are demanding and exert a high level of control
- Parents set strict rules and dole out punishments
- Parents give little consideration to their child's emotional needs or desires

If you disagree with the way your parents raised you, take a minute and identify their parenting style. Which parenting style reflects your upbringing? Which parenting style would you prefer? Trauma, again, plays a role when it comes to picking a parenting style. Mothers who experience symptoms of trauma are more likely to parent using authoritarian or permissive approaches.[17] But the ideal style, according to research is, you probably guessed it, authoritative parenting.[18] Authoritative parenting builds accountability, independence, and resiliency. Parents use inductive discipline to explain to children the consequences of their behaviors, which teaches their children kindness and empathy and promotes self-regulation.[19] They also use emotion coaching to help their kids understand and face strong emotions. Instead of telling children not to feel their feelings, like Andrea's parents did, emotion coaching validates feelings and helps children verbalize their emotions.[20]

Earlier in this book we talked about the pressure parents face to parent perfectly. Perfection is an unrealistic standard. You are going to make mistakes; everyone does. That doesn't mean you won't be a great parent, if you decide parenting is something you want to do. Parenthood is a lot of work, but it's with the unspoken assumption that the work starts once the kids arrive. In a lot of ways, that sets you up for failure, especially if you're someone who thinks they might want to have kids but fears they won't be a good parent. The work doesn't have to start once you get a positive pregnancy test or decide to open your home to a child. You can start preparing for parenthood whenever you want. Take a class, learn about different parenting styles, think about the type of parent you might want to be. But the best place to start, especially if you have unresolved trauma, is inward. Learn to regulate your emotions and develop your ability to cope with stress. Not only will it benefit you, but you'll also get to pass those same skills down to your children and perhaps their children, too.

> I lost my father after Christmas 2020, which jolted me from not wanting kids by choice to realizing I do want a family, but I still feel unsure sometimes. When I was a teen, I decided I didn't want kids due to the fear of passing down generational trauma. I wanted to be a successful artist living on my own and self-sufficient. Then, in my 20s, I met my partner, and we started dating. That's when I started to consider what having a family might be like.
>
> I've always heard the negative things about raising kids: the things you have to give up, the lack of sleep that

makes you more likely to yell. I wanted more time to work on my past family traumas and find what makes me happy before I committed to possibly never having the chance to figure that out.

I didn't think I would regret not having kids until my father's death. I realized I wanted to share my parenting experience with my parents to have that connection. Maybe that's a missing element to healing those past family traumas, in addition to my years of therapy.

Maryann, 36, New York, they/them, self-employed, nonbinary, pansexual, married

11

YOU'RE AFRAID OF PREGNANCY OR CHILDBIRTH

MEGAN ROSE DICKEY, 32, doesn't like being uncomfortable. It might sound like a strange statement; after all, who likes discomfort? But when she thinks about having children and the changes it would bring, she can't help but think about how uncomfortable it all seems. Megan, a journalist, lives with her partner, Katie, an engineer, in San Francisco. They've been together for two and a half years and have discussed having children but have no immediate plans to do so.

Megan's dislike of discomfort isn't unwarranted. Childbirth is notoriously painful, and Megan, who is six years sober, fears pharmaceutical pain management would threaten her sobriety. Epidurals commonly include fentanyl to balance out the numbing agents and allow birthing people the ability to move in bed during labor. It's also fairly common to get a prescription for opioids following childbirth. A study of 308,226 deliveries found that 27 percent of birthing people who delivered vaginally and 75.7 percent of those who had cesarean sections filled a prescription for opioids following childbirth. Among those prescribed opioids, 1.7 percent of those with vaginal deliveries and 2.2 percent with cesarean deliveries developed new persistent opioid use.[1]

In Megan's ideal world, Katie, 31, would carry their child; something Katie is open to. But the decision-making is complicated. Would they use Katie's eggs and a sperm donor? Who would the sperm donor be? Megan's brother, perhaps, or a Black donor from a sperm bank—a demographic sperm banks often lack. And do they even want to have a biracial baby since neither Megan nor Katie knows what it's like to be biracial? Megan would feel more comfortable parenting a Black child, which means using Megan's eggs and a Black sperm donor, but if Katie carries, that means doing costly IVF. For right now, it's all hypothetical, but what Megan does know is that she doesn't want to be the one to get pregnant.

Here's the thing: Not everyone dreams of pregnancy and childbirth. Fear, apprehension, even disgust (Come on, mucus plug? I mean, seriously.) are all relatively normal feelings. If you have a history of disordered eating or body dysmorphia, pregnancy can trigger weight-related concerns. For those who are trans, nonbinary, or gender nonconforming, pregnancy may lead to gender dysphoria. If you're a Black birthing person, the abysmal Black maternal mortality rate might leave you feeling terrified. Then there's tokophobia, a psychological fear of pregnancy. There are so many reasons to be less than enthused about the prospect of giving birth, you don't have to justify it.

The problem is we don't often get space to express these concerns. During interviews for this book, I mentioned to one doctor that a lot of folks I interviewed expressed concerns about giving birth. Her response: "Everyone says that, but by the end of pregnancy you'll be so ready to be done, and so eager to meet your baby, those fears will pretty much disappear." While that may be true—research shows feelings about a pregnancy change over time, generally becoming more positive between conception and birth and in the postpartum period—statements like that probably don't ease your anxiety.[2] They're dismissive. In fact, a lot of the way we talk about pregnancy and childbirth is. First, there's the gendered language around pregnancy that's not only exclusionary but idealizes pregnancy and motherhood as the most important thing one could ever hope to do with their life. Then, there's the competitive language that leads childbearing folks to believe they're a failure if they don't have a vaginal birth and breastfeed. Not to mention, the "no pain, no gain" mentality of just telling birthing people to tough it out and normalizing valid concerns as worth it for your "bundle of joy." This chronic invalidation doesn't ease people's concerns; it just stops them from expressing them.

Both my husband and I always wanted to have children. We are both teachers, so we like kids, and on some level there are also the assumed societal norms, too. I gave birth to our son right before we both turned 30. My pregnancy was blessedly easy. No sickness and barely any nausea, only uncomfortable toward the end. Birth was an intense but empowering experience. I was induced because he was a week overdue. I had an epidural and the whole process was about 18 hours. I was very nervous about childbirth. Lots of breathing and positive mantras helped. In hindsight, navigating the early times of parenting was far more difficult than childbirth.

Christina, 32, Oregon, she/her, teacher, Asian/
Hawaiian/white, cisgender, straight

UNDERSTANDING YOUR CHANGING BODY

During my first round of IVF, I googled "Do you really have to gain weight when pregnant?" I wanted so badly to be pregnant, but the reality of gaining weight during pregnancy found me spiraling into an old disordered eating mindset. Here I was spending thousands of dollars trying to conceive while searching for ways to avoid pregnancy weight gain—and I wasn't even pregnant! I felt ridiculous.

A few months later I brought up my weight gain concerns to a friend who was starting to think about having kids. "It's messed up that I would even think that way," I said, bracing for criticism. She was silent and then replied, "I think about that, too."

Identifying where the weight comes from helped me understand why weight gain is necessary during pregnancy. Growing a human is a full-body job. Even if you follow medical guidelines for eating well and exercising during pregnancy, you're still going to gain weight. Here's how it breaks down by the end of pregnancy:[3]

- Baby: 7.5 pounds

- Increased breast volume: 1 to 3 pounds

- Uterine growth: 2 pounds

- Placenta: 1.5 pounds

- Amniotic fluid: 2 pounds

- Increased blood volume: 3 to 4 pounds

- Increased fluid volume: 2 to 3 pounds

- Fat stores: 6 to 8 pounds

So no, pregnancy weight gain isn't from the late-night ice cream and pickle binges. It's your body doing demanding work. (Note: No matter what your weight is, doctors advise against losing weight during pregnancy as it can hamper the baby's growth and development. So don't beat yourself up if you don't fit the model scenario. Let your body do its job.) Still, thinking about your body changing, even if you know that four pounds of it is blood, can feel terrifying. Research shows pregnancy is a fraught time for folks with a history of disordered eating. The first 20 weeks of pregnancy and the first eight weeks postpartum pose the highest risk of relapse for those with a history of eating disorders. Those who relapsed were also more likely to experience severe symptoms of postpartum depression.[4]

An active history of eating disorders can also make it hard to get pregnant. Being underweight can stop menstruation and disrupt fertility. Fey, 29, spent over a year in a treatment facility for anorexia as a teenager. Though she considers herself largely recovered today, pregnancy is a concern, not just because her body will change, but because she might pass down the disorder or might not even be able to have kids. "I was always sort of afraid that I fucked my body up," Fey says. "What if I'm not even able to have children? My mother keeps reminding me I'm turning 30 soon. She's Mexican, so she's desperate to be a grandmother, and while she respects me and everything, I can feel the pressure growing. It's been so hard to build a positive relationship with my body, I'm just terrified it's all going to go to hell."

The birthing world can also be a hostile space for larger bodies. Larger people are often told their pregnancies are high risk before their doctor even examines them. While plus-size folks tend to have a higher risk of gestational diabetes, C-section, preeclampsia (a sudden spike in blood pressure), preterm birth, miscarriage, and stillbirth, the vast majority have healthy pregnancies and babies.[5] Because there are increased risks, however, it's important to seek out prenatal care even though weight biases in the healthcare system make it difficult for many folks to do so.

Ellen, 29, doesn't think she wants to have kids, but she keeps an open mind to the possibility in case she changes her mind like her parents did in their 30s. Among the list of deterrents keeping Ellen in the childfree camp is the way the medical system stigmatizes weight. An ob-gyn refused to see a pregnant friend of Ellen's because the friend had a higher body mass index (BMI), an outdated, imperfect, and controversial measure of health based on weight. "I'm already afraid of going to the doctor because most of the time they prescribe me weight loss and exercise," Ellen says. "I can't imagine being pregnant and being flat out refused just based on my weight or being told there's all these extra risks of being fat and pregnant and having to jump through hoops because of that."

If you think you might want to have kids at some point, you can help future you today by finding a gynecologist you like and trust. Many gynecologists are also obstetricians who deliver babies. Start the interview process now, Michela Crowley, a doula in New York City, says. Ask your gynecologist questions about weight and pregnancy and how they work with larger patients. If they're not someone you'd trust to deliver your baby, try finding a new practice. The longer you see your doctor before pregnancy, the more comfortable you both will be with each other.

I was 26 when I finally felt ready. I didn't want kids for a long time. I was helping my sister raise hers, teaching, and enjoying going home to just my husband and dogs. But I got to a point where we traveled a ton and did all of these adventures and I felt like kids were our next step as a family. I'm glad I chose to have them but I also understand others' reasons for not.

> With both of my pregnancies, I was very sick. I threw up all nine months with both. Medicines didn't work. My second pregnancy was the hardest because I also had a 1-year-old to look after. Childbirth was easy with both. I pushed for about 10 to 15 minutes and they were here. The healing process was fine, no tears or anything.
>
> **Carole,** 33, Oklahoma, she/her, teacher, Cuban American, cisgender, straight, married

NORMALIZE THE EXPERIENCE

Talking about pregnancy doesn't commit you to having kids. You can ask questions, do research, heck, you can even make a birthing plan before you start actively trying to conceive. While writing this book, I signed up for a webinar for pregnant folks on how to create a birth plan. I wasn't pregnant; I just wanted to learn. Did it feel weird? Yes. The "You got this, momma" language certainly didn't help, but I recognize I wasn't the target audience. There's this idea that pregnancy is an exclusive club that only members can inquire about, but pregnancy isn't some secret society, and you certainly don't need permission to access information to help you on your journey. It's your body; you deserve to know what it's capable of. Plus, learning about pregnancy before it happens might help you realize it is or isn't for you well before you feel pressure to decide.

One of the best ways to learn about pregnancy and childbirth is to ask birthing people about their experiences. The caveat here is that people tend to remember extremes: the best and worst things that happened to them. The mundane is less memorable, so if you have specific questions, ask. Asking your family members for their pregnancy and birth stories may also be beneficial.

"Most birthing people that I see who have prolapse or incontinence usually had no idea it could happen," urogynecologist Tirsit Asfaw, says. Prolapse occurs when the uterus and bladder descend into the vagina. It's also pretty common for the rectum to bulge into the vagina too. "Our mothers don't say,

'Oh, after I had you, I was peeing myself,' or 'I couldn't control my stool,' or 'My insides fell out.' These are not things that are talked about even within tight-knit circles, so not many people know that having a vaginal delivery particularly predisposes you to these risks."

You've probably heard a pregnant person say they pee when they sneeze or laugh. That's incontinence: urine leakage outside of the bathroom. "More than 40 percent of women have leakage just because they're pregnant and the uterus is pushing down on their bladder," Dr. Asfaw says. "And then, depending on which study you look at, anywhere from 25 to 50 percent of women can have leakage of urine after vaginal delivery."

If you have a strong family history of prolapse or incontinence, that also increases your risk. "There are a lot of us who said, 'You know what, vaginal delivery is not for me. I'm going to go for a scheduled C-section," Dr. Asfaw says. "There are side effects and risks associated with having a C-section that your obstetrician can then counsel you on."

It's important to prepare yourself for the ways your body will change. Remember learning about puberty? Pubic hair and menstruation probably sound terrifying to most 10-year-olds, but our bodies change, whether we like it or not, and we adjust. Stretch marks, enlarged nipples, constipation, hemorrhoids, and increased body hair are not selling points for pregnancy, and yet millions of babies enter the world each year.

If you have a concern, demystify it. Like postpartum hair loss, for example. While it's true that you do lose hair after having a baby, according to dermatologists, it's not "true hair loss"; it's hair shedding. When you get pregnant, your body produces more estrogen. At any given time outside of pregnancy, about 90 percent of your hair grows while the other 10 percent rests. Every two to three months the resting hair falls out. However, during pregnancy, increasing levels of estrogen pause your hair's natural growth and rest cycle, leading to less hair loss. When those high estrogen levels drop following childbirth, hair loss resumes and then some. Fortunately, this hair shedding doesn't last long. By the time your child's first birthday rolls around, your hair should return to normal.[6]

Pregnancy can also cause other seemingly unrelated symptoms like gingivitis, a form of gum disease that causes bleeding and inflammation, and carpal tunnel syndrome, a condition that causes pain and numbness in the wrists and hands, due to hormonal changes and increased blood flow. Despite the fact that they're super common in pregnancy—up to 75 percent of birthing people develop gingivitis and 31 to 62 percent experience carpal tunnel—there's a good chance you probably haven't heard of these side effects.[7] These changes might sound scary, but if we normalize them and promote people understanding their bodies, we can implement helpful changes, like practicing good dental hygiene, earlier. It's also worth noting that not all changes are bad. Doctor of physical therapy Amy Stein Wood, DPT, says she's noticed some of her pelvic pain patients, including those with vaginismus, which causes pain with penetration, have less pain during pregnancy due to increased blood flow.

If you have specific concerns about pregnancy, talk to a trusted medical professional. You don't have to wait until you're pregnant to ask. For example, if you take medication and are worried it might affect the developing fetus, ask your doctor if it is safe to take during pregnancy, or if there are alternatives you can take during pregnancy. It's typically considered safe to use certain types of antidepressants during pregnancy. Research shows a small to nonexistent risk of birth defects following antidepressant use in pregnancy. Untreated depression, on the other hand, can cause risks to both the parent and child, such as preeclampsia.[8] Prioritizing your mental health can also help you once the baby is born since depression during pregnancy is the greatest risk factor for postpartum depression.[9]

There are lots of things you can do now that will help you later. For example, you can reduce your risks of adverse events by learning how to push properly and strengthening your pelvic floor well ahead of time. "You really need to know how to use the pelvic floor muscles prior to childbirth," Stein Wood says. "You need to practice months before versus the day of or just a couple of weeks prior."

One of the main reasons people fear pregnancy and childbirth is because they don't want to lose control over their bodies.[10] Unfortunately, no matter how hard you try, you can't plan for everything. But if learning about childbirth before getting pregnant would help you maintain a sense of control, why not do it? Just like you can familiarize yourself with how your body changes during pregnancy, you can also learn about what happens during labor. If you plan on giving birth vaginally, you'll begin

How the Cervix Dilates During Labor

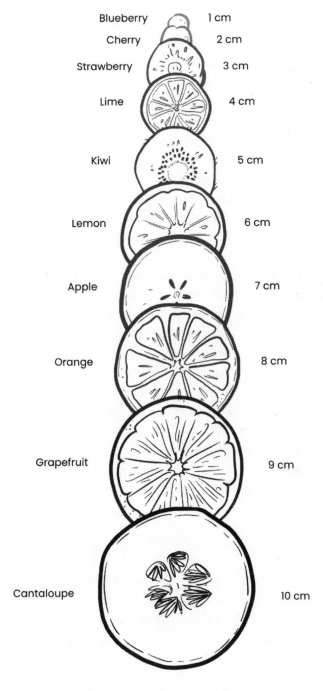

Blueberry — 1 cm

Cherry — 2 cm

Strawberry — 3 cm

Lime — 4 cm

Kiwi — 5 cm

Lemon — 6 cm

Apple — 7 cm

Orange — 8 cm

Grapefruit — 9 cm

Cantaloupe — 10 cm

pushing when your cervix dilates to 10 centimeters, but what does that look like? And how do you even know how dilated your cervix is? Your doctor or midwife isn't sticking a ruler up there; they measure with their fingers (and years of experience). And speaking of things that didn't make it into the *Miracle of Life* video you watched in sex ed class, diarrhea is a sign of impending labor and vomiting is a normal part of childbirth. Which leads us to the perennial question, "Will I poop during delivery?" Maybe, probably, who knows! If you do, you won't be the first and you certainly won't be the last. It's totally normal and very common. "No doctor ever will remember who pooped in labor and who didn't," Asfaw says. "Sometimes we actually give women an enema to help them empty out better to make sure there is adequate room in the pelvis."

Although you can't prepare yourself for everything, one very important thing you can do is build yourself a support system. Birth can be traumatic. Studies suggest that about a quarter to a third of birthing people develop traumatic stress symptoms following childbirth, and anywhere from 2 to 5 percent of people fit the criteria for PTSD six weeks following childbirth.[11] But there's one important risk factor that predicts both post-birth trauma and postpartum depression that you can control for: a lack of support. If you have a partner, get them involved early. If you are single, ask family and friends to accompany you to appointments. You can also hire a doula. Doulas help advocate for you and your birth plan in the hospital or birthing center. Having a doula present at your birth has been shown to increase spontaneous vaginal birth; decrease the length of labor, the necessity for a C-section, and the use of pain medication, as well as lower negative feelings about childbirth.[12] If you know you're someone who has a hard time advocating for yourself, enlist help early on. You'll be glad you did.

> First trimester was lots of nausea and heartburn. Second trimester was okay for like two weeks when I felt like a human. Third trimester was all about being giant and over it and nesting. I was apprehensive about giving birth, especially because I never attended any birthing classes.

The birth plan and what actually happened were very different. I thought I wanted to try an unmedicated delivery, but by the time we made it to the hospital, I was begging for an epidural, which took several hours to arrive. When my contractions ramped up, I squeezed the shit out of my husband's hand and demanded that he never let me forget this and that we never ever do this again (and he promised). Once my epidural kicked in, I got bored waiting for dilation to finish, and thought it might be good to take a nap. That's when suddenly the room was swarming with nurses, hooking me up to new things, administering medicine, trying to keep me conscious. Apparently, I was losing oxygen and so was my baby. But the staff stabilized us, and I stayed awake after that. Just as I was getting to 10 centimeters, the epidural wore off for half my body and I could feel everything down one leg, like a stinging pins-and-needles extreme discomfort. It took a while for the staff to fix that, but once they did, it was time to push. I didn't have the best coaching from the nurse, who told me to hold my breath while pushing, and finally, my husband intervened and told me to breathe the way I learned from martial arts. I did, and it worked, easy peasy, except for the whole second-degree tear that had to be stitched up. What helped was knowing that even if I was unconscious, my body would know what to do and deliver my baby. I couldn't really fuck it up, except when I started to panic and hyperventilate a little while waiting on my epidural. I could see one of the nurses assessing me and I did not want a C-section, although there's nothing wrong with having one! So I took deep breaths to calm my shit.

Speaking of shit, I was worried about pooping in front of my spouse during labor. In the moment, however, I didn't care. Neither did he or the nurses. It happened. It's normal. It's fine. Post-delivery cleanup is humbling. Everything hurts; there's blood fucking everywhere. Your baby is starving and latched to your boobs for like five hours at a time. Mental health suffers because your hormones are suddenly out of whack. It's rough. That first week is the worst. But if you can get through it, it gets easier. Promise.

Leslie, 32, Florida, she/they, corporate trainer, Puerto Rican, nonbinary, pansexual, married

GENDER DYSPHORIA AND PREGNANCY

The gendered nature of reproductive health care can make it hard to get care for yourself if you're nonbinary or trans. Although the American College of Obstetricians and Gynecologists encourages ob-gyns to make their practices inclusive to people of all genders, it's not always possible to get gender-affirming care, and it can be hard to know ahead of time what the environment might be like, especially if you live in an area with limited choices for care. Just sitting in a waiting room with pictures of pregnant cisgender women is enough to bring on feelings of gender dysphoria.

Pregnancy happens whether you're nonbinary, trans, or cisgender. Gender-affirming hormone therapy is not effective contraception, which means you can get pregnant even if you're not trying to and even when you're not menstruating. Many people taking testosterone do not want to use birth control because it contains estrogen. The dose of estrogen in oral contraceptives is typically small enough that little change in masculinization occurs, but there are other birth control methods, like IUDs you can use if you don't want to take that risk.[13] But what if you want to get pregnant? A survey study of trans men who became pregnant after coming out as trans found that two-thirds used testosterone therapy, or T, before pregnancy. Many of those surveyed became pregnant within four months of stopping T and 32 percent of these pregnancies were unintended.[14]

Because society genders pregnancy, you may struggle to conceptualize what pregnancy might look like for you. Van Ethan Levy, LPCC, LMFT, a trans and non binary mental health clinician, relates this difficulty to internalized transphobia. "You might think if I'm really a man, then I shouldn't be having babies, because that will lessen my manhood, which is false and wrong," Van says. "You have to get past your own biases and work through them." We'll talk more about how gender-affirming hormone therapies can affect fertility later in this book, but because it's generally recommended to freeze sperm and eggs before starting hormone therapy, it's worth taking some time to think about whether you want children early on in your journey.

"Really take the time to think about, if you didn't hate your body or believe that your body needed to look or engage with the world a certain way, what your thoughts around children would be," Van says. "If I had even stopped to ask myself that, I would have thought, if I was in a situation where I wanted children, that I would have wanted one of my own. I would have wanted to adopt, foster, and have a child, but I never gave myself the space. I thought if I had a child, it meant I was biologically female; I didn't know I could just be myself."

While working through any internalized transphobia can help you grow comfortable with the idea of pregnancy, it doesn't guarantee you won't experience gender dysphoria. Pregnancy can bring up feelings of gender dysphoria even if you're excited to be a seahorse dad or parent. "When you're pregnant, your breasts are growing, your hips are growing, there's more focus on your vagina. There's more focusing on these areas that we've appointed as a female, which brings more awareness to our own dysphoria of, *Maybe I'm not really nonbinary or trans* because there's so much focused on these experiences that have only been associated with cisgender women," they said. "It's a societal construct. A man wearing a skirt in US culture is considered a man wearing women's clothing, but if we look to Scotland, a man wearing a skirt is a man wearing men's clothes."

Another thing you might want to consider is whether you want to chestfeed. In some cases, trans men who undergo top surgery may not be able to chestfeed. If you think you might have a desire to chestfeed, it's worth discussing with your surgeon. If you don't want to chestfeed, that's great, too. Fed is best, whether that comes from you or a bottle. In a study of trans men who became pregnant, three out of nine people who had top surgery had minor chest tissue changes, three had moderate to significant chest tissue growth, and two had no change to their chests. Some were able to chestfeed but not all. Of the 16 people included in the study who chestfed, 9 did not experience gender dysphoria, which they credited to viewing nursing as a way of nourishing their child and nothing more. During pregnancy, only 9 out of 22 trans men said they did not experience gender dysphoria. However, they did experience distress when people misgendered them due to bodily changes.[15]

I'm a Black woman, and I've read so much about the mortality rates of Black women in this country. It was terrifying. So for our first pregnancy, we hired a doula, also a Black woman, and it was a game changer. She was so supportive and provided me with so many resources and knowledge to feel empowered. She helped me advocate for myself, and for the most part, I think my son's birth went well. There were still complications, but honestly, I think that was likely inevitable given my age and the fact that I had a complicated pregnancy. I have PCOS [polycystic ovary syndrome], so we were forced to do IVF, then I was nauseous until about 30 weeks, I had gestational thrombocytopenia, and my son was small for his gestational age for an unknown reason. But even with all of that, I felt empowered to speak up for myself. Also, I think the universe preps you for birth in the sense that you get so miserable toward the end that a lot of fears just leave you. I had a lot of anxiety about tearing originally—I don't know why, I just did—and by the end, it was the last thing on my mind. I just wanted to be done and get that baby out!

I am not someone who always knew they wanted kids. Don't get me wrong, I like kids. I was even a teacher for a while. But I had doubts about my abilities to nurture, questions about the future of society and this planet, as well as fears about a million and one other things. So, for me, deciding to have children was mostly about finding the right partner. If I found a partner who I felt would be an amazing parent and bring out the best in me, then I would consider it. When I met my husband, that was definitely the case. We got married when I was 30. We had our son when I was 33. Now I'm 36 and expecting our daughter in a few months. I can't imagine life without my kid (soon-to-be kids). At the same time, I sometimes also really resent not being able to sleep in, travel freely, and go out to fancy dinners when the mood strikes me—things I love to do. It feels like I've lost a bit of my identity as a new parent. Folks say it'll come back as the kids get older and I have more time, but for right now, I still mourn for that part of my life a bit.

Veronica, 36, North Carolina, she/her, works at a nonprofit, Black, cisgender, straight, married

THE BLACK MATERNAL MORTALITY RATE

When Megan thinks about the reasons she doesn't want to give birth, the first thing that springs to mind is not wanting to experience the discomfort of childbirth. The second is the Black maternal mortality rate. "If I'm being honest, I can't tell if it's mostly number one that's making me not want to have kids or number two, or maybe it's just a combination of both," she says. "I think of well-off Black women like Serena Williams and Beyoncé who had really scary childbirths. These people are wealthy and well-known and have all of these resources and still have all these issues while they're giving birth."

Approximately 55 in 100,000 Black birthing people die in the US during pregnancy, nearly triple the maternal mortality rate for white childbearing folks.[16] Black people are also 2.1 times more likely to experience serious pregnancy complications than white people.[17] And Black infants face increased risks largely due to preterm labor. The Black infant mortality rate is 2.4 times higher than the white infant mortality rate—about 13.3 deaths in 1,000 births compared to 5.6 in 1,000. Why do Black people have worse birthing outcomes?[18] The answer is simple: racism.

"African American women identify racial discrimination as a persistent stressor that occurs throughout their life span," Dr. Lynae Brayboy, a reproductive endocrinologist and infertility specialist, says. "Chronic stress activates the hormones that are involved in the stress response. If you're under chronic stress, it affects your brain, your pituitary, your adrenals—the organ that gives you your cortisol and your fight-or-flight response. If you always have that activated, that affects you and can affect a lot of functions such as your blood sugar control and high blood pressure. We know that Black women are more likely to have these chronic diseases going into pregnancy, so they're already high-risk."

The long-term psychological toll of racism puts Black birthing people at higher risk for preeclampsia, eclampsia, gestational diabetes, emboli, and postpartum depression.[19] Knowing that you have an increased risk of these conditions can help you be vigilant when it comes to your health, but it shouldn't be your job to be your doctor or make sure you make it out of childbirth alive. "As a Black woman, I don't believe the responsibility falls with Black women at all. It means fixing racism," Dr. Brayboy says. "Yes, there's definitely racism in health care, but racism is all around and it impacts BIPOC individuals every day."

So what can you do? Dr. Brayboy recommends finding a doula who can advocate on your behalf. You can also choose Black doctors or Black midwives; however, that option may not always be available. Dr. Michele Benoit-Wilson, an obstetrician-gynecologist, says a lot of her Black patients ask her about the maternal mortality rate and what their practice does to keep patients safe. While Dr. Benoit-Wilson, who is Black, gets these questions a lot, the white doctors in the practice don't.

If you decide you'd like to get pregnant, speak to your family members, mothers, and sisters especially, and get an accurate picture of their medical history and birthing experiences. Your doctor will want to know about any preexisting conditions you have and your family's medical history to help reduce the risk of complications during pregnancy. It's important to advocate for yourself or have someone with you who can ask questions on your behalf if you're not comfortable. Doctors don't always communicate effectively, Dr. Benoit-Wilson says. "I had one patient who was recommended baby aspirin to prevent preeclampsia by a previous practice, and they didn't explain why," she says. "Her perception was that they made a comment, 'Oh, because you're Black, we want you to start this baby aspirin,' and she felt offended by that. It wasn't really explained to her that, 'Yes, unfortunately, in this country, race in and of itself is actually an independent risk factor for certain pregnancy-related complications.'"

I was 29 when I had my daughter. My husband died when he was 34, otherwise we would have had more. We were married for two years and lived together for seven when I got pregnant. We both wanted children and felt we were ready. I did tons of research about childbirth and decided to go to a maternity clinic in New York City. I had a midwife and attended birthing classes. I wanted zero drugs. I loved being pregnant, other than morning sickness. At three in the morning, I started feeling labor pains, which first manifested as diarrhea and that was good cause it cleaned me out. My husband and I called the midwife who said, "Stay home until you can't talk through a sentence or your water breaks." We did that, and then it was time so we walked down five flights of stairs and two blocks to catch a cab. When we got to the center, I was only four centimeters dilated. I was bummed but suddenly the contractions were coming fast. I heard a woman in the next room screaming and for the first time I thought, *Oh no!*

My midwife and husband were encouraging. As I neared transition, I threw up, and then my water broke. That's when you get a bit crazy. I told my husband to get me a washcloth, and when he went to get one, I screamed, "Don't leave me!" At 10 centimeters, my midwife told me to start pushing. I had pretty bad back labor because my daughter was face up and her head was pounding my spine. I remember saying "fuck" a lot but no yelling. Pushing was intense. At that point, I could have cared less if my husband or the Queen of England were in the room. It was me focusing on that baby. It was the most remarkable, almost sexual, thing feeling her slide out. When she took her first breath, she unfolded like a flower. Then they put her on my chest, and after the cord stopped pulsing, my hubby cut the cord. That's when we saw she was a girl!

Jean, 67, California, she/her, white, cisgender, straight, widowed

PART III

HOW TO

HAVE KIDS

12

FERTILITY
101

WE ALL KNOW HOW babies are made, right? Genitals aside, you need an egg cell and a sperm cell and then, voilà! Baby.

While it's true that sperm and eggs are the key ingredients when it comes to making babies, eggs and sperm are as much a newborn as tomatoes and dough are pizza. When you learn about everything that has to go right in order to conceive, it starts to feel like a miracle that any of us are even here.

Most of what gets taught about sex in high school, if it gets taught, is about preventing teen pregnancy. Sex equals babies. No sex, no babies. So it may come as a surprise, when you get older and start trying to conceive that unprotected penetrative sex doesn't always equate to babies. And this doesn't even begin to factor in trying to conceive when you and your partner are the same sex.

We're taught it's easy to get pregnant when we're young, and for most young people, it is easy, but the ongoing messages we get about preventing pregnancy often give us an exaggerated view of fertility. A study of women over the age of 40 seeking fertility care found that nearly half were "shocked" and "alarmed" to learn that their understanding of the age-related decline in fertility was inaccurate.[1] News stories about celebrities and prominent figures makes having kids later in life seem commonplace, but US birth data tells a different story. About 52 children are born per 1,000 people assigned female at birth ages 35–39. The yearly rate drops to approximately 12 births per

1,000 females ages 40–44, and less than 1 birth per 1,000 for those 45 and older. If you look at younger groups, the number of births ranges from 66 out of 1,000 for the 20–24 age group, 94 out of 1,000 for the 25–29 age group, and 98 per 1,000 for those between the ages of 30 and 34.[2] While some of these differences might be explained by fewer people choosing to have kids in their 40s, research looking at cultures that reproduce until menopause shows that the average age of last birth occurs between the ages of 40 and 41.[3]

Understanding your fertility is a crucial family planning tool whether you're looking to get pregnant or avoid it. And if you decide you want to have kids, at some point, you're going to have to ask yourself how many kids you want, which also requires understanding the limits of your fertility. If you want to have two children without needing fertility treatments, research suggests starting around the age of 27 in order to give yourself a 90 percent chance of success.[4]

Everything in this and the next few chapters revolves around a not-so-basic understanding of the reproductive system. Consider this the intermediate user's manual to your reproductive system. And just as most people can figure out the gist of something without a user's manual, a lot of people end up getting pregnant without having to learn the ins and outs of their anatomy. Of course, you don't know what will happen until you start to try—either at home or in a lab—so you might as well get ahead of the curve.

Quick note before we get started: As inclusive as I try to be in describing reproductive systems, it's impossible to perfectly capture all of the variations our bodies have. I have two uteri (the plural of uterus), so I know how frustrating it is to read things that don't perfectly apply to you.

Let's start at the very beginning, back when you were a fetus. Fetal sex differentiation begins in the fourth week of development, but there are no observable differences in the urogenital system or external genitals until week nine. (Even though this differentiation starts early, it typically takes until weeks 18 through 20 to visualize a baby's genitals on an ultrasound.) During weeks six to seven, the Müllerian and Wolffian ducts form. How these ducts develop depends on your sex chromosomes and hormones. Typically, the Wolffian ducts become sperm maturation and transport system—the epididymis, vas deferens, and seminal vesicles—while the Müllerian ducts become the fallopian tubes, uterus, cervix, and upper part of the vagina. In most cases, if your Müllerian ducts develop, then your Wolffian ducts atrophy, and vice versa.[5]

However, not everyone is born with a typical "male" or "female" reproductive system. When it comes to Müllerian anomalies, some people are born with Mayer-Rokitansky-Küster-Hauser syndrome in which the uterus and vagina are underdeveloped or absent. Others experience issues with the Müllerian ducts fusing, which can lead to a smaller uterus, a uterine septum, a heart-shaped uterus, or two distinct uteri.[6] In rare cases, people assigned male at birth can also have fallopian tubes, a uterus, a cervix, and the upper portion of the vagina due to persistent Müllerian duct syndrome.[7]

The Different Types of Uterine Anomalies

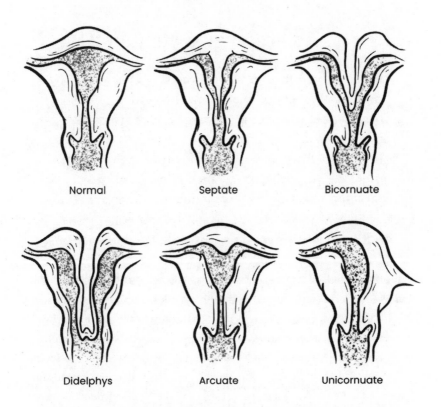

Normal   Septate   Bicornuate

Didelphys   Arcuate   Unicornuate

Intersex folks may have external or internal anatomy that doesn't match the standard expression of their sex chromosomes. Some people don't know they are intersex until they hit puberty or get diagnosed with infertility, although not everyone who is intersex is infertile. There are at least 40 different intersex variations including partial or complete androgen insensitivity, congenital adrenal hyperplasia, 5-alpha-reductase deficiency, vaginal or penile agenesis, Swyer syndrome, Klinefelter syndrome, Turner syndrome, and others. Given all the variability that can occur, researchers estimate that 1 in 100 people are born with bodies that differ from the male or female sex binary.[8] This does not include those who are transgender, nonbinary, or genderqueer.

We'll talk more about when and how reproductive differences can affect fertility later in this chapter, but for now, let's move on to eggs and sperm.

> I have always wanted children, but financial stability is a priority for me to start trying. Changes in the economy have impacted my income, and health issues with my partner set us further back. In my ideal world, my anxiety settles out, my income increases, and I have an ideal environment to raise functioning humans in.
>
> The pressure to have grandchildren has been a huge weight on my shoulders. My mother adopted two children from foster care recently because I haven't had children. My advanced age is always met with, "Those eggs won't last forever." I get unsolicited advice on how to conceive. I'm a petite person and get told I'll never conceive until I "put some meat on my bones." Not one of these people has ever asked if I'm actively trying to conceive. As a woman in my part of the country, it's expected of me to fulfill my "purpose." Having children should be a personal and private choice. Quit asking why.
>
> **Ashley,** 33, South Carolina, she/her,
> musician, white, cisgender, straight

EGGS 101

You are born with all of the eggs you will ever have. At around 20 weeks gestation, the ovaries of a fetus contain 6 to 7 million oocytes, or small immature eggs. That number drops to around 1 to 2 million at birth and then 300,000 to 500,000 by the time you reach puberty. The number of oocytes decreases every month until there are no more viable cells. At around the age of 37, you'll have about 25,000 immature eggs. After you turn 37, the rate of egg loss doubles. By the time you reach menopause, you'll have less than 1,000 oocytes remaining.[9]

While this might seem like a lot of opportunities to get pregnant, those tens of thousands of immature eggs won't all reach maturity. Each egg in your ovary is housed in a tiny sac called a follicle. These follicles must go through a lengthy process, called folliculogenesis, before ovulation can occur. Less than 1 percent of the follicles within your ovaries, about 400 to 500 follicles, will make it to ovulation.

The beginning stages of follicle development happen when you are just a fetus. At around 20 weeks gestation, your ovaries develop primordial follicles: teeny tiny sacs within the ovary that house a small immature egg, or oocyte. That tiny egg is frozen in a stage of meiosis, which you might remember from high school biology class as the process that gives sex cells 23 chromosomes (the structures that contain our genetic material) instead of 46. Egg cells have 23 chromosomes, and sperm cells have 23 chromosomes, and they come together to create a person with 46 chromosomes. (There are some exceptions to this, such as Down syndrome, which is a genetic disorder where people have a third copy of chromosome 21, giving them 47 chromosomes in total.)

Primordial follicles remain dormant until they reactivate and resume development through a process called recruitment. The number of follicles recruited per month varies with age. Recruitment starts when you are a fetus and continues until you reach menopause. Your body continues to recruit follicles on hormonal birth control and even in early pregnancy.[10] In your early 20s, you recruit around 1,400 follicles per month, and by your late 40s that number drops to less than 30 per month. The high number of follicles recruited each month in your younger years is how you go from having 300,000 follicles in your teens to less than 1,500 by the age of 50.[11]

Recruited primordial follicles go on to become preantral follicles, which develop into three classes: primary, secondary, and tertiary. There's a whole lot of science to cover here, but we'll skip to the important bits. Primordial follicles resume their growth and development at the start of recruitment. By the time the follicle gets to the secondary stage, the oocyte finishes growing and can resume meiosis. Meiosis doesn't end then and there, however; it continues to a point during ovulation and then finishes during fertilization. If this seems boring and irrelevant to the bigger picture, I promise you'll see why this is important in the next chapter when we talk about egg freezing.

After the tertiary stage, the follicle becomes what's known as a Graafian, or antral, follicle. If you get your fertility assessed, your doctor will do an ultrasound to tell you your antral follicle count (AFC). Your doctor counts these follicles to give you an idea of whether your ovarian function meets the expectation for your age group, as well as determine how many eggs you can expect to retrieve if freezing eggs or doing IVF.

In a typical menstrual cycle, only one follicle, the dominant follicle, makes it to ovulation. The rest of the follicles die. Dominant follicles contain higher levels of follicle stimulating hormone (FSH) and grow quickly during the follicular phase, which is counted from the start of your period up to ovulation. Once an antral follicle has enough FSH to become the dominant follicle, it produces estradiol, which keeps the other follicles from growing. Ultimately, the antral follicles that stop growing, die. Unless, however, you do fertility treatments, which rely on injections of FSH early in the follicular phase to save the nondominant antral follicles from their otherwise certain death.[12]

Once your dominant follicle reaches a certain size, it's time for ovulation. Which ovary you ovulate from depends on which ovary has the dominant follicle. It's thought that the ovaries roughly alternate sides, though some studies suggest the right side ovulates more frequently than the left. A study published in *Human Reproduction* found that eggs ovulated from the right side were more likely to result in pregnancy. Around 64 percent of the 682 pregnancies studied came from eggs from the right ovary.[13]

Ovulation typically occurs mid-cycle, day 14 in a 28-day cycle. (Note: Most people's cycles are not 28 days. Normal cycles can range from 24 to 38 days long.) Day 1 of your cycle starts with the first day of menstrual bleeding.

What Happens Inside Your Ovaries

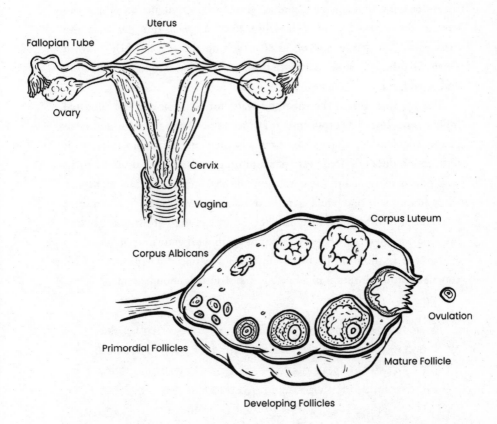

Your estrogen levels rise the closer you get to ovulation, but you don't ovulate until your luteinizing hormone (LH) surges. For some people the rise in LH is one short surge. For others, it's a peak followed by a slight drop and then a second peak. Less commonly, LH rises and then plateaus instead of dropping.[14] Ovulation typically occurs 24–48 hours after LH starts to surge or 10 hours after LH reaches its peak. About 40 percent of people experience some pain with ovulation, what's known as mittelschmerz (German for "middle pain"). The pain, which typically occurs around the time LH peaks, is one-sided and can last between 3 and 12 hours.[15]

Once it's time to ovulate, the egg bursts out of the follicle and gets picked up by the fallopian tube. Because of the way some diagrams are drawn, people tend to think the ovaries are connected to the fallopian tubes, but that's not the case. Ligaments connect the ovaries to the uterus. When you ovulate, the finger-like end of the fallopian tube sweeps over the ovary and little hairlike structures known as cilia pick up the egg and help move it down the tube with some assistance from contractions within the tube itself and tubal fluid.

The egg then sits in the tube and waits for fertilization. The ruptured follicle turns into the corpus luteum, which secretes progesterone and estrogen to thicken the lining of your uterus in preparation for implantation. If fertilization does not occur, estrogen and progesterone levels drop, 11 to 14 days post-ovulation, and the corpus luteum becomes the corpus albicans, a white fibrous scar that remains in the ovary for a few months.[16] When these levels drop, your body starts to produce more FSH to prep the next batch of follicles, and then the whole cycle begins again with your next period.

Now, if fertilization occurs, well, that's a whole different story. We'll come back to fertilization in a bit, but first, let's talk about sperm.

We had twins as a result of IVF. We had done several cycles and were both sick of it. After a promising cycle, we decided to put two embryos back to increase our odds of pregnancy. I sometimes wish we could have had two kids separately instead because it seems so much easier. You have to do the sleepless nights bit twice, but apart from that you outnumber the first kid, so the anxiety is lessened, and you have done it all before when the second one comes along. Twins are everything all at once in two different ways. The compensation, of course, is their relationship with each other, always having someone to play with and talk to. As they get older, and that relationship is intrinsic to the way they grow and experience the world, I enjoy it more and more.

I don't regret having kids, but I have regretted losing my friends and feeling like I've left my whole life behind. I've been depressed and, when extremely exhausted, on the verge of suicidal ideation. I've wished I was dead. But I have known that this was only part of how I felt, that I would never act on these feelings; I would never leave my family or hurt myself. I have to get through this, the hardest thing I've ever done, and see how it is gradually getting better. My depression was exacerbated by sleep deprivation and lack of social life, manifesting itself as a refusal to talk, angry moods, lack of energy. That's hard to deal with at any time, but when you also have two children who naturally have bad moods and cannot talk, it's a tough time. I got better medication, better therapy, but I had to be pushed to see that it was necessary and not a natural part of being a parent.

When kids can show you affection and appreciation, their bullshit becomes much easier to deal with. Also, they're really funny. My daughter's current catchphrase is, "Hola, buddy!" like she's Arnold Schwarzenegger.

Nick, 40, Virginia, he/him, editor, white, cisgender, straight, married

SPERM 101

Sperm production is the opposite of egg production in that it focuses on quantity over quality. Whereas you are born with all of the eggs you'll ever have, the same does not apply to sperm. Around 50–100 million sperm reach maturity per day.[17]

A lot of people think that sperm don't have a sell-by date. But the truth is a lot more complicated. Like eggs, sperm also age. The difference between the two is that all eggs reach a point where they are no longer viable, whereas sperm do not have such strict time limits. Some folks produce viable sperm well into old age. That's why you see more biological fathers in their 50s, 60s, and 70s, than birth mothers. But just because sperm last longer doesn't mean their quality stays the same. Age is associated with a decrease in semen volume, sperm count, and sperm movement and form; changes in hormone levels; and an increase in DNA fragmentation (abnormal genetic material within the sperm)—all of which can decrease your odds of conceiving.

Healthy sperm consist of three parts: head, midsection, and tail. The head contains 23 chromosomes, which combine with an egg's genetic material to create an embryo. The midsection houses the energy-producing mitochondria that power the tail, which allows sperm to move through the vagina and uterus and into the fallopian tube where fertilization happens.

Sperm production begins at puberty and continues throughout your life span. Sperm cells form and multiply through a process called spermatogenesis, which starts in the testes in clusters of tubes known as the seminiferous tubules. Different areas of the seminiferous tubules make sperm cells at different times, allowing the testes to continuously produce sperm. The process restarts within each sperm-producing section of the seminiferous tubules every 16 days. During this time, unique cells known as germ cells divide through mitosis and meiosis to become spermatids. This process turns the germ cells, which have 46 chromosomes, into spermatids with 23 chromosomes, while continuing to create more germ cells so the process can continue. Only 25 percent of the originating germ cells make it to the point of ejaculation. Of the cells that make it, more than half are deformed, leaving only 12 percent of sperm available for reproduction.[18]

After the cells finish dividing, they begin a complex process called spermiogenesis, where they go from round cells to formed sperm with an acrosome (the enzyme-secreting tip of a sperm head that penetrates the egg during fertilization) and tail. Once formed, spermatids begin spermiation. With the help of Sertoli cells (hormone-containing cells that regulate the environment of the seminiferous tubules), the spermatids disconnect from the tissue where they developed and become free cells known as spermatozoa. The entire process, from germ cell to spermatozoa, takes about 74 days to complete.[19]

The seminiferous tubules release upward of 25,000 spermatozoa per minute.[20] From the tubules, spermatozoa go on a 12-day journey through the epididymis, where they continue to mature and prepare for ejaculation. It's this journey that develops a sperm's ability to move once ejaculated. Abnormalities can happen at any stage of spermatogenesis, leading to a reduced sperm count, decreased motility, or an altered sperm shape.

Because the testes continuously produce sperm, semen always contains sperm, even if you ejaculate several times a day. The exception here is if you have a low sperm count or a condition known as azoospermia, where the semen contains zero sperm due to sperm production issues or a blockage in the vas deferens or epididymis.

In order for ejaculation to occur, the sperm must go from the epididymis up into the vas deferens, a muscular tube that goes from the scrotum to up behind the bladder. The sperm then pass through the seminal vesicles, prostate, and bulbourethral, or Cowper's, glands where they mix with other fluids to become semen. The average ejaculate contains around 180 million sperm.[21] However, sperm make up only 5 percent of the final volume of semen. Fluid from the seminal vesicles makes up about 60 percent of semen. This fluid contains fructose, a type of sugar, which gives sperm the energy to move once ejaculated. In the prostate, the sperm and seminal vesicle fluid mix with a milky substance that allows the sperm to thicken after ejaculation and then thin so that they can swim up the vagina, into the cervix, and toward the egg.

The final addition is made by the bulbourethral glands, which also produce preejaculate, the fluid you release before ejaculating when sexually aroused. This fluid helps lubricate and remove urine residue from the urethra. (If sperm is already in the urethra, left behind from an earlier ejaculation, preejaculate can contain sperm and cause pregnancy.) After all the components mix together, the semen passes through the urethra and out of the penis.

While the egg and sperm sections probably felt like a lot to take in, we really just scratched the surface of what happens within your reproductive organs. There are also delicate interactions that take place between the testes or ovaries and the hypothalamus and pituitary in the brain, and additional hormones and genes to consider. Do you need to know all of this in order to conceive? Probably not. However, if you find yourself struggling to get pregnant, you'll likely hear at least a few of these terms thrown around in the 15 minutes you get with your doctor. Fortunately, the more you understand what's going on in your body, the less overwhelming it tends to be.

I decided to have children because I had the financial resources, time, energy, and desire. I want to raise good humans for the next generation of social and global impact. I had my first at 32 and used IVF to conceive my second, who will be born when I'm 40. I enjoy parenthood, but the expense and childcare costs are big challenges. Plus, women carry the emotional tax and mental load when it comes to splitting responsibilities among parents. Fortunately, having kids hasn't changed my career trajectory as I work for a large employer that allows for generous maternity leave (five months) and supports working moms.

Heather, 39, Washington, she/her, marketing executive, Native American, cisgender, straight, married

THE MAIN EVENT: FERTILIZATION

Once inside, sperm travel up the vagina toward the cervix. The trip isn't far as sperm are typically deposited right outside of the cervix. After ejaculation, the semen coagulates, which restricts sperm movement. Over the next 20 to 30 minutes, an enzyme the semen picked up in the prostate liquefies the glob so the sperm can move. The vagina is acidic, so the sperm cannot stay there for long. In fact, the motility of most sperm diminishes after 30 minutes in the vagina, so whatever doesn't make it to the cervix has little likelihood of fertilizing the egg.

The cervix and its mucus both play a fairly critical role in fertilization. Cervical mucus stops atypical sperm from passing through and protects the sperm from being attacked by the immune system. Although it requires getting intimately acquainted with yourself, learning to distinguish patterns in your cervical mucus can help you identify your fertile period, which comes in handy when planning or avoiding pregnancy. Typically, the closer you are to ovulation, the more mucus, or discharge, you produce. Right before ovulation, you produce a thin, slippery, clear mucus, kind of like egg whites.

This mucus is most friendly to sperm. After ovulation, the discharge lessens and goes back to being cloudy and sticky, or there is none at all. (Note: If you use this method to track your fertility, you'll want to chart for at least a month before relying on it as contraception. Even then, proceed with caution as sex, be it arousal or any ejaculate left behind, can also change the consistency of discharge.)

The cervix also contains crypts that are thought to trap and store sperm for up to several days. Sperm live for three days on average but can survive up to five days under the right conditions. Vigorously motile sperm have been found in the cervix up to five days after insemination, but because it's hard to study, it's unclear whether sperm collected in the cervix for days have the potential to make it to the fallopian tubes to fertilize an egg.[22]

Sperm travel faster than you might think. But don't give sperm all the credit for getting there so quickly. It turns out that vaginal, cervical, and uterine contractions facilitate a lot of the transport. In 1973, researchers inseminated women undergoing surgery to remove their fallopian tubes and found it took 5 minutes for the first wave of sperm to get from the vagina to the tubes. Consistent levels of sperm were then found in the tubes for 15 to 45 minutes after insemination.[23]

The uterine contractions that push sperm through the uterus are not like the cramps associated with menstruation. Only one layer of the myometrium, the muscular layer of the uterus, contracts during sperm transport, whereas all three contract during menstruation. It's important that sperm pass through the uterus quickly because as time progresses, infection-fighting white blood cells build up in the uterus. It's thought that these cells attack damaged sperm, but they can destroy normal sperm too.

Even if they get there quickly, sperm cannot fertilize an egg immediately; they must first go through a process called capacitation. Studies looking at fertilization outside of the human body found capacitation time ranged from 3 to 24 hours.[24] It's an asynchronous process, meaning groups of sperm undergo it at different times to prolong their fertilization potential. Sperm also undergo hyperactivation, which causes them to swim vigorously in circular or irregular patterns giving them the ability to move through mucus in the tube and penetrate the exterior of an egg, called the zona pellucida.[25]

The fallopian tube provides a safe haven for sperm. How sperm stays within the tube for extended periods of time and how it makes its way toward the egg isn't clear due to how hard it is to study these mechanisms. Eggs only survive for up to 24 hours, which limits fertilization to a short window.[26] Typically, eggs are fertilized in the first few hours following ovulation. That doesn't mean, however, that pregnancy only occurs if you have sexual intercourse on that day. Since sperm can live up to five days, the window in which you can get pregnant starts five days before ovulation.[27] Research shows that having sex on the day before ovulation leads to the most clinical pregnancies (pregnancies in which a heartbeat is detected). Having sex on the day of ovulation has a slightly higher overall pregnancy rate, but a higher proportion of those pregnancies are not viable.[28] If you want to get pregnant, experts suggest having sex every one to two days to maximize your odds. Sex every day gives you slightly higher odds (37 percent compared to 33 percent).[29]

Although semen can contain upward of 200 million sperm, not many, comparatively, make it to the egg. About 10 to 1,000 sperm make it to the site of fertilization.[30] You lose thousands to millions during every step of the process. Some sperm are also lost to flowback, which is exactly what it sounds like: sperm just slip sliding back from whence they came. A five-year study found that flowback occurs after sex 94 percent of the time. Around 35 percent of sperm on average are lost to flowback, most of which happens within 30 minutes of having sex. In 12 percent of the intimate relations studied, almost 100 percent of the sperm inseminated were eliminated.[31]

This flowback is why some folks lie down or keep their hips arched for 10–15 minutes following intercourse. If you do artificial insemination, your health-care provider will likely advise you to stay reclined for 10–15 minutes just for good measure. Others trying to conceive sometimes put a menstrual cup in following sex to keep the sperm in the body longer. None of these things are mandatory for getting pregnant; they're just added security measures.

Once the egg is fertilized, it sits in the fallopian tube for 30 hours undergoing cell division. From there, it makes its way out of the tube and into the uterus. After five to six days, the embryo hatches out of its shell, known as the zona pellucida, and starts to embed in the uterus. A study published in the *New England Journal of Medicine* found that most implantation occurs on days 8–10. The later implantation occurs, the less likely the odds of a successful pregnancy. For pregnancies where implantation happened on the ninth day, 13 percent ended in early loss. The risk of miscarriage rose to 26 percent with implantation on day 10, 52 percent on day 11, and 82 percent after day 11.

After the egg implants, it starts to produce human chorionic gonadotropin (hCG), the hormone detected by pregnancy tests, almost immediately. The initial rise in urinary hCG happens 6–12 days after ovulation. The majority of successful pregnancies studied, 84 percent, saw levels rise on days 8, 9, or 10.[32] At-home pregnancy tests can only detect hCG following implantation. Early pregnancy tests can detect as little as 6.3 mIU/mL hCG, allowing you to test for pregnancy with some accuracy days before your missed period. Less sensitive tests may need up to 100 mIU/mL hCG to determine pregnancy, which is typically detectable within 15–20 days post ovulation, or the week of your missed period.

So now you know, in perhaps somewhat nauseating detail, the gist of how your reproductive system works. Approximately 80 percent of those trying to conceive will get pregnant within six months of unprotected sex, and between 40 and 60 percent of those under the age of 30 will conceive within the first three months of trying.[33] A study of nearly 3,000 American and Canadian couples trying to conceive found that 79 percent of couples ages 25–27 conceived within a year of trying compared to 55 percent of 40–45-year-olds.[34] A Danish study found that 87 percent of women between the ages of 30 and 34 conceived within a year, compared to 72 percent of those between the ages of 35 and 40.[35] So while you might not need the user's manual, it doesn't hurt to keep it around.

I never thought I wanted children. My husband did, but I was clear when we got engaged that I didn't, and he was okay with that. I thought if we decided to have children that we would adopt. All of a sudden, around 30, I began to really want a child. I still thought adoption was the best route since I believe in zero population growth and knew there were children that needed parents. However, adoption is expensive, invasive, and hard. The more I looked into it, the more I got discouraged, especially as a non-Christian. I stopped using all birth control methods and didn't get pregnant. We started actively trying and didn't get pregnant. My mother-in-law was willing to fund fertility treatments, so we started down that path. I felt guilty about having a biological child but also began to really want to experience pregnancy and have a child that was "ours" without any strings or conditions attached.

I was terrified of pregnancy and childbirth. I was especially afraid of losing control over my body and not being able to do the things I love. We tried so hard to get pregnant, and I had a miscarriage at eight weeks, which was devastating. It was emotionally and physically the hardest thing I ever went through. I was thoroughly surprised by how much it affected me. After that, I was so scared of everything that could go wrong and of not being strong enough to handle the emotional turmoil any longer. Once I got pregnant again, I was elated and terrified. My pregnancy was both easy and difficult. I absolutely loved feeling my son grow and move inside of me. I felt so connected to him right from the beginning. However, my entire pregnancy was during the pandemic. I ended up having vasa previa, which meant if I went into labor my baby could die. I ended up spending a month in the hospital being monitored before having a planned C-section at 36 weeks. By that point I was so in love with our son, and I didn't think I would survive if he didn't. Everything felt overwhelming, but he was fine, and I was fine. Navigating the fear and negative feelings was hard, but I was so hopeful at the thought of finally having a child after trying for 10 years. I clung to that hope and told myself whatever I endured would be worth it in the end.

Abbey, 39, North Carolina, she/her, teacher, white, cisgender, straight, married

13

GETTING YOUR FERTILITY ASSESSED

JILL, 34, KNEW THAT freezing her eggs could change her life, but she never anticipated just how much things would change. Jill's parents had a tumultuous relationship leading up to their divorce, the experience of which led her to think she didn't want kids—not unless she could provide a home different from the one she grew up in. Jill continued thinking she might not want children throughout her 20s, and then, when she was 31, she met her current partner. Quickly she realized he was someone she could see herself having kids with, but he had just finished medical school, so the timing wasn't right. Given the time needed to establish himself in his field, he wanted to wait six years before having kids. The math was easy. Waiting six years would make Jill 38, which lowered her odds of conceiving naturally. Rather than take the wait-and-see approach, Jill decided she would freeze her eggs. "Egg freezing is becoming so normalized that, at that time, it felt akin to just going to get your hair done. It's accepted, but so expensive," Jill says. "I was nowhere near the sort of financial status needed to even be able to consider it until I was probably 30."

Before Jill could freeze her eggs, she needed a fertility assessment. She had no reason to believe her fertility would be any different than the average 32-year-old; testing is just part of the process. It wasn't until halfway through her appointment that she realized freezing her eggs might not be as straightforward as she thought it would be. Her ovaries had fewer follicles than expected, two on the right and four on the left, and her level of anti-Müllerian hormone (AMH), a hormone used to determine egg reserve, was lower than typical for her age. Jill was shocked and confused. Forget freezing eggs, did this mean she couldn't have kids?

Learning about your fertility is often empowering, but it can also be terrifying. Most of us assume we can get pregnant, or impregnate someone, at any given moment, and so to be told otherwise often comes as a shock. Although infertility only affects a relatively small subset of people, especially in the years before age 35, what's considered normal varies. This variation tends to be stressful for folks who fall at the lower end of things, even if that's just the lower end of normal. Before you undergo any testing, it's important to understand what exactly gets measured and what those measurements say about your fertility. Hint: It's not as clear-cut as it's often made out to be.

WHAT FERTILITY TESTS MEASURE

Fertility testing, egg freezing, and fertility treatments are all numbers games. Nearly every step of the way there is a new number (and acronym) to learn, from your AMH to your FSH and AFC, all the way to the grading of your embryos. There's a lot to keep up with!

The first thing to know before you even set foot in a fertility clinic is that there is no perfect test of fertility. You can have infertility, which is defined as the failure to conceive within one year, with "perfect" numbers, and you can get pregnant even with abysmal ones. Fertility tests that measure your ovarian reserve don't predict your likelihood of getting pregnant; they predict how well your body will respond to fertility treatments.[1] These tests measure the quantity of eggs, not the quality. There is no test for quality; the best indicator we have is age. "Unfortunately, we don't have good tests that tell us what the egg quality is going to be until we actually use them," reproductive endocrinologist Aimee Eyvazzadeh says. "We take your age, your fertility levels, your egg or AFC, and use it to predict things ahead of time before you even freeze. But truly, you never know what you're going to get until you actually turn it into an embryo."

While this might seem scary, remember you only need one egg to get pregnant. If you ovulate, do not have any blockages in your fallopian tubes, and have a uterus, you can get pregnant on your own—whether that's through penetration or artificial insemination—even if your numbers are less than ideal. That doesn't mean you will get pregnant, however; there are other factors at play, too. But if you have those basic building blocks, you have at least a chance of getting pregnant, and that's really important to understand before undergoing any testing.

Bad numbers aren't necessarily a harbinger of doom, and good numbers, while promising, don't necessarily mean you are in the clear. "Don't go and say, 'Oh, because the test results are great, I can delay things,'" Janelle Luk, a reproductive endocrinologist, says. "That's not what it means. If you have high numbers, lots of eggs, and you're 28, then yes, it may be true that you can wait a couple of years, but I've seen patients with great numbers, who come back later because they're having a hard time getting pregnant."

So what do these tests tell us then? Let's break it down.

There are four hormone blood tests your doctor will likely order: FSH, estradiol (E2), LH, and AMH. If you use hormonal contraceptives, your doctor may not test for FSH, E2, or LH because the hormones in your birth control will prevent an accurate reading. Fertility-related testing of FSH, E2, and LH typically takes place on day three of your menstrual cycle. Because day one of your cycle starts with the first day of your period, testing on day three allows doctors to get an accurate baseline since day three is when all of these hormones are at their lowest.

FSH is a hormone secreted by the pituitary gland in your brain that causes the follicles within your ovaries to grow. On day three of your cycle, FSH ideally should be below 10 IU/L. To get an accurate representation of your FSH, your doctor will also check your E2, a form of estrogen mainly produced by the ovaries. Day three E2 levels should be less than 60–80 pg/mL. E2 suppresses FSH, so if your E2 levels are high, it can make your FSH appear lower than it is. High levels of FSH and high levels of E2 in the early days of your cycle are often indicative of diminished ovarian reserve or fewer eggs in your ovaries. LH is another hormone produced by the pituitary gland. It's the hormone that tells your body to ovulate. On day three it should be less than 7 IU/L. If your LH levels are higher, it may indicate polycystic ovarian syndrome (PCOS).[2]

AMH testing can occur at any time since it remains stable throughout your cycle. AMH is a hormone produced by specialized cells in your follicles called granulosa cells, which support developing eggs. A low AMH typically signals fewer remaining eggs. Unlike the other blood tests, you can test AMH while on birth control, which is helpful for those interested in assessing their fertility who don't want to stop taking oral contraceptives. You will, however, have to stop taking oral contraceptives during the egg freezing process. If you have an IUD, that can stay in.

AMH levels may be a bit lower when taking birth control; however, testing while on birth control should still give you a reliable enough assessment. If your levels are lower than what your doctor would expect for your age, they may ask you to stop taking the pill and go for a repeat test in a month or two, after which your AMH should return to its baseline.[3] Normal AMH levels range from 1 to 4 ng/mL. A study of 2,741 women looked at AMH levels and found the average AMH at age 25 was 5.41 ng/mL; at age 30, 3.53 ng/mL; at age 35, 2.58 ng/mL; and at age 40, 1.27 ng/mL.[4] If your levels are higher than average, it may indicate PCOS.

The last part of your fertility assessment is the AFC, which is the number of follicles recruited that cycle. Remember, only one follicle typically reaches maturity and becomes the dominant follicle for ovulation, unless you are on fertility medications. You will need a transvaginal ultrasound (an ultrasound done with a wand inserted vaginally) to determine your AFC. Your AFC typically correlates with your AMH level; the lower your AMH, the lower your AFC. An AFC of less than five to seven follicles is typically indicative of a diminished ovarian reserve. If you are freezing eggs or doing IVF, your AFC predicts the number of eggs likely to be retrieved that cycle. Dr. Eyvazzadeh says, "Patients will ask me, 'Is my number normal?' and I say, 'Your number is normal; it is your number. I can't compare you to someone else; that's just not fair. Egg freezing isn't a competition.'"

Research shows that neither low AMH nor high FSH nor AFC predict the likelihood of getting pregnant. Those trying to conceive with high FSH levels and low AMH values had similar odds of getting pregnant over a six-month period as those with normal levels, leading researchers to believe that "biomarkers indicating diminished ovarian reserve compared with normal ovarian reserve were not associated with reduced fertility."[5] High FSH values may signal lower egg quality, especially if you are over 35, but research has not definitively shown this. A study comparing women with high FSH levels to those with average FSH levels found that those with elevated FSH levels had the same implantation rates with their own embryos as their peers, implying that FSH does not significantly affect embryo quality.[6]

"These fertility tests only tell you quantity and not really quality of your eggs, and quality is what you need," reproductive endocrinologist Roohi Jeelani says. "When we freeze eggs and embryos, people think, 'We're set, we're protected,' and there's a chance that it can work, but there's also a chance it won't work because that quality parameter we have yet to understand. I always tell patients that if you're here to get tested, that means you're thinking about it and are not in a spot where you're ready. I would go ahead and proactively preserve any aspect whether it's eggs or embryos, just to have that chance."

I take a cautious approach to explaining these things not because your risk of diminished ovarian reserve is high—it's about 10 percent for people assigned female at birth—but because most people overestimate the ease and success of fertility treatments. Fertility treatments do not guarantee you go home with a child who shares your DNA. If you are under the age of 35, you need to freeze 24 eggs for a 94.4 percent chance of one live birth. If you are over the age of 35, 20 frozen eggs give you a 49.6 percent chance of a live birth.[7] Most people need at least two egg retrieval cycles, more if you are older, to bank at least 20 eggs.

"Typically, I would say, we get on average maybe at least 10 mature eggs from someone who's 30, and maybe about 3 to 6 mature eggs from someone who's 40," Dr. Eyvazzadeh says. "I have 30-year-old patients getting 2 eggs, but I also have 30-year-olds getting 25 eggs. It depends on your egg count and that's influenced by your age, genetics, and environment."

It's hard to hear that your follicle count or ovarian reserve is less than what you expected, which is why it's important to remember that these tests alone don't predict your ability to get pregnant; they predict how many eggs you'll retrieve. Unfortunately, there isn't anything you can do to increase the number of eggs in your ovaries. Your AMH level can fluctuate a little bit depending on when testing occurs, but you can't improve it; it is what it is. Similarly, there isn't much you can do to reduce your FSH level. FSH levels and AFCs can fluctuate from month to month, but typically once FSH levels fall outside of the normal range, they tend to stay there. People with higher levels of FSH tend to be "poor responders" to fertility medications, which use FSH to tell the ovaries to grow more dominant follicles, because their bodies are already accustomed to higher levels of FSH. Therefore, the medications don't have the same effect. Estrogen can lower FSH levels, which can be helpful before an egg freezing or IVF cycle or if your FSH increases to a level where your periods start coming less frequently, but it won't reverse your body's natural processes.

Because the likelihood of diminished ovarian reserve increases with age, the sense of urgency most people feel after their diagnosis comes from knowing they have fewer than average eggs left, which also increases the odds of going through menopause early. So while you do have eggs now, and you have a chance of getting pregnant now, if you have fewer eggs, you may not have as long to get pregnant as your peers. And if you decide to freeze eggs or do IVF, you may not retrieve many eggs. For those under the age of 35, diminished ovarian reserve can result from conditions like endometriosis, previous ovarian surgery, cancer treatments, and genetic abnormalities. Jill's first doctor didn't offer any explanation after her diminished ovarian reserve diagnosis, so Jill pressed further and did more testing with a different doctor. Genetic testing revealed a premutation of the FMR1 gene, a genetic abnormality related to fragile X syndrome, which can cause premature ovarian failure. Though there's a chance Jill can get pregnant—either naturally or through IVF—her numbers likely mean fewer eggs retrieved and an earlier start to menopause.

"It feels like a part of you is dying. We all die, we all know that we're going to die, but I didn't expect that this part of me was going to die younger than what I thought it was supposed to be," Jill says. "I started this whole journey for the purpose of preservation, and then I had someone telling me, 'Do you want to have a baby right now?' I ended up deciding that I didn't want to proceed with IVF because it would turn into the end of my relationship and me having a baby by myself. I would love to have a biological child, that's what I envisioned doing with my time, but the most important thing to me is that I'm doing that with someone that I love. You can't force someone to be ready for something, especially if it's a child."

I want kids more than I don't want kids, but due to fertility issues (low egg count and irregular cycles), I think it's better to not want kids to make it hurt less if I can't have them. Plus, the world feels like it's in shambles, I'm unmarried, and my partner and I don't have enough money and are hardly stable in our living situation. I always poo-pooed the idea of kids pretty aggressively until I was about 23 or so. I went to a gynecologist to ask about my irregular periods. He asked me some leading questions about my contraceptive practices and told me that it was great that I wasn't very consistent because I was in early menopause and if I wanted kids, I should have them immediately. That moment was really defining for me and changed my perspective. I felt that the option to have children was taken from me. As I have gotten older, children and family have become more important to me. Maybe that was initially because the option was stripped from me, but my desire for children grew as I attempted to work through the feelings. I'd love to have a child with my partner, and hopefully someday I will.

My last gynecologist recommended I freeze eggs as soon as possible, but the cost is too prohibitive. I'm 27, but I know my best chance of having children without medical intervention would be to have them as soon as possible. For that reason and some others, I'd like to have children before I'm 30. It's kind of an alarming thought. In less than three years I could be a mother. I can barely take care of myself. My boyfriend is aware of this timeline I've made for myself, and it is a source of some anxiety for him.

Nancy, 27, California, she/her, works in
HR, Asian, cisgender, straight, partnered

ASSESSING SPERM HEALTH

The other side of the equation is sperm. A semen analysis can help doctors assess sperm health. Though the semen analysis is the best sperm-assessing tool we have, it's not considered a comprehensive measure of fertility. A normal semen analysis doesn't necessarily mean you're fertile and an abnormal one isn't diagnostic of infertility, unless it shows azoospermia, meaning there is no sperm in the semen. If you have one abnormal test, your doctor will likely encourage you to get a second one a month later.

A semen analysis is a test that examines a sample of semen under a microscope. It evaluates things such as sperm count, activity (motility), and shape (morphology). When used as a fertility test, it looks at the pH level (too acidic and it kills the sperm), semen volume, sperm concentration (the number of sperm per milliliter of semen), sperm morphology (the size and shape of the sperm), sperm motility (how the sperm move), the number of live sperm in the sample, and white blood cells (a sign of infection). A semen analysis is only considered clinically significant if multiple parameters come back abnormal.

Normal vs. Abnormal Sperm

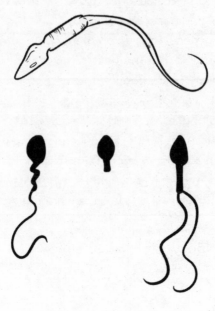

If your semen analysis comes back abnormal, your doctor may also recommend blood tests to check your FSH levels, which help control the production of sperm, and testosterone, which also plays a role in sperm production. FSH levels above 7 IU/L are considered indicative of a problem in the sperm production process.[8] Normal testosterone levels vary. Bloodwork to check testosterone levels should be done in the morning for the most accurate reading. Testosterone levels in the testes are much higher than those in the blood, which makes testosterone blood levels an unreliable predictor of infertility. Even those with low or borderline testosterone levels can have sufficient sperm production.[9]

Reductions in testosterone are a normal part of aging. Testosterone levels for those assigned male at birth drop 1–2 percent per year, and more than a third of those over the age of 45 may have below-normal levels of testosterone. Age-related declines in testosterone can lead to symptoms of andropause, the opposite sex equivalent to menopause, which can present as fatigue, reduced muscle mass, depression, anxiety, irritability, low libido, insomnia, and lowered fertility.[10]

Semen analyses follow the World Health Organization's reference limits for human semen. The numbers shown below are based on the lower limits, the fifth percentile, of fertile men whose partners became pregnant in 12 months or less.[11]

Semen Parameters	
Semen volume	1.5 mL
Total sperm number	39 million per ejaculate
Sperm concentration	15 million/mL
Vitality	58 percent live
Progressive motility	32 percent
Total motility	40 percent
Morphologically normal	4 percent

As long as you produce some sperm, you have at least a chance of having a biological child. In some cases, surgeries to retrieve sperm paired with fertility treatments may be necessary.

I always knew I wanted kids, probably more than most men I know. I am the oldest of three kids, and I have several younger cousins as well. I've always loved babies and taking care of kids, and I've always been good at it. I still love to hold every baby I meet! Having children was always a given for me, something I knew would be part of my life. That certainly contributed to the grief I experienced through infertility, wondering if I'd ever get to live out my dream of becoming a dad.

I chose not to undergo microTESE [microsurgical testicular sperm extraction] sperm retrieval surgery for several reasons. I was advised against it by my primary physician, I was fresh off of another failed surgery to repair a varicocele, and it was going to be an incredibly expensive procedure with poor odds with the absolute best case being the expensive and brutal process of IVF, again with poor odds. It was not an easy decision, because even though I never felt good about that procedure, I knew it was my only hope of having a biological child. I spent about a year grieving the loss of my genetics and of the child we could not have. We spent that time going to therapy and deciding on our next steps. Part of what made the decision to skip microTESE a little easier was the fact that we knew using donor sperm was on the table, and that we still had hope of becoming parents. We both knew that we wanted to experience pregnancy and childbirth and that shared DNA wasn't a requirement to love a child completely. After all that we had been through, I was just ready to be a dad, and in the end we decided that using donor sperm was the right choice for our family.

There's a lot of shame around infertility. I feel like many men really struggle to open up or process it at all.

There's a real feeling of emasculation and embarrassment that comes with the diagnosis, and almost every man I've ever spoken with about it has felt that way. I definitely felt it too. Using a donor was something that I really struggled with at first for that reason; I worried (and still do sometimes) that other people would think less of me for whatever reason or think less of me as a man, whatever that means. The advice I would give to other men in the same position would be to understand it's a medical diagnosis and not anything that you should feel ashamed of or emasculated by. There's much more to being a man, husband, or father than being able to produce sperm.

Alex, 33, Oklahoma, he/him, white,
cisgender, straight, married

GETTING AN INFERTILITY DIAGNOSIS

To get an infertility diagnosis, you need to be trying to get pregnant for at least a year without any success. Within six months of trying, most couples, about 80 percent, will get pregnant. For those who can't get pregnant, the first step typically isn't IVF. "Most people kind of fall in that gray zone where it looks okay, not bad. It's okay for your age group because that's where most fertility is," Dr. Jeelani says. "Most couples are not infertile; most couples are subfertile. Maybe with a little bit of time and a little bit of help, they'll get pregnant."

Most people misunderstand what causes infertility. A study published in the journal *Fertility and Sterility* found that 75 percent of people believed that infertility was caused by alcohol and/or drug use, and nearly 50 percent thought it was the result of family planning measures like oral contraceptives, IUDs, and abortion.[12] It's worth noting that there's no evidence birth control pills, IUDs, or abortions negatively affect fertility, and while smoking is associated with decreased fertility, the jury is still out when it comes to the relationship between alcohol and fertility.[13]

Infertility is thought to be split between the sexes. In heterosexual couples, one-third of cases are due to problems with the cisgender man, another third due to issues on the cisgender woman's part, and the last third related to both partners. About 20 percent of cases have no identifiable cause.[14] For those assigned female at birth, the likelihood of infertility increases with age with no fertility remaining by the end of menopause. Even in the years before menopause, it is difficult to get pregnant with your own eggs due to poor egg quality. Infertility for those assigned male at birth can also increase with age, but age is less of a factor. Between 2.5 and 12 percent of those assigned male at birth may experience infertility.[15]

Of course, there are factors beyond age that can impair fertility. Smoking tobacco and untreated sexually transmitted infections can affect fertility for both sexes, as can weight. It may be harder to get pregnant if your BMI (again, not a good measure of health, but it's what studies use) is above 30 or below 20.[16] Although weight can affect your fertility, research suggests weight does not affect embryo formation or quality. A study published in *Human Reproduction* placed women into four groups based on their BMI—underweight, normal, overweight, and obese—and found that the blastocyst quality was relatively the same for all weight classifications.[17] When split between the sexes, the major contributors to infertility are as follows.

Male Infertility

Most male infertility boils down to problems with sperm production or sperm transport. Issues with sperm transportation make up about 20 percent of male-factor infertility cases.[18] What treatments are available depends on the cause. In some cases, medication may help sperm production. Another option is surgery, which can repair issues related to sperm transport or retrieve sperm from the vas deferens, epididymis, or testes. Most male infertility cases come from the following:

- Azoospermia: A complete lack of sperm often caused by a hormonal imbalance (nonobstructive azoospermia) or a blockage in the sperm transport system (obstructive azoospermia). Azoospermia affects about 1 percent of people assigned male at birth and about 10–15 percent of those who are infertile.[19]

- Oligospermia: A low sperm count, typically caused by varicocele, an enlarged vein in the testicle, which makes the scrotum warmer than it should be and impairs the production and quality of sperm. About 40 percent of male-factor infertility is related to varicocele.[20]

- Certain chronic illnesses, such as diabetes, thyroid disorders, autoimmune diseases, and hyperprolactinemia (an overproduction of the hormone prolactin). Hormone imbalances like hyperprolactinemia and others make up about 20 percent of infertility cases.[21] Cystic fibrosis also causes infertility in those assigned male at birth as people with the disease are typically born without vasa deferentia. In some cases, male carriers of cystic fibrosis (those who have one copy of the gene but not the disease itself) may lack a vas deferens as well. Although they do not have the tubes to transport sperm, those with cystic fibrosis do still create sperm, which can be retrieved surgically.[22]

- Genetic abnormalities: Klinefelter syndrome (an extra X chromosome) causes infertility, as do microdeletions on the Y chromosome and balanced translocations. Those with Klinefelter syndrome typically do not produce enough sperm. Sperm retrieval may be an option as sperm are found in about half of those with the condition.[23] Balanced translocations occur when part of a chromosome breaks off and reattaches to a different chromosome. Most people do not know they have a balanced translocation until they have difficulty conceiving. A specialized blood test called a karyotype can diagnose genetic disorders.

- Retrograde ejaculation: An issue with sperm transport where sperm goes into the bladder instead of out of the penis. This may be fixable with medication or surgery to retrieve sperm.

- Cryptorchidism: Occurs when one or both testicles do not descend. The odds of infertility are less when surgery is performed early, before 1 year of age.[24]

- Injury to the testicles or testicular torsion (when the testicle rotates, disrupting blood flow to the scrotum). Prompt treatment of testicular torsion can help maintain fertility.

- Androgen insensitivity: An insensitivity to hormones such as testosterone, which disrupts sperm production.

- Cancer treatment such as chemotherapy or radiation, which can permanently or irreparably impact sperm production.

Female Infertility

Hormonal problems, issues related to ovulation, and other reproductive health conditions are the most common causes of infertility. Problems with ovulation account for about 25 percent of infertility.[25] "Polycystic ovarian syndrome is the most common diagnosis we see in females in the mid-20s to early 30s age group," Dr. Jeelani says. "PCOS is really variable; like endometriosis, its presentation can vary from person to person. There are some people that all you need to do is make them ovulate once and they get pregnant, and then there are people like me who take a long time to conceive and need IVF. I had my son through IVF and got pregnant with my daughter spontaneously while weaning off of breastfeeding, so it really varies." Needing IVF is not always the outcome of infertility. Fertility specialists typically try other treatment methods before jumping to IVF unless there is a structural problem that would prevent the egg from implanting in the uterus, or you are older. Most female infertility results from the following:

- PCOS: A hormonal disorder caused by excessive androgen production. Androgens are the hormones responsible for developing male sex characteristics. PCOS causes irregular ovulation and longer menstrual cycles, which makes it hard to identify your fertile days. The name is a misnomer as PCOS does not cause multiple cysts, but rather an excess of antral follicles.[26] About 15 percent of people assigned female at birth have PCOS, and about 40 percent of people with PCOS experience infertility.[27] Ovulation induction using oral medications can help people with PCOS ovulate. People with PCOS tend to have more eggs retrieved than those without the condition; however, they tend to form the same number of embryos and have the same pregnancy rate as those without the condition, suggesting a higher likelihood of lower quality eggs.[28]

- Endometriosis: An inflammatory condition where tissue resembling the lining of the uterus, also known as the endometrium, is found outside of the uterus. Endometriosis can reduce egg quantity and quality, warp the anatomy within the pelvis, and create scar tissue and inflammation that make it difficult to get pregnant. Endometriosis affects about 1 in 10 people assigned female at birth and can cause life-disrupting pelvic pain that typically is at its worst with menstruation. Around 30–40 percent of those with endometriosis are infertile.[29] Fertility treatment for folks with endometriosis will depend on the symptoms of their disease. Surgical excision of the disease can significantly improve pregnancy outcomes, but it is not without risks.[30] Ovarian surgery and removing endometriosis-related cysts known as endometriomas may in some cases lower AMH and negatively affect ovarian reserve.[31] For those who cannot get pregnant, IVF may be an option.

- Fibroids: Noncancerous tumors in the uterus that can affect an embryo's ability to implant in the uterus. Fibroids affect one in five people with a uterus and 50–80 percent of Black people with a uterus, but only make up 5–10 percent of infertility cases. Fibroids are more likely to cause infertility when they are larger than six centimeters, change the position of the cervix or shape of the uterus, block the fallopian tubes, or limit blood flow to the uterus.[32]

- Structural problems: Issues with the fallopian tubes or uterus can limit an egg's ability to successfully implant. Blockages in the fallopian tubes or hydrosalpinx (fluid in the tube) may be the result of an old infection or endometriosis. Uterine issues include fibroids, polyps (noncancerous growths in the uterine lining), Müllerian anomalies (e.g., a uterus with a septum dividing it), or adenomyosis (a condition where the lining of the uterus burrows into the muscle layers of the uterus). Some of these issues like fibroids, polyps, and a septum can be surgically removed. In some cases, surgery can also fix issues with a fallopian tube, but having a blocked tube usually necessitates IVF.

- Problems with implantation: Scarring in the uterus or a thin uterine lining may affect an embryo's ability to implant in the uterus. Progesterone medications can help thicken the uterine lining, increasing the odds of pregnancy.

- Certain chronic illnesses: Thyroid disorders and hyperprolactinemia can cause hormonal imbalances that disrupt ovulation. Medications can stabilize hormones depending on the issue. Autoimmune diseases can also negatively affect fertility.

- Genetic abnormalities such as Turner syndrome, fragile X syndrome, and Swyer syndrome all impact ovarian reserve. The natural pregnancy rate for Turner syndrome is about 2 percent.[33] Those with Swyer syndrome are intersex and do not produce eggs but can get pregnant using donor eggs. Balanced translocations can also make it difficult to get pregnant due to an increased risk of miscarriage.

- Cancer treatment such as chemotherapy or radiation can also deplete ovarian reserve.

Endometriosis, Uterine Fibroids, and Polycystic Ovarian Syndrome

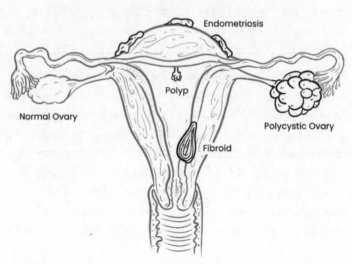

Endometriosis

Polyp

Normal Ovary

Polycystic Ovary

Fibroid

"Getting tested is about empowerment. I do see normal tests that go on to disadvantage patients who later can't get pregnant, so empowerment before and after is important," Dr. Luk says. "Ask yourself why you are getting the test to begin with. If you're here to just educate yourself, please go ahead. But if you get a number you weren't expecting, don't fret, talk to your doctor. If your reserve is low and you don't have a partner, I think it's better to know. Consider freezing, understand your resources, and maybe save up some money to preserve some eggs. That's the best you can do."

When I was 12, I thought I wanted 13 kids. I even named them. As I got older, I thought 3 seemed like a good number. I never imagined my kids would be over 21 years apart. I had my first child when I was 17. It was an unplanned pregnancy, so I finished growing up while raising another person. I did not marry my daughter's father, and we had a very contentious custody battle. I went to college and graduate school and then worked for a good 10 years while hoping to meet "Mr. Right" and have more children.

I finally met that guy and got married at almost 36 years old. We started trying to conceive four months later and had no success. Being over 35 means you are considered "advanced maternal age," so after six months of trying we went to see specialists. We ended up conceiving on our own, but I miscarried right away. I got pregnant the very next month and had another miscarriage at eight weeks. We discovered through testing that I had a gene for a blood clotting disorder. Plus, my eggs were older, and my husband had sperm quantity and quality issues. So odds were against us. We tried a couple rounds of unmedicated IUIs [intrauterine inseminations], two rounds of IVF, and two rounds of medicated IUIs. I had three more early miscarriages. In the end, I conceived fraternal twin boys at age 38, and they were born when I was 39.

Having children isn't for everyone. My brother and sister-in-law are childfree by choice and are happy with their decision. For those that do have children, it's beautiful, joyful, stressful, and exhausting all at the same time. You worry constantly about everything; at least I do. And it doesn't stop when they grow up. I have 8-year-old twins and a 30-year-old and I worry about all three just the same.

Mary Beth, 48, Pennsylvania, she/her, white, cisgender, straight, married

14

FERTILITY PRESERVATION

WHEN JENNY HAYES EDWARDS froze her eggs at the age of 35, she had no idea if or when she'd ever use them. After the financial crash in 2008, Jenny struggled to keep the three restaurants she owned afloat. People weren't taking ski trips anymore, which left the Colorado-based restaurants with a dwindling number of patrons, and working around the clock left no time for dating, which put a massive dent in her plans to settle down and have a baby. While Jenny's mind was elsewhere, her friend suggested freezing eggs. Her friend, who was 40, had failed to get pregnant following three IVF cycles. "If I had your 35-year-old eggs, you'd already be pregnant," her friend's doctor said, and so her friend passed along the message: Freeze your eggs. Don't wait until it's too late. Less than a year later, Jenny froze 16 eggs. Ten years later, at the age of 45, Jenny gave birth to a daughter using those eggs.

Think of egg freezing like an insurance policy for your fertility. If you don't see yourself having kids until your late 30s or 40s, freezing your eggs can help improve your odds of having a biological family later in life. Freezing eggs bought Jenny time to reinvent herself. She sold her restaurants, moved back east to be closer to family, and met her husband when she was 42. "I always thought if it's not going to work out for me to have my own biological children, at the very least I'd like to be a stepmom. I knew I wanted to be a part of a family in some way, and so when I met my husband, who had three teens at the time, I thought to myself, 'All right, maybe this is enough,'" Jenny says. "We talked about the fact that I worked really hard to go through the process of freezing these eggs, and gosh, it would be so freaking cool to just go through the process once. He was onboard. I didn't need a gaggle of kids. I did not need to use all my eggs. I just wanted to go through it once and experience being pregnant." All of Jenny's eggs survived the thaw. Ten out of the 16 fertilized. Four made it to the blastocyst stage, and all four of those embryos came back chromosomally normal. Jenny got pregnant with the first embryo she transferred.

Egg freezing is a numbers game. Your odds of success increase the more eggs you freeze. Below is a breakdown of your odds of achieving one live birth based on your age and number of frozen eggs.[1]

For those under the age of 35:

- Five eggs give you a 15.8 percent chance of one live birth.
- Ten eggs give you a 42.8 percent chance.
- Fifteen eggs give you a 69.8 percent chance.
- Twenty eggs give you a 77.6 percent chance.
- Twenty-four eggs give you a 94.4 percent chance.

For those 35 and older:

- Five eggs give you a 5.9 percent chance of one live birth.
- Ten eggs give you a 25.2 percent chance.
- Fifteen eggs give you a 38.8 percent chance.
- Twenty eggs give you a 49.6 percent chance.

Unfortunately, there is no way to ensure your frozen eggs will result in a live birth. Your odds of success depend on a number of factors including your age and how many eggs you freeze. The success rate of those eggs depends on many factors but mostly on the quality of the eggs, which generally depends on age. Fertility stays relatively stable between the ages of 28 and 33 but starts to decrease beginning in the mid-30s. The likelihood of achieving pregnancy within one menstrual cycle is about 14 percent lower for women aged 34–35 than it is for someone aged 30–31. By the age of 40–41, the odds of getting pregnant per cycle are less than half of what they would have been a decade earlier.[2] If you want to freeze eggs, the younger you are, the better. However, if you freeze eggs when you're very young, you run the risk of never using them, making the process an unnecessary expense. Dr. Eyvazzadeh recommends getting your AMH levels checked at 25 and freezing eggs by 32. If you have a family history of endometriosis or early menopause, plan to check your fertility earlier.

If you plan on freezing eggs, it's important to think about the future: how many kids you might want and when you plan on using those eggs. "If you want two kids, I want to make sure you have at least a 50 percent chance or more of having a second baby with the basket of eggs you froze for yourself," Dr. Eyvazzadeh says. "Someone who is 30 years old would need to freeze 14 mature eggs to give themselves at least a 50 percent chance of having two kids."

You also need to consider when you plan on using the eggs because if those eggs do not make enough viable embryos, you may not have much success retrieving eggs later on. "I think a lot of women freeze and forget, and then they come back to use their eggs at an age when they don't have any eggs left," Dr. Eyvazzadeh says. "It's heartbreaking when a patient freezes her eggs when she is 35 and thaws them all at 45, and there's no good embryo in there. I always tell young women, if you're going to end up using your eggs at an age where you don't have any eggs left, please do more egg freezing just to give yourself more options in case the first batch of eggs doesn't work."

I'm 42 and I always thought I would have kids by this age. I actually got pregnant when I was 22 and decided not to carry the child and keep it. I always call it the easiest hardest decision I ever made. I grew up not deeply religious, but I chose to get baptized when I was 14, which is very weird to think about now. So I did have some, not necessarily guilt, but just questioning whether it was the right decision. But I thought, *Oh, I'll have kids by the time I'm 30*, and then it was 35 and then 40. People had mentioned freezing to me, so I dug around, but of course, it was so damn expensive. It stayed in the back of my mind through my late 30s. And then I got dumped when I was 40 and that was an "oh shit" moment. But to go through this whole process was a huge relief once it was done. During the actual process it was such an adrenaline rush; I don't think I realized what my body was going to feel like. It felt like you could really feel your ovaries sort of fatten up.

A month and a half before I started the process, I met someone on Tinder of all fucking places. We had that first conversation where you gently throw out some of your red flags just to see if they run for the hills. His red flag was that he smokes, and I said, "Well, my big red flag is that I want to have kids one day. In fact, I'm planning on freezing eggs soon." And he didn't flinch, and that was huge to have somebody because I was going to do it by myself. I'm sure there may be other women that have maybe felt this way, but every time I thought about freezing eggs, I would start crying. It makes you think about all the decisions you made, and it makes you kind of wonder what if your life went a different way. I never think, *Oh, what if I had that child when I was 22? But what if I didn't prioritize my career?* I don't regret any of it, but it did make me think how it's really unfair that women have some sort of expiration date or rush to get things done.

I have had friends who were much younger than me who went through the process and got the same amount of mature eggs as I did. However, given their age, the chances of them not having chromosomal abnormalities are a lot lower. My AMH was 0.81, which at my age, 41 at the time, was considered low. They predicted they'd retrieve between two and four mature eggs. We got 16 eggs, 10 of which were mature. However, until I make an embryo, we won't know the egg quality. The doctor told me it would be good if I did another round, but it's just too expensive. If things are still going well in my relationship within the next year or so, I'm going to try naturally first. Pull the goalie, see what happens. If in a few months nothing happens, maybe then I'll call in the reserves.

Natalia, 42, California, she/her, anthropologist/comedian, white, cisgender, partnered

THE EGG-FREEZING PROCESS

Egg freezing is essentially one-half of the IVF process. If you decide to use those eggs later in life, you will need to do the second half, which includes fertilizing the eggs to create embryos and then transferring those embryos. According to data from the UK about a fifth of those who freeze their eggs return to use them.[3] Before you freeze any embryos, you will do a fertility assessment to check your hormone levels and AFC. Based on your numbers, your doctor will create a treatment protocol for you. There are several different types of protocols your doctor may use; however, protocols vary from doctor to doctor and patient to patient, so it's not exactly helpful to discuss the nitty-gritty here because the dosages used during your cycle will likely reflect a number of different factors, including how your body responds to the medications.

The medications and procedures used for an egg retrieval are relatively the same for both egg freezing and IVF. Ovarian stimulation typically starts on day three, give or take a day, of your menstrual cycle. Some clinics will have you take oral contraceptives or another form of estrogen prior to your cycle starting to suppress the ovaries and promote uniform follicle growth. The first medications you take are stimulation medications, or as they're more commonly known, stim meds, which help the follicle grow. Stim meds include injectable gonadotropin medications that act similarly to the FSH and LH your body produces naturally. Giving yourself an injection can seem scary if you've never done it before, but the injections are fairly quick and easy. The medication uses a tiny thin needle that goes into a small bit of skin pinched from your lower abdomen. If you don't feel comfortable doing this, enlist someone who can help.

Research suggests the optimal stimulation phase length to produce the most mature eggs is 10–12 days, but you may respond faster or slower depending on your body.[4] To start you may have appointments every few days, but as you get closer to the retrieval, you may be in the office every day or every other day. These appointments, called monitoring, take place in the morning and consist of bloodwork and a transvaginal ultrasound. The ultrasound measures your follicles as they grow. Once a follicle reaches 14 mm or your estrogen rises significantly, you will take another injectable medication, either a GnRH agonist or antagonist, to prevent your body from ovulating. You will take the ovulation blocking meds daily, using the same method you use to take your stim meds, until it's time for your trigger shot. Trigger shots use hCG, the hormone you produce when pregnant, to cause a surge in LH, telling your body it's time to ovulate.

If you are at risk of ovarian hyperstimulation syndrome (OHSS)—risk factors include PCOS or a high AMH—your doctor may use a different medication, an agonist trigger shot, instead. OHSS is an overresponse to stim meds that causes the ovaries to swell. It can cause abdominal pain, nausea, bloating, and, in severe cases, may cause fluid to collect in the abdomen. Symptoms of mild OHSS occur in one out of three cycles; severe OHSS is rare, occurring 1.4 percent of the time, and may require hospitalization.[5]

Some trigger shots, like stim meds, are done under the skin, while others use a larger needle that needs to go into the muscle, typically the glutes. Someone will likely need to help you with the intramuscular injection, though some people can do it themselves. Your doctor will want to wait to have you trigger until most follicles reach a good size. Follicles grow about 1.7 mm per day on average. Research suggests that follicles ranging from 12 to 19 mm on the day of the trigger shot are most likely to be mature.[6]

Follicles above 23 mm are more likely to be postmature, which can reduce embryo quality.[7] Your E2 levels can also predict how many mature eggs you'll get. A mature follicle produces between 200 and 299.99 pg/mL of E2.[8] Dividing your E2 level by 200 can give you some clues about how many mature eggs you will retrieve.

It is important for you to take the trigger shot at the exact time your doctor tells you to take it as the retrieval happens 35 to 36 hours later. Egg retrievals are typically performed under a light anesthesia, so you will be asleep for the procedure. Most retrievals are performed vaginally. The doctor uses a probe similar to the wand used for transvaginal ultrasounds, except this wand has a place to slide a hollow needle through. The needle goes through the wall of the vagina and into the follicle. It's a large needle, but you will never see it since you'll be asleep. The follicle is flushed with fluid, and then that fluid is drawn back through the needle. An embryologist examines the fluid under a microscope to find the egg.

Depending on the location of your ovaries, the doctor may perform the procedure abdominally, guiding the needle externally, atop of where your ovary sits in your pelvis. The procedure is generally not painful though you may have some mild cramping and bleeding after. Many clinics include the price of anesthesia in their fees, but some do not. When I did IVF, I opted to be awake for the procedure and save $500, since I was only having a few eggs retrieved abdominally. It was not painful, though I wouldn't call it pleasant either. It's a strange sensation, but you'll never feel it because you'll be sedated. (Most clinics prefer to sedate patients, and most patients prefer sedation.) You will need to stay in the clinic's recovery area until the anesthesia wears off, about an hour. You will also need someone to pick you up since you cannot drive after sedation. Plan to take the day of your egg retrieval off, and if you can swing it, the day after too.

What Happens During an Egg Retrieval

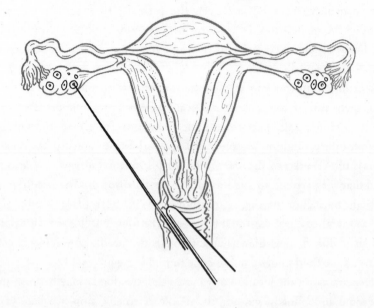

Shortly after you wake up from your egg retrieval, your doctor will let you know how many eggs they retrieved. This number will hopefully be the same as your follicle count going into the procedure, but it may be less, and in some cases, it can be more, if a smaller follicle grows large enough following your trigger shot. The trigger shot helps the egg complete the process of meiosis, which reduces the number of chromosomes in the nucleus from 46 to 23, allowing the egg to combine with the sperm, which also has 23 chromosomes, to make a 46-chromosome embryo.

Embryologists can tell if eggs are mature by looking for the polar body, which contains the excess chromosomes. The polar body degrades a few days after meiosis but is visible at retrieval. Typically, 80 percent of the eggs retrieved are mature. Sometimes, embryologists can get eggs to mature overnight in the lab. A study of 1,615 IVF cycles found that for those under the age of 35, at least 10 eggs retrieved led to an "optimal" pregnancy rate of 44 percent. For those with 1–4 eggs, the rate was 30.8 percent and for 5–9 eggs, 36.2 percent. For folks between 35 and 39, the best pregnancy rate (34.8 percent) occurred with 5–9 eggs retrieved.[9] Other research suggests 15 eggs in a cycle guarantees the best live birth rate and that higher egg counts did not produce more high-quality eggs. Of the 400,135 IVF cycles analyzed in that study, 9 eggs were retrieved on average with an average overall birth rate of 21.3 percent per cycle.[10]

The freezing process itself is quick and designed not to damage any eggs. Egg freezing requires a process known as vitrification, which uses liquid nitrogen to quickly freeze eggs. This process prevents ice formation and increases the likelihood that eggs survive their thaw. The vast majority of eggs tolerate freezing, but not all eggs do. The thaw survival rate for vitrification is 65–99 percent. A study looked at 3,146 egg donation cycles and found that 1.4 percent (45 cycles) had eggs that did not survive thawing.[11]

For the most part, prepare to spend a lot of money if you plan on freezing eggs. A round of egg freezing costs on average $15,000 to $20,000. This includes a clinic fee, which typically ranges from $10,000 to $15,000, and the cost of medications, which can be upward of $5,000, depending on how much medication you need. You'll also have to factor in storage costs, which range from $500 to $1,000 per year. Your first year of storage is typically included in the cost of your cycle. While the process is notoriously expensive, there are some cost-saving tips that can help you spend less.

To save on clinic fees, look for high-volume clinics (facilities that take a lot of patients) as they tend to be less expensive. Some of the larger clinics advertise costs as low as $6,000. If you choose a larger clinic, expect fewer interactions with your doctor since they have a lot of patients. Most facilities, regardless of size, rely on nurse coordinators for much of the contact, so no matter where you go, you likely won't end up speaking to your fertility specialist as much as you'd expect. Your doctor might not even be the person performing your retrieval, as doctors typically rotate schedules and not all providers perform retrievals.

Sometimes, insurance companies will cover some of the costs of egg freezing. However, this benefit is typically limited to fertility preservation for people with medical conditions associated with infertility, such as those with reproductive conditions like endometriosis or PCOS or those undergoing treatment for cancer.[12] If you have insurance, it's worth seeing what, if anything, they cover. Though the billing staff at most clinics will call your insurance company to see what they cover, you should also make the call yourself since some clinics don't take insurance or only take insurance for certain procedures. Calling your insurance directly gives you a better idea of what they cover overall as opposed to what they cover at a singular clinic.

When insurance companies provide coverage, it's usually limited to "monitoring." Monitoring includes all of the bloodwork and ultrasounds leading up to your egg retrieval. In most cases, you will likely have to pay for the egg retrieval and your fertility medications out-of-pocket. A growing number of companies have begun to offer egg freezing as part of their benefits package, so take a look at your offer letter or employee handbook. Depending on where you live, it may be less expensive to go to a clinic that's a bit farther away. If you find a more affordable clinic out of state or far from home, ask if they are open to working with patients who do their monitoring at local facilities and only come in for the egg retrieval. The clinic fees tend to be less in this arrangement because you only pay for the retrieval, freezing, and storage. The monitoring fees go to whatever nearby facility you choose.

Though traveling can save money, it tends to be a lot more work for you. First, you have to find a facility near you that does same-day bloodwork and ultrasounds. If you have a good relationship with your gynecologist, they may be open to doing your ultrasounds. For bloodwork, most laboratories offer same-day testing if you go early. In addition to getting yourself to those appointments, it also becomes your job to make sure that everyone has the documentation they need. The fertility clinic typically sends you the prescriptions you need for your imaging and tests, and then the facilities you go to send the ultrasound and lab reports back to your clinic. This all has to happen in a timely manner since your medication dosages and timing depend on your results. If you choose this arrangement, you'll want to figure out the clinic fees, monitoring costs, and the cost of travel plus accommodations since you'll likely need to stay nearby for at least one night, two if you want to recover after the procedure.

Other money-saving options include loans, grants, and clinic-sponsored giveaways you can apply for. Some grants and giveaways have an application fee or are limited to people actively trying to conceive. Clinics may also have payment plans or risk-sharing programs. However, risk-sharing programs and package deals are typically offered to those most likely to succeed, and so there may not be much cost-savings in the end.[13]

There are also ways to save on medication. One way is to order medications from overseas. However, these savings are not without risk, as importing medication for personal use is technically illegal. This is due, in part, to rules and regulations maintained by the FDA in the US that the agency cannot enforce internationally. Although importing medication is technically illegal, current law directs the FDA to allow personal importation when the medication is "clearly for personal use and does not appear to present an unreasonable risk to the user."[14] If you run out of medication, sometimes clinics have extra doses donated by other patients that you may be able to use. You can also shop around. Prices tend to differ from pharmacy to pharmacy. You can also ask your doctor if there is a pharmacy they work with. Sometimes clinics set up package deals for patients with specific pharmacies.

When buying medications, be sure to ask what the self-pay price is. If your insurance plan has a lifetime maximum for fertility treatments, it may benefit you to pay for drugs out-of-pocket as self-pay costs may be less than what's billed to the insurance company. If you can't afford the medication costs, you can also try doing a "mini cycle," which uses less medication. However, in most cases, this will also retrieve fewer eggs. Some studies suggest that people with diminished ovarian reserve and those who are older respond to mini cycles just as well as they do traditional cycles, so this may be a way to bring your cost down if you will need to do multiple cycles to get eggs.[15]

Joey: I was diagnosed with stage four pancreatic cancer in the summer of 2015 when I was 25. I would eventually be told that I had 18 months to live. There was a fair amount of fertility talk, everything from freezing sperm to chemotherapy affecting fertility, and obviously, end-of-life type of talk and treatment. We ultimately made the decision not to freeze any sperm for a variety of reasons, the main one being that it's expensive for something that only might work. But the other reason was that if we did get to a point in our lives where we wanted to have kids, we would adopt, if anything. The desire for a biological child wasn't too much of a priority for us.

Sammy: We were 2,000 percent forced into discussing it. We had not been dating that long, eight months. It was very bizarre. My parents offered to help pay to freeze sperm, and I was like, "You haven't even met him yet!" And then his parents were talking to me about freezing his sperm. It was a lot. We had all these conversations about having kids when we didn't even know if he was going to live. I thought, *I don't want to have this guy's baby if he's going to pass away and then I'm going to have to be a single mom.* Grieving the loss of him and then having a baby sounded crazy to me. Joey has been in remission now for two years, but we're still waiting for him to get to a point where he's been cancer free long enough that we can do things like move away from where his doctors are.

There were definitely points in our journey where someone would ask me, "When are you going to have kids?" And I would just cry because I hadn't even had time to process what the fuck was going on. I think if adoption was more accessible, we'd be thinking about it more, but the fact that it's so complicated and choosy means they can reject us just based on Joey's cancer diagnosis.

Sammy and Joey, 32 and 31, Washington, she/her and he/him, sexuality educator and bartender, white, cisgender, married

ENOUGH ABOUT EGGS, WHAT ABOUT SPERM?

When we think about fertility preservation, it may help to think beyond eggs to sperm. After analyzing 40 years of research on fertility, researchers recommended that those looking to delay parenthood should ideally freeze their sperm by age 35; 45 at the latest. Older sperm, as in sperm from those

45 and older, has been linked to negative outcomes for newborns and those giving birth. A study examining more than 40 million births found that newborns conceived using sperm from those 45 and older were more likely to be born premature as well as have a low birth weight and low Apgar score (a test used to determine newborn health). The risk of preeclampsia and gestational diabetes for those impregnated by older sperm were also higher. Older sperm has also been found to increase the risk of congenital diseases, neuropsychiatric disorders, and cancer. Sperm age can also contribute to miscarriage risk, especially if the pregnant partner is 35 or older.[16]

Freezing sperm is relatively straightforward: you go to a fertility clinic and "give a sample." There are also start-up companies that let you provide a sample within the comfort of your own home. The cost up-front is typically less than $1,000 to assess and freeze sperm. After that, you have a yearly storage fee, which runs a couple of hundred dollars on average. Frozen sperm does not have a sell-by date as long as it's properly stored in a liquid nitrogen tank. "There's no such thing as frostbite," Dr. Eyvazzadeh says. "You're gonna lose some sperm from the thaw, that's just natural, but the quality of the sperm should still be just as good with frozen as fresh unless the sperm quality was extremely poor to begin with."

Do you have to freeze your sperm? No, but it certainly doesn't hurt. Dr. Eyvazzadeh recommends freezing sperm around the age of 25, if you have a chronic illness such as diabetes, Lynch syndrome, a family risk of cancer, a spine injury, childhood issues related to the testes, or are in the military. "I can tell you that when my sons are 25, I'm going to tell them to just freeze and forget it," she says.

Ultimately, egg quality determines success more than sperm quality. A large study of IVF cycles found that more than 80 percent of success was dictated by the age of the eggs.[17] "Men have the ability to remake sperm every 90 days, so tests of sperm at one point aren't necessarily reflective of what their future may be," Dr. Jeelani says.

TRANS FERTILITY PRESERVATION

For a long time, trans folks viewed losing their fertility as the "price to pay" for gender-affirming care.[18] Fortunately, today, that's not the case, although the price tag associated with preserving your fertility may dictate otherwise. Many trans folks report wanting to start a family. Half of trans adults say they would like biological children.[19] However, studies suggest that less than 5 percent of trans adolescents pursue fertility preservation.[20] Cost is a big barrier for many, as is the invasiveness and gender dysphoric nature of care and concerns that fertility preservation would delay the start of hormone therapy.[21] Nonbinary folks who wish to use hormone therapy can also benefit from fertility preservation.

Although transgender men are often told to freeze their eggs before starting testosterone therapy, or as it's more commonly known, T, a study of trans men taking testosterone suggests that doing so does not significantly reduce the number of eggs you have. T slightly decreased AMH, but levels remained within the normal range after a year of initiating T. T did not affect the AFC of those studied at any point in time. Four men included in the study fathered biological children after utilizing T for up to 12 years. The only caveat to this research is that the majority of men studied were young—most ranged from 19 to 31 years old—so it's not clear if and how T might affect ovarian reserve in the face of age-related ovarian decline.[22]

Case studies show successful egg retrievals have been performed on trans teens as young as 15, including those who were originally on puberty blockers. In four cases of trans men ages 15–21 undergoing egg retrievals at Brigham and Women's Hospital in Boston, all four patients were able to get at least 10 mature oocytes, giving them a 69 percent chance of having a live birth.[23]

"I was concerned going into egg freezing because people framed it as you're injecting yourself with tons and tons of female hormones, and I thought that would make me feel really dysphoric," Arthur, who froze his eggs, says. "But the reality of it is that a lot of my dysphoria was about things that were not going to change from the experience of egg freezing. Egg freezing is not going to make your voice higher pitched, and it's not going to make your hips larger. In those moments, you might feel hormonal and that might not feel great, but the level of female hormones doesn't matter so much as like the absence of testosterone. It's important to make sure you're in a good social space. It was important that the clinic was willing to gender me as male. Make sure the person doing your injections respects your trans identity and the journey you're on."

Something that helped Arthur, 23, deal with gender dysphoria while freezing eggs was removing the notion that organs have a gender. As you might remember from the beginning of chapter 12, we all start out with the ducts that form the epididymis, vas deferens, and seminal vesicles and the ducts that form the uterus, fallopian tubes, cervix, and vagina. There are also things you can do in your doctor's office to help reduce dysphoria. You can ask for external or abdominal ultrasounds instead of internal ones and ask not to be positioned for the procedure (it's a posture somewhat like being in stirrups) until after you've been sedated.

Trans women can also freeze sperm. It's best to freeze sperm before starting hormone therapy. Sperm can be frozen at any point following puberty, including after puberty blockers. Young trans women tend to have lower morphology but otherwise normal sperm. It may be possible to freeze sperm after starting hormone therapy, but it would depend on how long you've been on hormone therapy, and you would need to stop taking estrogen in order to do so. A trans woman taking spironolactone along with E2 for just over two years had no motile sperm after coming off of hormone therapy, so the success of freezing sperm following gender-affirming therapy is likely small.[24]

Trans women on estrogen can also breastfeed. There are reports of trans women successfully inducing lactation through a combination of hormones and pumping, who go on to breastfeed continuously for at least six months.[25]

> For a while I just assumed that I would not have kids because I didn't want kids for a long time. There's also the complication of not being able to have kids the same way that a cis couple would be able to. I briefly contemplated adopting, but I wasn't really a huge fan of that idea. I wanted to have the option to have biological kids. I didn't even really know about egg freezing until I did some research online.
>
> The process of finding a doctor wasn't as hard as I thought it was going to be. I emailed a few places and found a place nearby. I will say that the whole experience

was just kind of uncomfortable because of the fact that I am a trans man, and that's just not something you commonly see in those types of doctors' offices and whatnot. I had to do a lot of explaining to each doctor that I saw. If you are trans or nonbinary, you should be prepared to constantly have to explain yourself because people don't really understand. I don't necessarily blame them, but there will be a lot of moments that are probably triggering to a lot of trans people that are just uncomfortable. I know I wasn't necessarily prepared for that. I knew there were going to be some procedures. There are a lot of ultrasounds, and I had to get a pap smear for the first time in my entire life. I kind of just walked blindly into the whole process. You have to just keep telling yourself that it's going to be over eventually, and you have to keep the end goal in mind. If it's all worth it, you should be able to get through it.

As of right now, I just have a very tentative timeline because I still personally feel like I'm not fully an adult yet, even though I'm 23, and my mom had me when she was 22, which is crazy to me because I don't feel like I'm ready to have kids. I think before 30 would be my ideal time to get married and then I think, around 30, or after that, like mid-30s, maybe, I think that's when I would consider having my wife use the eggs. But I still don't know 100 percent if or when I will be having kids. I mostly just froze eggs so that I'd be able to have the option of biological kids at some point.

Shane, 23, Connecticut, he/him, YouTuber/
freelance editor, Hispanic/Latino and white,
transgender, straight, in a relationship

15

FERTILITY TREATMENTS

SIONE, 29, GREW UP wanting to have big beautiful kids, as many as possible, as is customary in Tongan culture. Sione's dad grew up one of nine, and most people in his family have more than six kids each. Sione never expected anything different for himself, so he was terrified when he and his wife couldn't get pregnant.

Sione and Courtney decided to start trying when they were 25. In the Midwest, where they lived at the time, having kids at 25 was considered old. Most parents started having kids in their early 20s, but Sione wanted to wait until he finished school. "Everyone and their mom was having a baby," Sione says. "Everyone would ask, 'So when are you having kids?' and it was a punch in the face every time."

A few years into his engineering program, they started trying. After several months with no pregnancies, Courtney grew concerned. She knew people with infertility and wanted to be proactive. They went to see a fertility specialist who told them to return if they weren't pregnant within a year. Since 90 percent of people get pregnant within a year of trying, fertility specialists typically require people under the age of 35 to try a year of unprotected sex before starting fertility treatments, six months if you are 35 or older. It's also a common requirement mandated by insurance companies before they'll approve any treatment.

At home, Courtney tracked her cycles and bought ovulation kits, and everything was timed according to what she read. And whatever she read, they tried: eating better, cutting chemicals out of their shampoos, vitamins like CoQ10. They did everything the books suggested, but they still failed to get pregnant. A year later they returned to the clinic looking for answers. They had done everything right, but the problem wasn't something that could be remedied at home: Sione had azoospermia—no sperm in his semen.

Without any sperm in his semen, Sione's best option was a sperm retrieval surgery. His doctor did a testicular biopsy and took multiple samples. The first sample had plenty of sperm. It was great news, his doctor said, that meant they could do intracytoplasmic sperm injection (ICSI), a procedure where they inject the sperm directly into the egg. They sent the remaining samples to Courtney's fertility clinic; meanwhile Courtney prepared for an egg retrieval.

Courtney's procedure was a success, 26 eggs retrieved. A relieved Sione and Courtney thought they were through the worst of it, and then shortly after arriving home, their phone rang. The embryologists could only find 10 sperm in Sione's sample. "Talking with my doctor, they said the first sample must have somehow been a good pocket. Unfortunately, they threw it away because they thought the other samples would be good," Sione says. "That first group of sperm was the first good news we received in the entire process, and then it just got taken away."

They used all 10 sperm, regardless of the sperm quality, to fertilize Courtney's eggs, and froze the remaining eggs. Only one egg turned into a blastocyst. They transferred the egg, and it took. They were ecstatic and immediately told family and friends, and then, a few weeks later, Courtney miscarried. "There was no happiness left; everything was blank," Sione says. "I truly felt like I was nothing in that moment."

The pair took some time to recuperate and decided to sell everything they owned and move to Hawaii. Another sperm retrieval procedure produced more sperm but not many. They fertilized Courtney's remaining eggs and were left with three viable blastocysts. They transferred two embryos, and both took. A few weeks later, Courtney started bleeding.

They lost one fetus, but the other was still there and stayed there for eight months until Courtney gave birth to a big beautiful baby.

When most people think of fertility treatments, they think of IVF, but IVF isn't the most common fertility treatment out there. About 85–90 percent of cases respond to conventional therapies, such as medications or surgery.[1] If you still are not pregnant after one year of trying, or after six months if you are over 35, a fertility doctor can investigate potential issues. A fertility workup includes blood tests for both partners, a semen analysis, a transvaginal ultrasound, and a hysterosalpingogram (HSG). During the HSG the doctor passes a thin tube or a small instrument through the cervix that slowly passes dye detectable by X-ray imaging into the uterus. If the fallopian tubes are open, the dye then passes through and out of the tubes. A blockage will cause the tubes to stretch. The fluid can cause cramping, so your doctor may prescribe you a muscle relaxer or recommend taking over-the-counter pain medications before the procedure. You won't feel the dye passing through; the radiologist performing the test will see the dye using X-ray imaging.

Your doctor may also have you do a hysteroscopy, a procedure where they look inside the uterus for polyps or abnormalities, which is typically done under sedation in case they have to remove or biopsy any tissue. Or they may ask that you get a saline infusion sonohysterography in which the uterus is filled with saline to assess its shape and detect abnormalities such as fibroids, polyps, or scar tissue. You may experience some cramping during the procedure as the catheter passes through the cervix and the uterus fills. If you are concerned about pain during any of these procedures, ask your doctor about pain management. You shouldn't have to just "tough it out."

You can also go to a fertility clinic earlier if you are in a same-sex relationship and plan on doing intrauterine insemination (IUI). Unfortunately, insurance won't cover fertility treatment since you haven't been trying "naturally" and therefore, by their standards, do not have infertility. (If you fail fertility treatments down the road, insurance coverage may kick in after a certain number of failed attempts.) How you proceed will depend on those causes. Your options are typically timed intercourse, IUI, and ICSI/IVF.

I had my child at 36 in the middle of the pandemic. I made the decision to start trying at 31. I always knew I wanted to have children, even as a young child. I was hell-bent on making sure I had children at the right time. I was financially stable and had lots of travel experiences. I knew it was time when a friend announced her pregnancy, and I was jealous. It was a new feeling for me, almost like my inner self was saying, *Go ahead, it's your turn now.* It took nearly five years to get pregnant.

It was very difficult to enjoy parenthood at first. I had a very difficult birth and initial postpartum experience. Pregnancy was hard. Shortly after a successful IVF transfer, I got deep vein thrombosis in my leg, so I had to continue blood thinner injections throughout my entire pregnancy on top of all the injections for IVF. No one saw my bump because we were in lockdown. My blood pressure was high due to stress, so I was at risk for preeclampsia. Birth was hard. I was determined to have a healthy baby, so I made sure I voiced my feelings often and stated boundaries, but it was really hard.

I'm a pretty big believer in the idea that people should trust their gut. Parenthood will never be an easy road, so if it's not your jam, that's perfectly okay. I lived a fulfilling life before children, and now I feel like I get to start over and enjoy it all over again.

Kari, 36, Washington, she/her, video game
executive producer, Asian and white,
cisgender, bisexual, married

Timed intercourse is the least invasive and cheapest approach. In most cases, your doctor will give you oral medications, either letrozole or clomiphene citrate, to induce ovulation. These drugs work by lowering your estrogen levels, which in turn causes your brain to produce more FSH and

LH, promoting the recruitment and ovulation of a follicle. Because these medications promote follicle growth, they also increase the risk of twins. The risk of twins is 7.4 percent on clomiphene citrate and 3.4 percent on letrozole. A study of women with PCOS found that letrozole has a higher pregnancy rate (27.5 percent) compared to clomiphene citrate (19.1 percent).[2] Your doctor will have you come into the office to check for an LH surge around the time you should be ovulating, or they may have you do at-home ovulation tests, which work similarly to pregnancy tests, to detect a rise in LH. Or your doctor may have you do a trigger shot once a follicle grows large enough. Ovulation typically occurs within 24–48 hours of the LH surge. Since the egg is only viable up to 24 hours following ovulation, your highest odds of success occur if you have sex the day before ovulation.

If timed intercourse isn't an option, or doesn't work, the next step is typically an IUI. IUIs only work if your tubes are open. For IUIs you typically take the same medication as timed intercourse. The major difference is that instead of having sex at home, you get inseminated at your fertility clinic. Alternatively, some queer people and single people skip the fertility clinic altogether, buy donor sperm, and do intracervical insemination (ICI), a.k.a. the "turkey baster method," at home. There are specialized syringes you can buy specifically for ICI, but a syringe without a needle can work too.

If you choose to go the clinic route, your partner "provides a sample," or you provide the clinic with donor sperm. In the early days of artificial insemination, IUIs were painful because the sperm wasn't filtered beforehand. Now clinics perform what's known as "sperm washing," a technique that removes a number of different cells present in the semen that aren't necessary for fertilization and gets rid of nonoptimal sperm. While you won't have any pain with the IUI itself, you may have some cramping as the catheter transporting the sperm passes through your cervix and into your uterus. The success rate of IUI is thought to range from 5 to 15 percent per cycle. Generally speaking, your odds of success depend on your age and the cause of infertility. IUI can be a good option if your partner has a low sperm count, but the success rate tends to fall if there are less than nine million motile sperm.[3] If you don't have infertility and are doing IUIs because you are queer, asexual, or don't have a partner, your success may be higher.

A study from 2014 comparing lesbian couples doing IUI with donor sperm to single women using donor sperm showed higher pregnancy rates for lesbians compared to single women, who tend to be older. After one cycle, the lesbian women had a clinical pregnancy rate of 14 percent compared to 8 percent for single women. After eight cycles of IUI, 70 percent of lesbian couples and 47 percent of single women were pregnant.[4] Most successful IUIs happen within three to four cycles, so if you don't see success, especially if you are 35 or older, your doctor may recommend you move on to IVF.[5] Some people stick to IUIs, however, since they are significantly cheaper than IVF. The insemination procedure itself ranges from $150 to $400, but there are additional fees such as medication, bloodwork, and ultrasounds. Those fees may be covered if you have insurance.[6]

I haven't decided whether I want kids. I actually tried artificial insemination when I was 35 and single, because I was afraid of getting older and not finding someone. It didn't work the two times I tried, and after reflection, I realized I didn't really want to have a child alone. I was just reacting to societal pressure and norms.

I love kids; my nieces and nephews, friends' kids, and, as a teacher, I love my students, too. I always thought I would eventually have kids but didn't meet my wife until I was 39 and she was 40. It's hard to know if our current exhaustion is from surviving the pandemic or that we both work in education, but we are so tired it doesn't seem sustainable to start trying to have a baby in our early 40s. We also haven't come to an agreement on whether or not to use an anonymous donor. I had a few students in the past who struggled mightily not knowing who their biological parent was, and that was a choice their other biological parent made for them, but I know there are also issues with using a known donor. It's an added layer of complication that needs to be well thought out for the child, for certain.

Think of IVF like playing a video game. If you get to the egg retrieval and retrieve mature eggs, congrats: you've reached a save point. Hopefully, those eggs create enough embryos that you don't have to go back to the beginning and start over. There are multiple save points throughout IVF. If you're lucky, you'll beat the level on the first try, and get your baby—but for many people, it's not that easy.

We discussed the egg retrieval process in the previous chapter, so if you skipped over it, give it a read. In egg freezing, you freeze eggs after the retrieval. When you are ready, you can thaw those eggs and fertilize them. You can also freeze any embryos made from those eggs. When you transfer eggs is up to you. However, the American Society for Reproductive Medicine (ASRM) recommends doctors limit embryo transfers to 50 years of age for mothers with health conditions and 55 years of age for those without health conditions.[7]

With IVF and ICSI, you fertilize eggs *before* transferring or freezing them. In ICSI, the embryologist injects a singular sperm into the egg. IVF exposes the egg to multiple sperm, and one of them fertilizes the egg. ICSI is traditionally used to circumvent issues with the sperm. Using ICSI when sperm-related issues are not present does not increase the success rate.[8] The average IVF cycle costs between $12,000 and $17,000, and ICSI can cost an additional $800 to $2,500. Fortunately when insurance covers IVF, it also tends to cover ICSI.[9] If your partner is nervous about giving a sperm sample the day of your procedure, ask your clinic if your partner can do the collection part at home.

Sometimes people have a hard time performing on the big day, so if there is a chance nerves might get in the way, plan ahead of time.

Sometimes surgical sperm retrieval is needed to get enough sperm for IUI, IVF, or ICSI. For those with nonobstructive azoospermia, microdissection testicular sperm extraction, or microTESE, can retrieve any available sperm from the testes. However, sperm removed from the testes haven't finished maturing, so you will need to do ICSI with any sperm retrieved. Those with obstructive azoospermia have more options for retrieving sperm. There are different types of sperm extraction and aspiration procedures for both the epididymis and testes. Sperm retrieved following a vasectomy typically comes from the epididymis. Sperm from the epididymis is mature and can be used for IUI or IVF if enough is collected. The likelihood of retrieving sperm is greater than 90 percent for people who have obstructive azoospermia and up to 63 percent for those with nonobstructive azoospermia.[10]

Lesbian couples interested in IVF can also do reciprocal IVF, or RIVF. RIVF lets both partners get involved in the process. One partner provides the eggs, and the other partner carries them. This is something Gena Jaffe and her partner opted for. Gena's wife had an egg retrieval, and Gena carried their embryo, which was fertilized with donor sperm. "After having our son, DNA didn't mean as much to me," Gena says. "I didn't need to have a genetic child; our son couldn't have been any more mine, and so when we went to have a second baby, I said, 'Let's just use the embryos we have left.'"

Another reciprocal type option that is a bit less expensive than IVF is INVOcell. INVOcell bypasses the embryology lab. The egg and sperm go into a device about the size of a champagne cork, and that device is then placed vaginally, so it can go in the nonegg providing partner. A trans woman can also incubate the INVOcell if they've had bottom surgery. However, Dr. Eyvazzadeh, cautions that the success rate for INVOcell is half of what it would be for IVF.

A very important thing to understand about IVF is the rate of attrition. Retrieving 12 eggs doesn't mean you get 12 embryos. You lose eggs and embryos with every step of the process from retrieval to transfer. Sticking with this example, let's say you retrieve 12 eggs. About 80 percent of those eggs will be mature, giving you 10 eggs to fertilize. A day after your egg retrieval, you will get a fertilization report. About 80 percent of eggs typically fertilize, so now you have eight embryos. The next report you might get is on day three. Most embryos that fertilize make it to day three. Today most embryo transfers are day-five transfers, but embryology labs didn't always have the knowledge and technical ability to grow embryos to day five, which is why, before the 2000s, all embryos were transferred on day three. We'll get back to the difference between day three and day five in a bit, but first, back to the embryo math. Let's say all of your embryos make it to day three. The next critical checkpoint is day five. Only 30–50 percent of embryos make it to day five. This leaves you with four day-five embryos.

Early Embryo Development

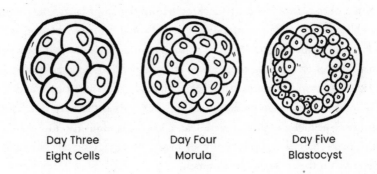

Day Three	Day Four	Day Five
Eight Cells	Morula	Blastocyst

By day three, an embryo is typically 6 to 10 cells. Sometimes, clinics will transfer embryos on day three, the cleavage stage, if there were very few eggs retrieved or if the previous embryos did not make it to day five. If transferring on day three, you will get a number grade for your embryo in addition to its cell count. Grades for cleavage-stage embryos go from 1 to 4 with 1 being the best. If the cells in the embryo are an equal size and there is little-to-no fragmentation (broken-off bits of the cell's cytoplasm), the embryo gets a grade of 1 or 2. The more fragmentation or unevenness of the cell size, the lower the grade.

Embryos graded 1 or 2 are most likely to make it to day five and most likely to transfer successfully. Good quality day-three embryos—seven to nine cells with 10 percent or less fragmentation—have the highest likelihood of success with a 40 percent birth rate.[11] Without factoring in embryo quality, statistics from the CDC show the live birth rate for day-three embryos is 34.4 percent for those under age 35, 28.6 percent for those 35–37, 20.8 percent for those 38–40, 12.5 percent for those 41–42, and 5.1 percent for those 43–44.[12]

The embryos that make it to day five are known as blastocysts. Depending on how developed the blastocyst is, it can be called an early or expanding blastocyst, an expanded blastocyst, or a hatching blastocyst. Which stage it's in determines how many cells it has. Early blastocysts can have 50–75 cells, while expanded and hatching blastocysts will have upward of 100 cells. The cells differentiate to form the inner cell mass (ICM), the part that becomes the fetus, and the trophectoderm, the part that becomes the placenta. In order to implant in the uterus, the embryo must "hatch" out of its "shell," called the zona pellucida.

Sometimes blastocysts start hatching before the embryo transfer. Sometimes blastocysts don't form until day six, so if you don't have a blastocyst by day five, the clinic has the embryos culture another day or two. Blastocysts' grades depend on how big the embryo is, its expansion, and the quality of the ICM and trophectoderm. The expansion grade goes from 1 to 6, and the ICM and trophectoderm grades go from A to C. Six is the most developed blastocyst (the highest number grade), and A is the best quality. Your fertility clinic's embryologist will give you your blastocyst's grade on day five or six, depending on the embryo's development.

A study of 1,766 single embryo transfers showed that good embryos (3–6 with either AA, AB, or BA) had an implantation rate of 55 percent and a birth rate of 46.8 percent. Fair embryos (3–6 BB) implanted 47.2 percent of the time and had a birth rate of 39 percent. Poor embryos (3–6 BC or CB) implanted at a rate of 43.6 percent for a birth rate of 34.1 percent.[13]

Looking at it from an age rather quality perspective, the live birth rate for blastocysts not genetically tested is 49.4 percent for those under 35, 42.1 percent for those 35–37, 32.1 percent for those 38–40, 21.4 percent for those 41–42, and 10.9 percent for those 43–44.[14] Depending on the age group, blastocyst transfers are 1.5 to 2 times more likely to lead to a live birth. When it comes to transfer with donor eggs, 51 percent of fresh transfers resulted in a live birth, regardless of the age of the recipient.[15]

If your embryos make it to day five, you can choose to get them tested for genetic abnormalities. If you decide to test embryos, you must freeze them first. The lab will take a tiny sample of the embryo before freezing it. Genetic testing costs $3,000–$5,000 on average and insurance does not cover it.[16] Preimplantation genetic testing (PGT-A) looks for aneuploidy, or embryos with more or less than 46 chromosomes. Essentially, you want your embryos to be euploid, meaning they have 46 normal chromosomes. Sometimes embryos come back as "mosaic," meaning they have a mix of euploid and aneuploid cells. Some clinics will transfer mosaic embryos if there aren't any euploid embryos because it's believed that the aneuploidy might self-correct as the embryo continues to grow. For low-level mosaics that had less than 50 percent of aneuploid cells, the ongoing pregnancy rate was 40.1 percent, for high-level mosaics it was 28.4 percent, and for entirely euploid embryos it was 52.3 percent.[17] And because chromosomes determine sex, if you do PGT-A, you will also know the sex of your embryos.

Chromosomal abnormalities are the leading cause of first trimester miscarriages, so selecting out aneuploid embryos can help improve your chance of a live birth. Research presented at the annual meeting of the ASRM found that three tested-normal embryos provide a 95 percent chance of a live birth. The study looked at 4,515 patients ages 31–39 who had up to three consecutive single euploid embryo transfers and found that 94.9 percent of the group achieved a pregnancy. Pregnancy rates were highest for the first transfer (69.4 percent). The second two transfers had implantation rates of 59 percent.[18]

However, newer research suggests that genetic testing does not significantly improve the live birth rate compared to the traditional grading system discussed above for those 37 and younger with three or more good graded blastocysts, although there may be some benefit for older prospective parents.[19]

Genetic testing isn't the only reason to freeze embryos. Stim meds change your hormone levels, which can thin the lining of your uterus. For embryo transfers, clinics like to see a trilaminar (three-layer) endometrium with a progesterone level between 10 and 20 ng/mL, which may not be possible following stim meds, especially if you have symptoms of OHSS. It is not safe to transfer an embryo until OHSS resolves.[20]

You can proceed with a fresh transfer if your lining and progesterone levels look good—your clinic will give you intramuscular injections of progesterone to facilitate this—or you can choose to wait and freeze. If you wait and freeze, your clinic will also give you medication, typically intramuscular progesterone and estradiol, to fluff up your lining for the frozen embryo transfer (FET). Or you can do a natural cycle FET, which uses only a trigger shot to induce ovulation and puts the embryo back days later.[21]

Because most trigger shots contain hCG, the hormone detected by pregnancy tests, you will need to wait a few days for the trigger to leave your system before you can test for pregnancy following a fresh transfer or any protocol that uses hCG. About 90–95 percent of blastocysts survive the thaw compared to 70–80 percent of day-three embryos.[22] FETs tend to perform better than fresh embryo transfers. The CDC compared all fresh and frozen embryo transfer from 86,266 cycles and found a 45.9 percent live birth rate for frozen transfers compared to 36.3 percent for fresh transfers.[23] Keep in mind that data is for all ages and all embryo days combined.

Once you have the embryo transfer, you typically need to continue taking progesterone for another 8–10 weeks. Studies show that progesterone increases the pregnancy rate following IVF and helps decrease the risk of miscarriage.[24] Your clinic will have you come back to test for pregnancy about 10 days later. However, if the transfer works, you may be able to detect pregnancy as soon as 5 days post five-day transfer (5dp5dt in fertility lingo).

In "natural" conception, embryos typically implant in the uterus on days 8–10. So five days following a five-day transfer is day 10 of that window. Once you get a positive pregnancy test, you'll want your hCG levels to double about every 48 hours. Levels that do not double or drop most often indicate a miscarriage. While it's most important that your levels double, research suggests that pregnancies with hCG levels that reach 100 mIU/mL within 10 days of a five-day transfer or 12 days following a three-day transfer are the ones most likely to result in a live birth.[25]

And that's it, you're pregnant! Easy, right?

> I've always wanted to be a mom, but after years of fertility treatments and six losses in four years, I didn't think it was going to happen. We stopped trying when I decided to go to nursing school. I was tired of the pain and loss and thought that maybe motherhood was just not for me.

About three months into nursing school, we conceived on our own, which in itself was a miracle given that I only had one fallopian tube and a 1 percent chance to carry to term. We did months of progesterone shots to keep that little one inside. Our daughter was born after five years of agony and loss.

We suffered another ectopic loss about two years after our daughter was born. In a way it was a blessing because we had no other choice but to go through IVF to get our second daughter. We implanted three embryos and got one perfect little girl. I still get sad that we can't have more children and that I couldn't have a "normal" pregnancy, but I am blessed to have two perfect daughters.

Jessica, 43, Nebraska, she/her, registered nurse, white, cisgender, straight, married

16

MANAGING THE GRIEF OF INFERTILITY

EVERY TIME DIANDRA, 32, decides to move, she gets pregnant. And every time moving day comes, her pregnancy ends. What might seem like a bad omen has happened three times now. It was too much. It would be too much for anyone, and it broke Diandra.

"I legitimately had a nervous breakdown," Diandra says. "It wasn't just the losses; it was the hormones going up and down in my body. I honestly think I had a form of postpartum depression. I wanted the hospital to remove the tube I had an ectopic pregnancy in, my last remaining tube, and they wouldn't take it because it was a Catholic-based hospital. They said, 'You're in your prime years of reproduction.' I had to basically wait until the critical time passed, and then I could write a letter and plead my case. But I was too busy having a mental breakdown, I never got around to it. I admitted myself to intensive outpatient care; I did a partial hospitalization, and then I just started making changes. I started making boundaries and looking at my life a lot differently after that."

Diandra has been trying to conceive for eleven years. She and her husband started trying soon after they got married. When Diandra was younger, doctors told her she had PCOS and that getting pregnant would be difficult, and they were right. She knew it would be hard, so they started trying, and she got so caught up in trying that she never stopped to ask herself if it was what she really wanted.

"It wasn't until this year of not trying and focusing on my health first and really putting myself first for once that gave me the space to realize having kids was something I actually wanted," Diandra says. "I got to ask myself, *Do I want this because we had losses and it feels like I've got to fix something or do I want it because I really want to be a mom?*"

Infertility and pregnancy loss come with their own unique brand of emotional whiplash. Infertility can cloud your desires or make you jump full steam ahead into something you aren't ready for, like Diandra. And if you miscarry, it's the billowing highs of pregnancy brought crashing down by loss. Or maybe it's the other way around: relief that a pregnancy you didn't want or weren't ready for is over, or, alternatively, the realization that you wanted a pregnancy you initially felt ambivalent about.

It took a miscarriage for Lia's husband to realize how much he wanted kids. Lia always saw a future with kids in it. The same could not be said for her husband, Evan. In the early days, kids were a big question mark. When Lia was 12, doctors cautioned that she might never have children. At the time, they thought she had PCOS. Lia shared this and her concerns about possible challenges in conceiving with Evan from the beginning, but her disclosure didn't change his burgeoning feelings. Less than six months later, Lia, 24 and Evan, 29, were engaged.

Though she grew up hyperaware of her fertility issues, Lia couldn't shake the feeling kids were in their future. Evan wasn't as certain, but he loved his wife and his wife loved kids, so they began trying. Six months later, Lia's gut feeling proved right. She was pregnant. The pregnancy, unfortunately, was not viable. Instead of implanting in her uterus, the embryo burrowed into her fallopian tube, an ectopic pregnancy. Lia would need surgery to remove the tube. With that operation came a new diagnosis: endometriosis, an inflammatory condition known to cause infertility. PCOS, the doctors now believed, was a misdiagnosis. The pair spent all of 2017 trying to conceive with no luck. At that point they resigned themselves to the fact that IVF might be their best option.

Lia's health went further downhill following her pregnancy. In 2018, she had surgery to address the damage endometriosis had wrought within her pelvis.

Scar tissue fused her remaining tube and ovary together behind her uterus. Doctors told her she wasn't getting pregnant because the disease completely warped her anatomy. It felt counterproductive to everything she wanted, but she began to accept that kids might not be in their cards. Sure, IVF was an option but the expense alone was enough to talk them out of it. The focus had to be on Lia's health, which meant another procedure with a more skilled surgeon in 2019. The surgery offered more than some much-needed pain relief; with it came hope. Six months later, Lia was pregnant again.

Unfortunately, like the first time, the pregnancy was not viable. This time, Lia had a miscarriage. "That loss was worse than the first one, which feels really terrible to say, but it's the truth," Lia says. Grief wrecked both Lia and Evan. Before meeting Lia, Evan couldn't picture himself as a dad. But the two pregnancies had given him the opportunity to do so, making him excited for fatherhood.

Miscarriages, which are pregnancy losses before twenty weeks gestation, happen more frequently than you might think. Up to 26 percent of pregnancies end in loss. Approximately 80 percent of all pregnancy losses occur during the first trimester, so the further along you are, the less likely you are to miscarry.[1] About 50 percent of those early losses are due to fetal chromosomal abnormalities, which become more likely as you get older. Clinical pregnancy loss rates, or losses following a detectable fetal heartbeat, also rise with age. Between the ages of 20 and 30, the chance of pregnancy loss is 9–17 percent. By the time you're 35, the risk of miscarriage is 20 percent. The risk doubles to 40 percent at age 40 and 80 percent by age 45.[2]

Many people who miscarry go on to have healthy pregnancies; however, some face an increased risk of additional pregnancy losses. You have a 20 percent risk of miscarriage following one pregnancy loss. After two consecutive losses, the risk is 28 percent. More than three losses in a row, and the risk jumps to 43 percent.[3]

Though society is starting to encourage people to openly share their difficulties conceiving or maintaining a pregnancy, people are still typically told not to announce their pregnancies until they are twelve weeks along, which is when the risk of miscarriage drops. The idea behind that recommendation is to save people the pain of having to tell friends and family they miscarried, but instead it stigmatizes pregnancy loss and forces people to endure their grief in silence.

Beyond stigma, part of the reason infertility and miscarriage-related grief is so complicated is because the losses are ambiguous. Coined in the 1970s by psychologist Pauline Boss, PhD, the term *ambiguous loss* was first used to describe the sense of loss felt by the families of pilots who went missing during the Vietnam War. Without a body or confirmation of death, the grieving process was frozen. Since then, our understanding of ambiguous loss has expanded to include a variety of other losses like infertility.

In the introduction of this book, I mentioned how many of us think about our future children. We give them names, imagine them with our partner's nose and our eyes, we look at tiny shoes and imagine their feet in them. They are, to us, very much a person—even if they don't exist yet. And then one day, you are told they may never exist. That person you've yet to meet, but already love, is gone, as is the life you pictured for yourself. There is no tangible physical loss; it's an ambiguous loss. And it can be hard to grieve fully if, like the families waiting for their loved ones to return home from war, you're waiting for a person to arrive via fertility treatments or adoption. Ambiguous loss freezes your grief, making it harder to move on.

Grief comes in many forms. If a baby cannot grow in your uterus, you may struggle with feelings of inadequacy. For people who identify as a woman, part of your grief may include feeling like your femininity has taken a hit. If you don't identify as a woman, but have a uterus, its lack of function can stir up gender dysphoria. If you are in a same-sex relationship, you might be hurting if you are the one who wanted to get pregnant but can't.

For those who identify as a man, infertility can feel emasculating. "When it comes to feeling like you're losing your manhood or feeling less than a man, just remember who you are, all the things that you still have, the people who support you, all the things you've accomplished in your life," infertility therapist Brandon Johnson, MHS, LGSW, says. "You still have these accomplishments that you've done that you can still look back on and say, 'Hey, I am a good man. I am a man. I am more than my fertility.'"

Another type of grief you may experience is disenfranchised grief, or grief that's viewed as "less legitimate" by society.[4] People unfamiliar with the pain of infertility will be quick to tell you there are alternatives to your dream: you can use egg or sperm donation or adopt. While it's true that you have other options (this entire book is about all of the different ways you can be a parent!), these comments and others, like, "You're lucky you don't have kids" or "I don't know why you're putting yourself through all that when there are so many children in need of a good home," devalue the very real emotional pain infertility and pregnancy loss causes.

You're entitled to share how others' words or actions make you feel, even if they're "well intentioned." Sometimes, it's hard for people to accept what they view as criticism when they are "just trying to help." A great way to approach tough conversations is through what mental health professionals call "I statements." Instead of focusing on the hurtful action, explain how it made you feel. Rather than saying, "Don't tell me I'm lucky I don't have kids," try communicating how the comment hurts you. "When you tell me I'm lucky I don't have kids, I feel sad and like no one understands how much I want to be a parent. It makes me feel like I can't open up about how much I'm struggling."

GRIEVING ISN'T LINEAR

As important as it is to recognize your grief, it's also crucial to realize there is no set timeline for grieving. You may be familiar with the five stages of grief, developed by psychiatrist Elisabeth Kübler-Ross. The science behind it is not perfect (it was never rigorously studied); however, a lot of people find comfort in its explanation of the different emotions that can accompany grief. Within the grieving process are denial, anger, bargaining, depression, and acceptance. There is a common misconception that these stages proceed in a chronological fashion, but in reality, they are not linear. You can go from depression to anger to denial back to anger and then to acceptance. You may spend years in certain stages and not experience others at all.

While grief gets better with the passage of time, it may never fully heal. There's an analogy that comes from a therapy session Twitter user @LaurenHerschel had that helps explain the phenomenon of why grief doesn't resolve completely with the passage of time. Picture a box with a button inside of it. The button represents your grief. Now imagine a ball inside of the box. The ball just fits inside the box. With little space, the ball repeatedly hits the button. The ball represents your infertility or miscarriage. Newly diagnosed, your infertility causes you unrelenting sadness. It's the large ball hitting the button over and over again.

Over time, the trauma of your pregnancy loss or infertility diagnosis decreases and the ball shrinks. As it shrinks, it hits the button less. It's the difference between crying for weeks after your diagnosis to years later only crying on Mother's Day. Time may decrease your triggers, but it doesn't erase your memory. You may have a child, but find yourself back in the throes of a familiar sadness when a coworker casually tells you it only took one month to get pregnant. Or you might find the ball swelling back to its original size when you realize you want a second child, but fear you may not be as fortunate as you were with your first.

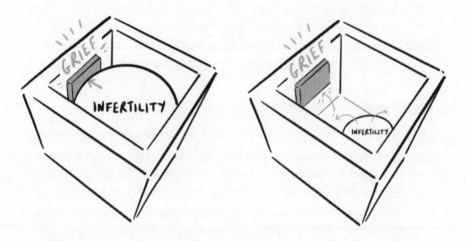

There is no timeline for grief. A small study of women living without children after infertility found that it took three to four years on average for infertility to no longer feel like it was their primary identifier.[5] The grief of infertility followed Regina Townsend, whom you met in chapter 3, even after her son was born. "It's hard because there are pieces that just kept getting robbed. I didn't get the experience of saying I think I feel funny, let me take a test. And then when he was born, they had to induce so I didn't even get to just go into labor, and then they did a C-section, so none of this felt natural for me," Regina, who runs Broken Brown Egg, a space for Black women facing infertility, says. "There's still a disconnect sometimes and I need to remind myself that I am his mom because so many parts weren't what I envisioned."

My military doctors told me because of my age, I was 35, that I needed to be induced because that was their policy for everyone 35 and older, but they literally never told me why. They never said, "There's an increased risk of stillbirth." I was being a know-it-all, and my midwife said, "Oh, that's not necessary." So I kind of went with what the midwife said because that's what I wanted to do. I lost my son at forty-one weeks exactly. I went in for a stress test, and there was no heartbeat. The doctor came over and told me there was no heartbeat, and I just started screaming.

I'm kind of a weirdo in the community because I adamantly hate being told it's not my fault. I really feel like it is my fault. I'm not beating myself up about it, but it is my fault. It's a decision that I made that led to his death, and I'm okay with that fact. I think that makes a lot of people uncomfortable when I say that, but it's also really important to me to acknowledge what really happened.

I did deal with a lot of grief and regret in the beginning, and it was hard to talk about it because people would automatically say, "Oh, it's not your fault. You need to stop thinking like that." So a big thing I try to advocate for is don't tell people how to feel. Whatever you're feeling is whatever you're feeling. It just is. I remember being awake at two in the morning, and just screaming at the ceiling.

I sent out an email about a week after my son died. It was a very short email, and I sent it to literally everyone I knew. I said, "I cannot handle having this conversation multiple times, so everyone's on the BCC line, here you go." I remember being surprised at the responses because people that I thought were going to be really great said the platitudes, and then people who I wasn't expecting as much from were just really sweet. One person said,

"You know, I know that this is a difficult and awkward time, I want you to know that I'm here and if you want to call me on the phone and just sit in silence, I'm okay with that." I know that that sounds odd, but that was really meaningful to me.

I still don't know the perfect thing to say to someone who is grieving. The best things you can say are the simplest: I care about you, I'm here, I love you, and I'm sorry. Keep it simple and try not to draw meaning where there isn't any.

E. Miranda Hernandez, 40, California, she/her, runs Adrian's Elephant in honor of her son, cisgender

INFERTILITY AND YOUR MENTAL HEALTH

While time and having a child may ease the pain of infertility, there's a lot you can do in the interim. One of the first and best things you can do is connect with others. It might not seem like it, because society is pretty *hush, hush* on the infertility and pregnancy loss front, but there are plenty of other people who understand your pain.

"Talking to other people with infertility definitely helped throughout that process," Sione, whom you met in the previous chapter, says. "If I didn't have anybody to talk to, it would've been worse. It can be hard to open up for men. It's a pride thing; you feel like you're less of a man because of it, and I guess those are some things I felt in the very beginning. I thought, *This is my issue. I'm going to deal with my issue.* But talking with our friends who were also going through infertility helped immensely."

In addition to connecting with people who get it, you also need to take care of your mental health. During the darkest days of your infertility journey, you will be convinced happiness no longer exists. Infertility can cause depression, anxiety, and even PTSD. A study presented at the American Psychological Association's annual meeting showed that 46 percent of people undergoing fertility treatments developed symptoms that met the official diagnostic criteria for PTSD.[6] Another study found that women with infertility reported the same levels of anxiety and depression as those diagnosed with cancer, hypertension, and heart disease.[7] It's not all bad news though. With counseling and adequate support, research shows the challenges of infertility can lead to post-traumatic growth and positive psychological change that promotes resilience.[8]

Infertility is an expensive diagnosis, so it's understandable if you can't also afford therapy, but if you can, now would be a great time to go. "I will really say seek therapy first and deal with the emotional aspects," Brandon, who has experienced infertility himself, says. "We put so much emphasis on the medical concerns that we forget about the emotional concerns, and we're not prepared for them."

Several studies have shown that cognitive behavioral therapy (CBT) and support groups reduce anxiety and depression in people with infertility.[9] The pregnancy rate was also higher for those who utilized CBT, support groups, or couples counseling.[10] If you have insurance, check and see what coverage your plan offers. If you don't have insurance or good mental health coverage, look for a local clinic with therapists who offer appointments on a sliding scale. While there are benefits to going alone, i.e., more time for you and your needs, you can also go to a marriage and family therapist for couples counseling.

It's important to have people on your team that you trust. Diandra likes to remind herself and the people she works with as a community health specialist that medical professionals work for you. "You are a consumer; you are paying for their services," she says. "If you were shopping for a new mattress, would you buy the mattress from the person being an asshole to you? Because I wouldn't. I wouldn't buy a mattress from somebody who told me I was too fat. Why would I continue paying for services? You deserve and are worthy of being treated with the utmost respect. You deserve to be listened to, and you deserve compassion."

Infertility can also place a major strain on relationships—financially, emotionally, and sexually. At first, all of that trying (sex) may feel like it's bringing you closer together, but when you're ovulating on a night you're not in the mood to have sex, getting the job done can feel like a herculean task. It's important to keep open lines of communication with your partner, if you have one, because they are likely grieving too. Even though it's largely cisgender women talking about infertility, they aren't the only ones who go through it. In a study of 200 couples being seen at a fertility clinic, 50 percent of the women and 15 percent of the men said that infertility was the most upsetting experience of their lives.[11] However, male rates of depression and low self-esteem tend to be the same as females when it's the male partner diagnosed with infertility.[12] And though science and research tend to stick to the gender binary, it's important to note people across the gender spectrum experience infertility and its related grief.

Ultimately, it's not your job to counsel your partner through infertility. If your partner doesn't want to talk about it—it happens, everyone grieves differently—ask if there is anyone they would feel comfortable talking to. If your partner constantly offloads on you, remind them that you are struggling too and suggest alternatives for them like a support group or couples counseling. If they aren't willing to seek help elsewhere, it's up to you to assert your boundaries.

"Just be there and give him the space to open up as he feels necessary," Brandon says. "Whether this is coming out or given in one or two sentences about how they feel at that moment, which was me. Sometimes you just have to let them deal with it when it comes to things like donor sperm or choosing an option. Give them space with a small nudge because given too much space, you'll be waiting forever."

My first pregnancy was an accident at 31. I was terrified. It's no exaggeration to say that about eight weeks in, the day I caved into caring for the life inside me and my desire to be a mother, I miscarried. The subsequent three pregnancies, including one ectopic, created such confusion, anxiety, and ambivalence about the prospect of having children. After we finally decided to stop with any procedures (I had just had the final two miscarriages from IUI), I became pregnant naturally. It was my fifth pregnancy. I had my son at 36.

> Pregnancy, for me, was terrible. I expected a loss at any moment. The trauma of the miscarriages and the medical system that ignored my ectopic symptoms until it almost killed me will never go away. I didn't navigate them, really, I just stared at the ceilings during ultrasounds. I cried constantly. My friends scolded me and told me to enjoy myself at the depths of my pain. It was a nightmare. After tentatively leaning into pregnancy around the eighth month then finding out your kid has a condition no one saw and only finding out postpartum was the worst day of my life. Thinking about it all now, even with a super happy 4-year-old, is incredibly hard.
>
> **Nadine,** 40, New York, she/her, works at a nonprofit, white, cisgender, straight, married

EVERYONE HAS BOUNDARIES

Setting and understanding your boundaries will be one of the most important things you do when it comes to preserving your sanity throughout your infertility journey. Personally, I don't dwell in spaces where I know babies will be present. Right now, I can't. I've set that firm boundary and decided it has to be okay.

A lot of people do some version of this, whether it's calling in sick for Take Your Child to Work Day, muting someone on social media because they're posting too much about their pregnancy, or declining an invitation to a friend's child's birthday party. It's easy for loved ones to confuse asserting boundaries with "diva-like" behavior. People assume you could do something—like be around children—but you just don't want to. Unless you have a family member or friend who has experienced infertility, it can be hard for those around you to understand the depths of your pain.

It shouldn't come down to you having to put on some display of emotion to get your loved ones to respect your wishes. Ultimately, you have to respect your boundaries before you can expect anyone else to. If you tell your friend it's too painful for you to discuss their pregnancy, don't ask them 500 questions about being pregnant. They won't understand the boundary, which means they can't respect it. Only you can decide what your boundaries are. A good way to figure out your needs is to identify what makes you upset and then find ways to minimize that trigger. For example, if photos of your friend's pregnancy make you jealous, unfollow their profile. (This is not the same as unfriending; they won't know you unfollowed them.)

It's important to note that some of your boundaries may face blowback. If you tell your friend you'd prefer to hang out without her children present, she may take it personally. You can try to minimize this by saying something along the lines of, "Friend, when I see your kids and how you interact with them, it makes me want what you have and that is really painful for me right now as I'm going through fertility treatments. Maybe we can do something when the kids are at school or when your partner can watch them?"

It can be hard to stand up for yourself and your needs, but if you don't, chances are no one will. If it helps to think of it this way, make taking care of yourself, mentally and physically, your first task as a parent. If your child needed something, you'd move mountains to do it. If you are going through fertility treatments or adoption, you're already moving mountains just to meet them. Afford yourself that same love and care.

RECONNECT WITH WHO YOU WERE BEFORE LOSS

At some point in your fertility journey, you'll hear a doctor or well-meaning family member ask you what you are doing to manage stress—as if you can downward dog your way out of depression. Someone will tell you about their uncle's cousin's brother's niece who stopped trying to get pregnant and then magically did. Yes, there is scientific evidence that stress negatively impacts your body, but fixating on it won't help you get pregnant. And, as a counterpoint, it's also worth noting that plenty of people are still able to get pregnant during traumatic, highly stressful times—rape survivors and refugees of war get pregnant. Even people in concentration camps during the Holocaust got pregnant.[13]

You need something that can balance out all of that heaviness, especially if you can't afford therapy or find a support group that meets your needs. You might be thinking, *I'm physically, emotionally, and financially exhausted, and you want me to find joy? Are you kidding me?* I hear you, I do. I know how intoxicating the misery can be—the times where it feels like everyone is moving on except you. It threatens to take every ounce of joy you have, but you can't let it.

"Infertility is bigger than babies. When we hear the term, our immediate thought process jumps to the baby. Infertility is so many things; it's financial status and socioeconomic background; it's faith in religion, family, culture, cultural identity, sexual identity, gender expression—so many things. A baby is just one part," Regina says. "My biggest thing is just reminding people that their feelings are valid, their feelings are important. They deserve attention because the moves that we make are predicated on those feelings. If we don't validate them, identify them, and address them, we waste time. We lose people, and we lose ourselves."

I knew I wanted the experience of raising children and also felt drawn to the experience of pregnancy. I wanted to know that my body could do it. Having lived a life in contention with my body, I wanted to celebrate it rather than admonish it. I was so desperate for a pregnancy and child that I "made deals" with the universe that I would never complain if I could just get pregnant. I wouldn't say that I fully upheld my end of that deal, but I definitely worked on appreciating we got as far as we did. I was 34 when my daughter was born.

I love being a parent. I am regularly in awe of the fact that my daughter exists in the world. Because we didn't start trying until several years into our marriage and then experienced unexplained infertility for two years, I spent a lot of time wondering if a biological child would ever be here. I would close my eyes and picture her walking through our house, smiling at me—just being. Now we have been trying to get pregnant with our second for nearly two years, and the interventions that worked last time, IUI, are not working this time. Before my first pregnancy, my "deals with the universe" included saying I would be content if I could have just one child. Now, I'm yearning for a second. We are considering other methods of parenthood such as fostering or adopting, but I have a deep desire for a biological child that I thought would be "fulfilled" after my first. It's a lonely and confusing place not knowing when or how we will get a second child but knowing our family feels incomplete.

Amanda, 36, Wisconsin, she/her, works at a nonprofit, white, cisgender, bisexual, married

17

ALTERNATIVE PATHS TO PARENTHOOD

WHEN ALISEN AND KAITLYN thought about building their family, they never imagined themselves becoming parents through IVF. Growing up, Alisen wanted a sibling and begged her parents to consider becoming foster parents after learning about the foster care system when she was 8. Over a decade later, an adult Alisen would sign up to learn how she could foster. It was hard to believe that she, a single, queer, 24-year-old, could become a foster parent, but there she was with her first placement.

Over the next two years, Alisen would go on to foster five kids under the age of 4, first by herself and then with her now-wife Kaitlyn. Kaitlyn lived two hours away and would drive down to where Alisen lived in Florida to visit her and her foster child. Alisen's passion for fostering is part of what drew Kaitlyn to her. Alisen and Kaitlyn never planned on adopting, but the closer they grew to their foster kids, the harder it was to fight those feelings. "I didn't go into fostering saying, 'Wow, I hope that I can foster these children and then they never leave and I get to adopt them,'" Alisen says. "I went into it thinking I was going to help children but then you fall for them. So as much as I'd like to give advice to someone else and say, 'Don't go into fostering with the attention to adopt,' I can't because I didn't mean to either.

It wasn't something I could control, you know, the feelings just followed. You can say going into it, 'I'm not gonna let my guard down' and try not have any expectations, but sometimes people's minds change."

Dealing with the child welfare system in Florida was difficult. Things were constantly changing, and it was bad for everyone involved. After their last placement left, Alisen and Kaitlyn decided to close their home and move on with just adoption. They applied to adopt a 14-year-old-girl and were not selected. Then they applied to adopt a sibling set of three: a 6-year-old, a 4-year-old, and a 2-year-old. They were not chosen as an adoptive home for them either.

Alisen never had a desire to give birth or have biological children until after the couple's experience with foster care and adoption. She had some health concerns she feared would not be compatible with pregnancy. "I wanted a child that we could love that wasn't going to leave, and if that meant that I had to sacrifice my health, then that was something I was willing to risk," she says. Kaitlyn had no interest in being pregnant. Being butch and more masculine than Alisen, she didn't want to be visibly pregnant and carry a child. Alisen did two at-home inseminations with donor sperm and then two IUIs at a fertility clinic. The clinic process was not easy. Alisen felt like their infertility caused by Alisen's PCOS was not taken as seriously as fertility concerns of heterosexual couples. They had one doctor who could not understand why Kaitlyn didn't want to carry and made a point that she should be the one to do it at three separate points during their appointment. Then, after all four of their IUIs failed, they moved to IVF. Alisen got pregnant from her first frozen transfer. And though they are both on the birth certificate, they plan on doing second-parent adoption, even though it's expensive, and despite fears they might get a homophobic judge who denies them both legal parentage.

Things get complicated real fast when you can't have a child naturally or choose alternative paths to building your family. There's an analogy that explains this difference very well, even if that wasn't the original author's intention. In 1987, *Sesame Street* writer Emily Perl Kingsley penned an essay titled *Welcome to Holland* about her experience parenting a child with a disability. In it, Kingsley compares preparing for parenthood like planning a trip to Italy: you learn some of the language, buy guide books, and dream about the places you'll go. But as the plane lands, the flight attendant announces you're in Holland, not Italy. Holland, or as it's more commonly known today, the Netherlands, is a beautiful place, but it's not the trip you planned. You don't speak the language, you don't have an itinerary, and, perhaps most pressingly, it's not the place you wanted to go. In Kingsley's story, the protagonist realizes that Holland (having a child with a disability) is different from Italy (having an able-bodied child) but not less. There is beauty to be found where you landed, even if that wasn't the journey you planned for.

I think about this story a lot when I think about adoption, fostering, and donor conception. While having a child with a disability is often a surprise to parents, building your family through adoption, foster care, or donor conception is not. Using alternative means to grow your family may not be how you initially envisioned parenthood, but you can prepare yourself for this new journey. You can learn to speak the language and appreciate where you are going, even if it's not the destination you originally set out for. If you don't, then you're the person in the cafe shouting for a panino when you should be asking for a boterham. Learning the language isn't for you, it's for your kids, so that you can communicate effectively.

This chapter and the next are about the kids who come from donor conception, adoption, and foster care. In these chapters, I lean heavily on the experience of people who grew up in these systems for two reasons. First, their perspectives aren't often considered, or they're seen as secondary to recipient parents (those who adopt or use donor conception). And second, if you plan on adding children to your family through these systems, who better to advise you than those who know what it's like to be adopted, fostered, or donor conceived. But before we talk about the kids, we need to talk about the adults who use these systems to build their families.

Not everyone comes to third-party reproduction the same way. Adoption, fostering, or using donor cells is a different path to parenthood regardless of whether you're queer, single, dealing with infertility, or just choosing not to have biological children. Different doesn't mean bad, wrong, or less meaningful than conceiving a child using your DNA, and it doesn't affect the love you'll have for your child either. What it means is that your child comes with a backstory, a history that differs from yours, and as their parent, it's your job to honor that.

For Cora, whom you met in chapter 3, that meant discovering the identity of the egg donor she and her husband used so they could have a second child. It's been a learning process for Cora, learning what her daughter might need and taking steps early on so her daughter never has to ask to connect to her biological roots. To Cora, what good was a child-led approach if her child might grow up and somehow fear offending the parents who raised her by asking to meet her genetic mother. "I didn't have any issue with my daughter not being genetically mine, but the term *mom* was so important to me. Going into this, I never would have thought that I would have been calling my egg donor (her genetic mom), *mom*, or her *other mom*, and now it's not an issue," Cora says. "But I had to grow and center my daughter and think about how she's going to see it and how she should be able to see it if she wants to. Had someone told me at the start that I had to raise her this way right now or don't do it, I wouldn't have been able to. Looking now at how magical this all is and how good it all feels, I wouldn't want it any other way. But I had to grow into that, and I think that going into the process with the idea that you're going to need to grow for the sake of your child and really look at your ability to be able to do that and your openness to do that is really important."

Cora's daughter will never have to ask to meet her genetic mother because she already knows who she is and will grow up having as much access to her as she'd like. And while Cora is biracial, she's not part Puerto Rican like her egg donor, and so she's made sure her daughter has access to her Puerto Rican roots as well. "I feel like there are a lot of recipient parents who feel that as long as they do everything right, it will diminish their child's need to go out and look for that person or a relationship with that person," Cora says. "I feel like that's such a terrible way of looking at things. I feel like if you've done everything right, you have provided the tools for your child to figure out whatever works best for them, and if that is meeting or knowing them and having a relationship, you've made it possible for that to happen."

I'm an adoptive mom. My husband has a child from his previous marriage and his ex kind of stepped out when kiddo was 2. I knew my husband had a child when we started dating and that his ex wasn't really in the picture. I made it very clear that the moment he introduced me to his child, I would consider that a marriage proposal because I wasn't interested in breezing in and out of a child's life. They're too fragile, especially given his history of his mom leaving. I came in when kiddo was 5, and I've been his mom ever since. (He's 9 now.) After we got married, we decided to let me be stepmom for about two years before doing adoption paperwork so that it would go smoothly with the courts. We completed adoption proceedings, and I am legally kiddo's mom now.

I'm autistic. My husband and kiddo are also autistic. On one hand, it's nice to be with people who just let me be me. On the other hand, people with autism spectrum disorder usually have a whole host of comorbidities, and parenting with health issues is exhausting. I've known since childhood that I never wanted to be pregnant and give birth. My mom miscarried a couple of times and almost died giving birth to my little brother. I have a lot of body trauma due to my health issues, and the idea of passing my genetics on is a little horrifying. Pregnancy has always seemed kind of gross and painful. I had written off becoming a mom because adoption and surrogacy are so expensive. Becoming an adoptive parent of my husband's child wasn't something I expected or looked for, but it worked for me.

Erin, 35, Oregon, she/her, works in IT, white, cisgender, straight, married, disabled

WHO DESERVES CHILDREN?

When the birth rate dropped following the pandemic, so did the number of adoptable children. Some people saw this as a win; others, largely hopeful adoptive parents, not so much. Following some difficult conversations within the adoption community came one salient point: adoption is about finding homes for children, not the other way around.

A spectrum of opinions exists when it comes to alternative paths to "natural" conception. When I interviewed adoptees and donor-conceived people and asked what they wanted intended parents—people who plan to adopt or use donor conception—to know, all stressed the importance of self-reflection, but a few took it a step further stating prospective parents should ask themselves why they feel "entitled" to children.

It's a tricky and uncomfortable question. It's also an unfair one. When we talk about who "deserves" kids, we imply that there are acceptable and unacceptable parents. This kind of thinking harms all parents. The idea that there are acceptable parents already exists in that we use such justifications to take children away from "unacceptable" ones. And while, yes, there are cases where children need to be removed from their homes, such as instances of abuse and neglect, historically most removals target parents of color and low-income families whose parenting looks different from intensive parenting norms. Some of these people, if given proper resources and support, could easily parent on their own.

How, then, should we answer that question? Do we make biology the sole determinant of parenthood? If we say yes, we push forward bioessentialism, the idea that all children need a cisgender biological mother and father, which disadvantages those who are queer, infertile, or single. If we ignore the blatant discrimination that pushes forward—which we shouldn't, but let's decimate this argument so we can move on from its hideousness—how do we enforce such a prescribed notion of parenthood? Do we outlaw divorce? What happens if a parent dies? Should parents who walk out on their families be shackled to their homes? Obviously this argument falls apart pretty quickly.

Why someone feels "entitled" to children shouldn't be a question for those who need alternative routes to parenthood, it should be a question for all people considering children. The underlying implication is that it's selfish to have children, a departure from pronatalist norms that say that *not* having children is selfish. When you look at studies of people considering parenthood, most of their reasons have nothing to do with the child. People want to leave a legacy, reach milestones, gain a sense of achievement, have new experiences—internal reasons mostly to do with themselves. And these reasons are rarely, if ever, questioned when reproducing within the confines of your bedroom. If the idea behind questions of deserving and entitlement is acting with intention, how do we define good intentions?

Adoption, foster care, and donor conception will never not exist. People would desire children and find ways to have them even if these systems were to disappear. Just look at those who go outside of the regulated sperm donation system. There are men who have fathered dozens of children through posts shared in online groups. Biology does not make good parents; care does. And while it's true that caring for your child can look quite a bit different when their roots differ from yours, we can improve these systems so that they uphold the dignity of both parent and child without abolishing them or admonishing people who need such systems to become parents. We can fight to keep parents with their biological children whenever possible while finding more affordable ways to help people have children through assisted reproductive technologies without depriving those children of their genetic roots. It will take work, but isn't that true of all parenthood?

I have always wanted to be a parent. I grew up with small children always in the house, from siblings to cousins to the kids my mother did daycare for. I've been a teacher of children in one form or another my whole life, and I love the journey of discovery inherent in each child. Our journey was a long one, but ultimately worked out. Our baby is one month old now. We started by using frozen sperm from a sperm bank, but ultimately went with a known donor, which turned out to be way less stressful and free.

> I still don't know what title I will use as a parent. I use she/her pronouns as well as they/them, so most adults are referring to me as a mom, mother, mommy, and mama. I think I like it, but I'm also really intrigued by the idea of using a gender-neutral title. I feel like my gender identity is always in a bit of flux, and I don't feel super attached to my own gender labels, nor do I feel turned off by them. I will probably just let the kiddo decide what they want to call me and go with that.
>
> **Kiona,** 32, California, they/she, Black, multiracial, genderqueer, nonbinary, pansexual, married, polyamorous, neurodivergent

QUEER FAMILY FORMATION

The idea of "families of choice" comes from the queer community. Those who identify within the LGBTQIA+ umbrella tend to have a broader definition of parenting, placing less emphasis on pregnancy and genetic parenthood and more focus on the act of parenting and raising children. A study comparing infertile heterosexual couples and infertile lesbian couples found that queer women were less attached to biological notions of parenthood and had easier transitions from trying to conceive to adopting.[1] This approach results in a spirit of openness and a sense of pride that doesn't always exist for heterosexual folks.

"Family formation stories are a huge part of LGBTQIA+ families because there's no 'natural biological way,'" says Jordan Budd, the executive director of COLAGE, an organization for the children of queer parents, a.k.a. queerspawn. "There's obviously some story about how this child came to be, whether that's through donor conception, adoption, previous marriage, or what have you. Those narratives are part of what we talk about a lot. The level of openness is such a common thread among LGBTQIA+ families because you're constantly having to justify your family to the outside world."

"Something I worked on for years was, how, as an LGBTQIA+ person, am I going to have a family?" Al says. "A lot of that was realizing in the end, I'm not going to be alone." Al, 26, met Angela, 28, back when they were both college students. They've been together for five years and plan on having Angela start fertility treatments soon. The pair spend a lot of time thinking about what their family might look like and the roads that might take them there. They'll start with IUIs, and if that doesn't work, they'll move on to IVF, and maybe down the road they'll adopt. The beauty is that they get to choose free of heteronormative ideals, which is why it bothers Al when people assume they'll be the "dad" just because they are nonbinary and present more masc. But when it comes to their kids, Al doesn't care what they call them. "I really like Baba, but they may call me mom, they may call me mama, and they may call me dad some days."

Like Al, some nonbinary parents choose amalgamates of "mom" and "dad" like mapa or baba. Others create something unique to them. Choosing what your family calls you gives you something special that makes you feel connected and that you don't have to share with the rest of the world, Van Ethan Levy, a trans and non binary mental health clinician, says. Van's recommendation: find what works for you. Van doesn't have children, but says if they did, they'd probably use "vandeti," the name their brother's children call them. Van's family lives in Puerto Rico and in Spanish *tio* means "uncle," *tia* means "aunt," and *titi* is gender-neutral.

An important part of building your family when you're queer includes protecting that family. If you are in a relationship where one or both parents are not the genetic parents, second-parent adoption, sometimes called stepparent adoption, is a must. Second-parent adoption gives nongenetic or nonbirthing parents legal protections should their parentage be called into question. "It doesn't matter if both parents are on the birth certificate," Gena Jaffe, a lawyer who had her children through reciprocal IVF, says. "A birth certificate is not a legal document so it doesn't hold any weight. It is unconstitutional to disallow same-sex parents to go on the birth certificate, but these birth certificates are being challenged," Gena says. Another option is a voluntary acknowledgment of parenting, but Gena advises against this because a court can overturn it. The document, which gets signed by both parents in the hospital, can be called into question, leaving it up to the court to decide. It offers nowhere near as much protection as a judgment of parentage or an order of adoption, which is irrevocable once issued by the court. (Jaffe also recommends heterosexual parents who use donor conception go through the second-parent adoption process to protect their rights and to avoid inheritance issues following a parent's death or custody battles in the event of divorce.)

"Second-parent adoption can be expensive and time-consuming. It sucks, so let's just put it out there and acknowledge that it sucks that we have to go through this, that we already often have to spend a ton of money on fertility treatments and are told that we have to do more to protect our family when we already feel marginalized and discriminated against," Gena says. "That being said, I try to remember that we've made a lot of progress in the past decade even. This is something we're legally allowed to do now, and we weren't allowed to do this not long ago. We couldn't even legally get married, let alone be considered the legal parents of our children. So while this is annoying and another expense, it is the greatest thing that we can do to protect our family. It is a great gift that we have to give ourselves to ensure that our family is protected and will stay intact."

While times are changing, queer parents still fight for recognition of their parenthood. Even with legal documents and the right to adopt in all 50 states, the last state of which only changed its law in 2016, discrimination abounds. In 2021, the Supreme Court ruled in favor of Catholic Social Services, an agency hired to provide foster care services in Philadelphia that would not certify same-sex couples as foster parents due to religious objections.[2] And even when parents get on the birth certificates, those documents don't always honor their gender or lack thereof.

"Having me is a radical act of defiance," Emily Harnett, a donor-conceived person whom you'll meet in the next chapter, says. "I'm not just a child that's entering into the world with a mom and a dad. My parents had to think about how it was going to be in school for me, how I was going to be discriminated against, how they were going to be discriminated against; and so, because these acts are so intentional, it makes me feel really special in my moms' eyes."

I have always wanted kids. Ideally, I would have a husband and give birth to my children but I'm asexual and autistic, which complicates this scenario. I also have cerebral palsy, which means my body doesn't always do what I want it to, which could further impede my having a healthy pregnancy.

As a heteroromantic asexual, I've always had the idea of getting pregnant via artificial insemination, either with a husband or donor sperm. I am a sex-averse asexual, so having children via sex has never been on the table for me. Recently, though, concerns about my ability to have a healthy pregnancy and birth have led me to lean more toward surrogacy. I have sensory defensiveness due to my autism, as well as GI problems, that may make pregnancy more uncomfortable for me. My cerebral palsy sometimes messes with my body in ways I don't expect, which makes me nervous about both pregnancy and childbirth. All of these options are very expensive, so I worry that by the time I can afford to start a family, my choices will be limited due to my age.

Shannon, 25, Florida, she/her, graphic designer, white, cisgender, heteroromantic asexual, single, disabled

WHAT COULD YOUR FAMILY LOOK LIKE?

Around the time she was 25, Rachel realized her only motivation for seeking out relationships was so she could have a family someday. Asexuality wasn't a word Rachel, now 29, heard very often growing up. She didn't realize that there are people like her who just don't desire romantic and sexual relationships. Choosing to become a single mother was hard for her to conceptualize at first, but after a while she realized it may be the best choice for her, or, at least, the only thing that made sense in her mind. After four rounds of IUI, Rachel became a mom.

"I love being a mom, so it worked out for me," Rachel says. "I wish I could've heard from more people in similar situations. Maybe that would have eased some of that fear of whether I was doing the right thing so I didn't have to be so freaked out through the whole thing."

It's understandable why Rachel would freak out. Single parents face higher levels of stress and often struggle to maintain a work-life balance. Knowing this, Rachel prepared by saving money before doing IUIs. She also had support from her parents, who live close by and were happy to help out when needed. Emily, on the other hand, has found single parenthood brutal. Emily was 26 when she had her son. Emily had never wanted children and was surprised to find herself excited when she got pregnant. Most of the challenges Emily, now 44, faces have nothing to do with her son. It's the discrimination single moms face. Employers don't want to hire single moms, she says. "I have two master's degrees, yet I've lived in poverty most of my child's life. My career ended when my son was 2, and now I'm 'too old' due to rampant ageism to rebuild in the sector my degrees and experience are in."

Research shows single parents are more likely to experience work-family conflict, greater parenting strain, and more sadness, stress, and exhaustion when spending time with children.[3] Given the cost of living and the blurred boundaries of work these days, it's hard for moms to make it on their own—but many do. Michelle, 31, got pregnant with her daughter when she was a junior in high school. There were many panic attacks when she first learned she was pregnant, but she decided to raise her daughter. Her daughter's father was largely unsupportive, and so Michelle did not press for child support because she didn't want him to try to get custody. (Note: if you father a child, even if you want nothing to do with them, you will have to pay child support if the birthing parent takes you to court.)

Michelle lived with her parents at first, but she was largely on her own. "I didn't have the support of a husband where I could say take the baby while I take a nap for 30 minutes," Michelle says. "If I got to the point where it was too much, everybody there would help out, but it was lonely. I graduated from high school early and immediately started college. So I was working and going to school and had her—it was a lot." Today, Michelle has two children, 11 years apart. Her second child, a son, she had with her husband.

For people who want to have children but don't have a partner and don't want to do it alone, there is always co-parenting. When most people think of co-parenting, they think of divorced parents raising their kids, but that's not the only type of co-parenting. On websites like Modamily and Just a Baby people can connect with others looking to have children. Sometimes it leads to romantic relationships, and other times it's just a legal agreement to share custody of a child both parties create through assisted reproductive technologies. Of course, not everyone feels a strong desire to parent, and not everyone needs a genetic connection to their kids.

Nick, 38, is happy being a stepparent. Having kids never crossed his mind, but he's glad things turned out the way they did. Nick and his wife Marjorie, 34, were friends for 10 years before they decided to date. When Marjorie's son was 2, she moved to be closer to Nick and see if the two could make things work. Nick hated his stepmother growing up and knew he wanted to do things differently. He approached his new role like a "ball of clay," ready to be molded into whatever was needed of him.

Research suggests that stepparenting might be more stressful than parenting biological children since there are no rules about what roles stepparents hold. However, other research finds that stepparents living with minor children face no more distress than their childless peers.[4] When stepparents do feel strain, it tends to be stepmothers due to gender roles and challenges to their authority.[5] "Co-parenting was quite an adjustment at first," Nick says. "I had my own complexes and misgivings about parenthood, but I knew I needed to learn my place and do anything and everything that I could to make it easier for Marjorie, her ex, and their son."

Nick and Marjorie have no plans of having biological children together, but Nick dipped into one more parent-type role before getting a vasectomy: he donated sperm to a lesbian couple who are friends of his. "It's an honor to have been such a part of their life," he says. And while he's not their daughter's dad, he's happy to answer any questions she might have as she grows up.

18

USING AN EGG, SPERM, OR EMBRYO DONOR

EMILY HARNETT, 23, HAS 20 half-siblings. They all share the same biological father—an unknown man Emily calls "donor dad." Emily knows the identity of 17 of their half-siblings. It's a puzzle they're always finding new pieces to: one they've had to accept and that they might never solve.

Emily is one of a growing number of people conceived from donor sperm, eggs, or embryos. The US doesn't maintain records of births resulting from donor sperm insemination, but estimates suggest some 30,000 to 60,000 people are born each year using these methods. The birthrate from egg or embryo donation is much lower, about 11,000 births per year. When it comes to pricing, donor sperm is typically the least expensive, costing about $1,000 per vial.[1] Donor eggs can cost anywhere from $12,000 to $20,000, while the medical costs associated with donor embryo transfers range from $4,000 to upward of $10,000.[2]

Though egg and embryo donation are fairly new, artificial insemination has been around for centuries. Unofficial historical claims suggest the first case of artificial insemination occurred in the mid-15th century to impregnate Joan of Portugal, wife of Henry IV, king of Castile and León—either that or she had an affair. The first documented case of artificial insemination took place in the 1770s. A merchant with hypospadias, a condition where the opening of the urethra is located on the underside of the penis instead of the tip, was instructed to collect any semen that escaped during sex, put it in a warm syringe, and then inject it into his partner's vagina. More tests using postcoital sperm took place in the 1800s. Only 1 in 55 inseminations was successful, but this was likely due to the belief at the time that ovulation occurred during menstruation.[3]

The development of practical methods for artificial insemination began in the early 1900s, but not in humans. The methods we use today came from research on how to artificially impregnate domestic farm animals. Reports of human insemination using similar techniques followed in the 1940s and '50s. In 1953, the first sperm-cooling methods were developed, and the first pregnancy from frozen sperm occurred later that year.[4] In 1978, came the first child born using IVF, which helped refine sperm processing techniques and led to an increased interest in artificial insemination. The 1970s also saw the start of the sperm bank industry.

Egg donation followed in the 1980s. The first child conceived using donor eggs was born in Australia in 1983.[5] A 29-year-old woman altruistically donated four eggs to a 25-year-old woman with premature ovarian failure. The 25-year-old ended up conceiving using the donor eggs; however, the 29-year-old could not get pregnant with her own eggs.[6] The first US child born from donor eggs came a few weeks later in January 1984 in California.[7] Today, the average egg donor is 28, and the average recipient parent is 41.[8] Fifteen years after the first egg donation, the first donor embryo-conceived child was born in the US.[9] Embryo donation (remaining embryos created during another person's IVF that are then donated to someone else) is less common than egg donation, resulting in about 1,000 births per year.[10]

The stigma attached to using donor conception added to the shame many people with infertility already felt about their diagnoses. There was concern in the early 1900s that donor sperm would promote eugenics. Meanwhile, the Catholic Church decried sperm donation as a form of adultery that deprioritized the importance of marital sex and promoted the vice of masturbation. (Many religions still prohibit donor conception with the exception of Judaism, Shi'a Islam, Hinduism, and Buddhism.[11])

Shame and stigma surrounded donor conception throughout the 20th century. The first pregnancy with frozen sperm in 1953 wasn't announced until 10 years later due to public opinion about artificial insemination at the time.[12]

The pressure to keep donor conception hidden even shaped the way doctors performed artificial inseminations. In the past, doctors would mix donor sperm with their patient's sperm, despite no evidence of medical benefit, so that couples could "entertain the delusion that the previously infertile husband [was] the father of the child."[13] Doctors would tell their patients to proceed as though the child was biologically theirs and would deemphasize telling children their origin stories. While the sperm mixing trend died out in the 1990s, the secrecy and shame around donor conception persisted.

The thing is, there is no such thing as anonymity these days. The rise of direct-to-consumer genetic testing in the late aughts obliterated any prospect of anonymity. Even if you steer clear of ancestry sites, it's virtually impossible to keep your entire extended family off them. Losing the option for secrecy isn't the issue though; the need for secrecy is the problem, and that's what donor-conceived people, or DCP as they're also known, want to change, not just for themselves but for their children, too.

The views of DCP vary somewhat, but they all agree on one thing: you must tell your kids where they came from. "The voices of donor-conceived people often illustrate that a child may have a different perspective, desire, and need than their parents, and the child doesn't have any say in how they're created," therapist Maya Grobel, LCSW, who had her daughter through embryo donation, says. "We need to move the needle in terms of assisted reproduction away from a shame-based model to more of an empowered model where people can come to the table as parents with confidence so they feel pride in their decisions of how they're building a family and less shame, so that disclosure is easier. Secrets in a family don't end well."

Choosing donor conception requires what Emily calls "radical honesty." You need to tell your child how they came to be, starting at birth using age-appropriate language. There also needs to be a spirit of openness when it comes to connections they might want to have with their genetic parent or half-siblings. And it's not enough to just tell your kid, say other DCP. You have to tell the whole family. Your child should feel free to speak openly about their identity, which means they shouldn't be the one breaking the news to family and friends. As the parents, it can be difficult to have these conversations, and if the reason you are using a donor is because of infertility, sharing can feel invasive. People often don't know the right thing to say and words hurt. But if you don't want your child thinking their existence is some shameful secret, you need to show them it's not by celebrating their origin story.

Discussing your child's conception doesn't have to be, and shouldn't be, some big dramatic event. Emily grew up knowing they were donor conceived. As a young child, Emily's moms would tell them they had "special ingredients" to make them. Emily later learned that special ingredient was donor sperm.

Emily's moms were open to any connection Emily might want to have with those who shared the other half of their DNA. When Emily was 8, their mom signed them up for the Donor Sibling Registry, a website that helps people connect with their genetic parents (donors) and half-siblings. Immediately after signing up, Emily's mom found Jessica, a half-sibling. Before telling Emily, their mom reached out to Jessica's mom to see if there was interest in the siblings meeting. There was, and to this day Emily and Jessica remain close, as close as any siblings would be.

But having over a dozen siblings has not always been easy. The siblings all communicate through a Facebook group, and at one point during Emily's sophomore year of college, it got to be too much. "It was hard to sometimes wake up, you know, maybe I'm having a rough day, and I wake up and see, *Oh, my gosh, I have two new siblings, and I'm finding out in a Facebook group,*" Emily says. Though Emily maintains connections to their siblings, they have no desire to find or meet their biological father.

KNOWN VS. ANONYMOUS

There's an analogy some DCP use to explain why they want to meet, or at least know the identity of, their genetic parent. Imagine having a child and learning later in life that the child you raised wasn't biologically related to you.

Wouldn't you want to meet your biological child? Wouldn't you be curious who they were or if they looked like you? Catie, 27, had to cover all of the mirrors in her apartment after learning through direct-to-consumer genetic testing in her mid-20s that she was donor conceived. She couldn't look at herself without wondering whose features were reflected back at her. She's since found and met her genetic father and maintains a good relationship with the parents who raised her, but she would have liked to have known from the beginning.

It's not hard to understand why so many DCP want to know who their other genetic parent is. Millions of people send their saliva to genetic testing companies, hoping to learn more about their genes and heritage. For DCP, half their DNA is a mystery—it makes sense they might want to know something about it.

Lauren Weiner, 23, doesn't remember a specific conversation about being donor conceived. Her parents were open with her well before she could talk. Still, Lauren wondered who her genetic father, or "sperm daddy" as she calls him, was. She tried reaching out to him through the sperm bank where he donated, but the bank said he didn't want any contact. Lauren eventually found some of his relatives through genetic testing websites and used Facebook to connect the dots. Although she now knows his identity, she's refrained from messaging him since he doesn't want contact. "I don't want anything from him. He didn't raise me, and he's not a part of my family," Lauren says. "But I'm curious; I wonder if I sat down with him, would we have the same hand movements when we talk."

Anya Steinberg, 23, also wants to know who her biological father is. Anya doesn't have a relationship with her social, or nonbiological, father and grew up largely without a connection to her Korean heritage. Her social dad is half Korean, so he and Anya's mother chose a Korean sperm donor. "Not having a connection to half of my heritage makes me feel like I'm unanchored in the world," Anya says. "White parents raising children who are people of color don't usually do a good job passing down cultural knowledge. That isn't my mom's culture. What could she tell me about being Korean? She has no idea. She didn't grow up Asian in America."

As much as Anya obsesses over the idea of finding her biological father, she's also terrified. Her father donated anonymously, which means she may never find him. The sperm bank sent him a letter on her behalf, but he doesn't have to respond. The bank only offers DCP two chances to reach out. If he doesn't respond to either attempt or doesn't want to connect, the bank will cease all contact regardless of Anya's wishes.

A survey of DCP run by We Are Donor Conceived, an online space for DCP, looked at the views of nearly 500 DCP, mostly millennial females raised largely by heterosexual couples using sperm from an anonymous donor with no identity disclosure agreement, and found that most, 76 percent, do not support anonymous donations. About 80 percent of those surveyed who were able to find their biological parent tried to communicate with them and in only half of those attempts was the person "happy" to hear from their child. Five people got a cease and desist letter. In most cases, DCP did not want a parent-child relationship; some hoped for a friendship, and others a more mentor-like bond. A study of 76 25-year-olds raised by lesbian parents published in *Fertility and Sterility* in 2020 found that donor-conceived young adults had largely positive feelings about their donor conception status. About 40 percent of those studied were conceived using unknown donor sperm. and most felt neutral or comfortable not knowing the identity of their genetic father. Another 40 percent knew their genetic father's identity, and two-thirds of that group maintained ongoing relationships with their genetic fathers. About half considered their genetic father an acquaintance, and nearly half felt good about the relationship, while others felt more neutral or conflicted.[14]

What nearly all DCP want is access to their biological parent's complete medical and family history. Sarah Blythe Shapiro, 21, got to meet her biological father when she was 19. Sarah's mother is a single mother by choice and picked someone who she thought was half-French and half-Iranian because she thought he would look like her Jewish family. He was an open ID donor, meaning Sarah could reach out when she turned 18, which is exactly what she did. "I didn't realize that open ID means you may or may not be able to reach them," Sarah says. "You can reach out when you're 18, but there's no guarantee they'll be receptive, which is not something they tell you at a lot of these banks. They could not want a relationship, and nobody can force them."

Sarah's biological father was open to contact, but the messages came through a mediator from the sperm bank. Her father got to keep his identity anonymous, but Sarah figured out who he was through bits and pieces about his life. About a year later, they made a plan to meet. He would be in Chicago for work, and she would come from her college in Minnesota to meet him. She took a bus eight hours to get there. While she was right about his identity, he was not who she thought he was. He was not half-French, and he lied about his medical history. Learning about her father was "horrifying," Sarah says. "I learned French growing up, because I thought I was French. I told him and he said, 'Yeah, I thought that nobody was going to choose me if I just said Iranian.'"

After they met, Sarah thought they formed perhaps a relationship of sorts. And then, her father made a podcast about his life and recorded an episode about donating sperm. He donated multiple times resulting in at least 11 half-siblings that Sarah knows of. On the podcast he talks about Sarah and his experience meeting her. "He published it with my name, talking about how much he did not like me, and he just eagerly sent it to me. I could not believe my ears. I was so angry and sent him this huge text asking how he could do that to me," Sarah says. "His texts were so cold. It was devastating, and now I have him blocked."

Although it's not always possible, the best option, according to DCP, is a known donor, someone whom your child has access to throughout their life. Some DCP like the idea of the donor being a family member, like a sibling of the social, nonbiological, parent. This allows the child to stay in their social parent's gene pool. Jenna and her partner, Christine, plan on using Christine's brother's sperm to build their family. Christine and her brother are very close, so there was never any doubt that he would play a large role in their child's life. It seemed kind of simple, then, to simply ask him to donate.

"It was very uncomfortable to bring up because we've done years of research, and you want to summarize that in a 15-second description that doesn't freak them out," Jenna says. "We gave him the info, and he listened. He asked some questions and made some jokes, and we toasted to him thinking about it. We gave him some time and then, about eight weeks later, my wife texted him to see if he had any questions. He said he'd definitely given it some thought and was willing to move forward."

I didn't get the issues surrounding donor conception until I found out I am donor conceived. My mum told me when I was 33. My child, who is also donor conceived, was 3 months old at the time. I'm disappointed with my parents for not telling me. Identifying the donor can be time-consuming and exhausting. I worry whether or not he'll be receptive to the letter I wrote him, which has sat on my laptop for months.

I told my kid he was donor conceived when he was a baby. Just general talking, and we read a book. Sometimes he picks it, sometimes I do. I don't want him to not know like I didn't know. Anonymous donation causes a lot of strain for donor-conceived people. I want recipient parents to know that you cannot define the relationship your kid wants or has with the donor. The biological link is important. It doesn't mean that they love you any less, but this mysterious donor person and any half-siblings are a big deal for many of us. Help your kid form relationships with half-siblings early. Developing relationships as an adult is hard.

Lou, 36, United Kingdom, she/her, cisgender, heterosexual, partnered

MATTERS OF LANGUAGE

When Janelle and Bird decided to have children, they were faced with a choice: go through the sperm banks to find an indigenous donor who shared Bird's roots or bypass the banks and pick someone they knew. They opted for the second route, but because they did IVF, they still had to follow the requirements set by their clinic: a legal contract declaring Janelle and Bird the parents, which they would've done regardless, and a six-month quarantine as recommended by the FDA to test the sperm for transmissible illnesses (some clinics will waive this requirement if the donor does blood tests within seven days of their donation).

"The more we thought about the kids, the more we would try to assume what would be best for them in the long run or what they would potentially prefer once they're cognizant beings with opinions," Janelle says. Jack, a friend of Janelle's, reached out to them and offered to donate. Jack is gay and in a committed relationship with no plans of having children of his own, but he was excited by the prospect of helping his friend and being involved in an "uncle role."

"In the contract, we have to be very clear about disassociating Jack from any parental rights, obligations, or responsibilities, which was interesting because Jack's only request out of the whole process was that if something were to happen to both Bird and me that he be named the children's guardian rather than one of our family members. We discussed it, and we all decided if Bird and I die, it should be what the kids want, but right now Jack is in the contract," Janelle says. "In the contract, it says no one can call him dad, but we had a very candid conversation about what if that's what the children want or need to call him. We all agreed that it's important for us to respect the kids' needs and perceptions of what their relationships are. Our baseline always just comes back to whatever they are going to want or need is just what we all have to do. That's why we're doing this, so that we can create people that feel like they have what they need."

One of the hardest things to discuss in the donor conception community is who the parent is. Most DCP prefer to call their biological parent exactly that: their biological parent. The donor provided sperm, eggs, or embryos to you, not to them. Genetically, the donor is their parent. Acknowledging that connection, although hard, doesn't mean your child will love you any less. "Just as parents can have room in their hearts for multiple children, the same can be true for children with their parents," Alex, 33, says.

Alex's daughter is just shy of 2 years old, and he is already preparing for the possibility that she will want to meet her biological father. Alex and his wife decided to use a sperm donor after learning that Alex has azoospermia. "At first I was very uncomfortable with that idea because it felt threatening to my status as her dad. What if she has a better connection to him?" he says. "I have grown to understand how much that connection may matter to her, and I will fully support whatever relationship she decides to pursue with him. Now that I'm a parent, I know a deep bond can exist without genetics.

My love for her is very real. I am who my daughter looks to for love and support. I am who she comes to when she is hurt or scared. It doesn't get any more real than that."

It's not just heterosexual parents who struggle with the meaning of parenting titles. Same-sex parents have long fought the idea that their children need a dad or a mom. In some ways it can feel like a step backward to acknowledge that there is another person involved. "It's like, my God, again, another thing that we have to go through as LGBTQ people," Gena Jaffe says. But the person who donated sperm to Gena and her wife is not their children's dad, he is their biological father. It doesn't make them any less parents or mean that their children need a dad. It means that his genes make up 50 percent of their children's DNA, which means they may want to know who he is one day.

"I think just having an open dialogue with my kids about it is really important," Gena says. "It's a chance to bring us closer and to really grow together. Like DCP say, 'There's more family to love our kids.' Why wouldn't we want that?"

19

ADOPTION AND FOSTER CARE

OPEN ADOPTIONS WERE RARE in the early 1990s when Torie's family adopted her as an infant. No adoption agencies in Ohio, where Torie's family lived, facilitated open arrangements, so they moved to Kentucky to adopt through an agency that did. Torie's adoptive parents wanted her to know her biological mother—and she did. Her first mom came to birthday parties, carved pumpkins on Halloween, and helped decorate for Christmas. By all accounts, Torie had a happy childhood.

Although closed agreements were the norm in the 1990s, prior to 1940, most adoptions were open. Adoption has always existed with communities and kin taking care of children when their parents could not, but these were informal agreements. Adoption as we know it got its start in the 1850s. In 1851, Massachusetts passed the first modern adoption law making adoption a legal determination based on child welfare rather than adult interests. Several years later the New York Children's Aid Society began its orphan train program, creating one of the first blueprints for the modern-day foster care system. Over the course of 75 years, up to 200,000 impoverished children were taken from the streets of New York and other large Northeastern cities and put on trains to Western states where families would give children homes in exchange for their labor. Building off of the initial perceived success of the program, more formal child placement programs and protections followed suit.[1]

By the mid-20th century, adoption became an acceptable way of building a family. But gone were the days of informal agreements and community-based arrangements. Placing children with married couples was seen as a solution for children born to unwed mothers, and adoption records were sealed due to the stigma surrounding many of these births. Meanwhile, deceptive practices grew alongside transracial and international adoptions, serving to remove children of color and foreign-born children from their communities and into the homes of white middle-class families. For most of the 20th century secrecy prevailed. The lack of disclosure affected more than just court documents; many adoptees were not told they were adopted or didn't learn about it until later in life.

As with donor conception, the earlier people learn about their origins the better the outcome. Those who learned they were adopted before the age of 3 reported greater psychological health and life satisfaction than those who found out later in life.[2] But it's not just open lines of communication about the adoption itself that adoptees want, it's supportive relationships with their adoptive parents that allow for contact with birth or first parents.

"I would say that my open adoption was successful because both of my mothers were very communicative and emotionally mature," Torie, now 28, says. "I think it can be really hard to share a child and to validate both biological and adoptive maternity, but they both did it really well. It didn't come without struggle, but their ultimate emphasis was on my well-being."

As successful as her adoption was, there were things Torie needed, beyond access to her birth mother, that she grew up without. The older she got, the more apparent the missing pieces became. Torie is a transracial adoptee. Her biological father is Black, and her birth mother and adoptive parents are white. Growing up, Torie and her adoptive sister were the only people of color in their neighborhood. Although she describes herself as a happy and carefree child, within her bubbled questions about her racial identity. At church there was a mural of a group of children sitting on Jesus' lap. One day, Torie asked her adoptive mother why none of the children Jesus welcomed onto his lap were brown. Soon after, her mother got the mural changed to include children of all races and ethnicities.

It wasn't until college that Torie found the words to voice how she felt growing up with little to no Black or biracial representation within her community, what she calls "racial imposter syndrome." "I felt as though I didn't have a right to claim Blackness because I wasn't raised in it," says Torie, who is now working on her doctorate in sociocultural anthropology with a focus on race and the US adoption system. "I didn't feel fully comfortable in white spheres because I was expected to behave as a white person even though I didn't have the same beliefs as my white peers."

As Torie learned what her Blackness meant, so did her parents, highlighting one of the crucial problems of adoption and well-intentioned child-led approaches. Rather than growing up with the resources she needed to understand herself, Torie had to educate her parents on what it means to raise a Black biracial daughter. And while they're now learning in their 70s, they recognize the harm that came with failing to proactively educate themselves earlier.

I was adopted when I was five months old from South Korea. My oldest aunt adopted her two children from South Korea, and that went really well, so when my dad and my mom wanted to grow their family, they saw adoption as a way to have children. They adopted my nonbiological sister, who's three years older, from South Korea and then they adopted me.

I vaguely remember being sat down when I was maybe in kindergarten and being told about my adoption. All I remember is just wanting to go back to watch my TV show. I didn't think much of it. My mom is pretty Scandinavian looking so we really didn't look alike. But there was never any weirdness, probably because I was used to seeing my cousins look Asian and not look like their parents. The fact of being adopted and being different due to being a transracial adoptee really didn't hit until elementary school. It wasn't so much about being adopted but rather being Asian in a white suburban area. I was teased because I couldn't say my *r*'s and because I had an eye patch. Kids would pull their eyelids apart and make fun of my eyes.

I found an opportunity to teach English abroad and wanted to do it in my home country. While I was there, I was fortunate enough to find and meet my birth mother. We had a translator. I remember when she walked in, it was more like meeting a long-lost aunt; it wasn't this immediate connection. She was beautiful, absolutely stunning. And I found out that she had actually looked for me when I was 10. All she knew was that an accountant in the US adopted me. That was the only information she was given.

My dad said he thought we would ask to visit South Korea as kids, but I never realized that asking or going was an option when I was younger. Every adoptee is different, but I think it's better to open doors than waiting for your kids to knock on them. I don't think my brain was developed enough or mature enough emotionally to understand the opportunities that I could have.

Chloe Edwards, 28, Minnesota, she/her, founder of Pineapple Mindset, Korean American, cisgender

THE PATHWAYS TO ADOPTION

Despite how frequently we hear about it, adoption is not a common path to parenthood. About 1 percent of cisgender women and 2 percent of cisgender men choose to adopt.[3] Placing a child up for adoption is also uncommon. Most people faced with unintentional or mistimed pregnancies choose either to parent or have an abortion. Approximately 33 percent of pregnant people will have an abortion within their lifetime. Only 1.3 percent will choose to place a child for adoption.[4] No agency tracks private adoptions in the US, but estimates suggest there are up to 18,000 infant adoptions and 55,000 adoptions from foster care each year.[5]

There are four main options when it comes to adoption: private agencies, public agencies, independent adoptions, and international adoptions.

When most people think of adoption, they think of infant adoption through private agencies. Private agencies work with intended parents and first parents to facilitate adoptions. Susan Dusza Guerra Leksander, LMFT, a first mother, transracial adoptee, licensed psychotherapist, and clinical director of Pact, an Adoption Alliance, estimates there are 30 to 100 prospective parents per every infant available for adoption. Birth parents cannot provide final consent for an adoption until after the child is born. State laws differ on the time needed to give or revoke consent. Private adoptions also tend to be among the most expensive, ranging from $20,000 to $45,000.[6]

"A lot of adoption professionals are very hesitant to turn away preadoptive families. They want to smooth the path for them and make adoption as attractive as possible and give them as much hope as possible, speaking to that emotional place of people who want to build a family," Susan says. "Oftentimes, adoption professionals will paint this very rosy, optimistic picture and not have the hard conversations because they don't want to turn people away or discourage them from giving them their money and trying to adopt a child through them."

Money is much less of a factor when adopting through the state. Public agencies manage adoptions for children in foster care. While fostering can be a pathway to adoption, the goal of foster care is typically reunification with the birth parents. There are more than 400,000 children in the US foster care system, a quarter of whom are waiting for adoptive homes. The foster care system takes in children of all ages, including infants. Adopting through foster care is typically free since the state subsidizes the costs.[7]

Some people choose to forgo agencies altogether and adopt independently. Those who go the independent route find a pregnant first parent on their own or through an adoption facilitator. Once a connection is made, a lawyer then finalizes the adoption. There are no licensing requirements or regulations for adoption facilitators, which means the tactics they use to recruit first parents are not subject to oversight, making their services riskier for both sets of parents. Independent adoptions can be just as expensive as private adoptions, especially if you're using a facilitator since you will need to pay for both the facilitator and a lawyer. Independent adoptions can also include adopting a relative or stepchild in the case of their parent's death or the termination of their parental rights.

International or intercountry adoption is less common than it was decades ago due to changing international policies regarding adoption and the US's ratification of the Hague Adoption Convention in 2008, tightening regulations around adoption. International adoptions also make it harder to adopt ethically due to the language barriers and geographic distance from the child's first family and community. No matter which route you choose, all adoptions must go through the appropriate legal channels, which depend on the state or country you adopt from. Most adoptions also require background checks and home studies where a social worker comes to your home to make sure it is a safe environment for a child. Some stepparent adoptions do not require home studies.

Although adoption is about finding families for children, the predominant narrative looks at it the other way around, centering on the adults instead of the children in need of homes. "If you're looking to adopt a child because you're focused on you and growing your family, that's often not the right approach to take," Ruchi Kapoor, a Colorado-based lawyer focused on child welfare, says. "A better approach would be to remember that this kid is coming from somewhere. A lot of people assume kids are blank slates."

If you decide to parent an adopted child, you need to hold space for their story rather than try to rewrite it. The adoptions Ruchi has seen go well are those where the adoptive parents are open to and maintain a relationship with the first parents. "That's the most ethical and the most sensible way of doing it," she says.

But getting to a place where you put aside your expectations of adoption is not easy. "I always tell parents that choosing to adopt a child is not the same as making a family by conceiving a child," Lesli Johnson, MFT, an adoptee and therapist in California, says. "That family is going to be the healthiest if the adoptive parents have done their own work around why they've chosen to adopt and grieve any biological child they might have originally wanted."

If adoption is the most feasible route for you to build a family, it can be hard to put down your notion of parenthood and replace it with a new kind of family building—one that honors everyone in the equation. Parenting an adoptee requires a different skill set than parenting a biological child. Adoptive parents need to acknowledge the trauma of being adopted, even for children adopted shortly after birth, and celebrate their child's biological race, ethnicity, and heritage. "If you had a child with diabetes or a child with learning differences, you would learn everything you could about that phenomenon, and then you would invoke the services that you need to support it," Jemma Elliot, LMFT, LPCC, a therapist and adoptee, says. "Adopting a child requires the same mindset."

Yes, it can be hard work. And yes, it's more than the baseline expected from most parents. It's okay to feel frustrated or overwhelmed, especially if you can't have biological children of your own. But it's important to process those feelings so that you can choose adoption rather than settle for it.

"There are so many people who come to adoption who have not done any critical reflection [on what they will do] when their child becomes old enough to articulate any kind of complex criticism of adoption. They choose to silence their child to defend their choice of adoption and uphold their ego," Torie says. "It is so much more effective if you start to reorient your value system before you adopt and meet your child where they're at and engage with them after having done some of that proactive self-analysis and excavation."

I got pregnant the summer after my freshman year of college. I was 19, and the birth father and I had only been dating for a couple months at the time. Unfortunately, I did not see a future with him. I grew up in a very conservative Christian home, so this was a very difficult situation for all parties involved. It was a big shock to my family. I used to lead worship at our local church. I didn't get into trouble growing up. I was a good kid and got good grades.

When I found out I was pregnant, adoption was the first option that came to mind. I knew I didn't feel comfortable with the idea of parenting with the birth father, and being in college, I didn't think I would be able to provide her with the future that she deserved. I wanted her to have two parents who were committed to one another.

I went through so many profiles and had a long list of requirements. I knew what I wanted, and I wasn't going to waver on that. After looking at many profiles, I finally found a family that had everything on my list. The birth father was part of that process, and he agreed on the family too. The agency I placed through were good advocates for me. You can't sign your rights over until either 48 hours after the baby is born or until you're discharged from the hospital. I was discharged a little bit early and signed my rights over. The revocation period for Florida is a little bit different. Basically, when I signed those papers, that was it.

It is a semi-open adoption. At first, I thought I wanted a closed adoption because the adoption world was completely different 10 years ago. Open adoptions, where you're basically like an aunt, are a new thing in the adoption world. I got letters and pictures at different points in time, the bare minimum required from the adoptive family. But all of this is just a gentlemen's agreement. None of it is set in law. I just prayed that these people would follow through and thankfully they did.

Knowing what I know now, I would advocate for an open adoption. It's important that adoptees and their birth parents have a connection. Having communication with biological family is healing in so many ways. Being in a semi-open adoption, there's a lot of testing boundaries. I've never had any issues with it with her adoptive family, but I definitely don't want to step on any toes. I'm always minimizing my pain or my situation because I don't want them to feel overwhelmed or obligated or anything like that. I chose this for my birth daughter, she did not. Therefore, I kind of feel like I have to suck it up.

Jessie, 30, Florida, she/her, white, cisgender

SHEDDING YOUR EXPECTATIONS

Victor Sims's favorite type of foster parents are the ones who are afraid they aren't cut out for it. Those who fear they won't be "perfect" are the ones he encourages to foster because they try the hardest. And he would know. Victor grew up in the foster care system and was adopted when he was 12. Today, he works in child services. He's run a group home, served as a foster parent, and helped prospective foster parents get licensed. All in all, he estimates that foster care has touched most of his 25 years of life, save for the first year. In short, he's an expert.

Victor knows firsthand just how imperfect the child welfare system is. It wasn't a rosy experience that made him want to dedicate his time to the child welfare system. He's there because he wants to make the system better for the children it's meant to serve. And that's why it makes him angry when people choose not to engage with the system because it's broken.

"The system is the way it is because the resources aren't there. If you have quality foster parents or quality communities, you're able to build something better, you're able to build something stronger," Victor says. "It's actually a beautiful thing to foster. The idea that we believe the alternative for kids who can't stay in their homes would be placing them in a group home or sometimes in psychiatric placements isn't the better option to me, no matter how bad the system is."

Arguing that adoption shouldn't exist isn't helpful either, says Imani Gandy, 48, an adoptee and the senior editor of law and policy at Rewire News Group. "I think the idea that there wouldn't be any adoption if everyone had access to everything they needed is a really flawed way of talking about it," she says. "I don't like that framing because it kind of makes me feel superfluous as an adoptee. It's pie in the sky thinking because no one's ever going to have access to all the family planning they need because that's the society we live in."

While we can't change the child welfare system overnight, we can change the way we think about and approach foster care and adoption. Engaging with the foster care system requires challenging what we're taught makes a "good" and "bad" parent. Today's cultural ideals set unrealistically high standards for low-income families. Many families struggling to get out of difficult situations are not able to do so no matter how hard they try. Children make it harder to rent a home and increase the risk of eviction.[8]

"A lot of the time when we think of the child welfare system, there is this shame and blame, and that is an incredibly harmful narrative," Ruchi says. "A lot of the parents who find themselves at the point where they're entangled with child welfare are truly at the lowest point in their lives. They might be homeless, struggling with a substance abuse disorder, or trying to make it work as a single parent, and this is a system that wasn't really designed to handle a lot of the things that pull people into the foster care system."

Becoming a foster parent means you have to challenge your biases. It's not fair to say a child is better off in your care because you have economic resources their parents lack. If you struggle with this, try reframing the situation and put yourself in the parent's shoes. If you fell on hard times, would you want your children taken away? What about if they were put in a more affluent home, would that change your mind?

You will also need to challenge some of the stereotypes you may have heard about the types of children in foster care. While many people associate foster care with teens, the average age of a child waiting to be adopted is 8 years old.[9] "Kids in foster care are just like kids who aren't in foster care," Victor says. "The difference is there's just more documentation that follows a foster child. When a child in a family sneaks food into their bedroom, it's not considered stealing, but in the system of care, you took it without permission and now you're considered a kleptomaniac."

The behaviors of foster kids make sense when you take the time to analyze them and remember what it's like to be a child. "The language of trauma is behaviors," Victor says. "When you find out why the behavior is happening, the child's response often makes sense." Victor remembers one case where a foster child kept running away. Instead of simply labeling the child as a "runner," Victor took the time to learn why the kid kept running away. It turned out he was grieving and wanted to visit his mother's grave. Instead of pathologizing the behavior, Victor suggested they just pick him up and take him to his parents' graves. It shouldn't sound revolutionary, but no one thought of doing that.

Being a safe space for children in the child welfare system means meeting them where they are as opposed to trying to find or mold your ideal child. As a child in the foster care system, Victor remembers trying to make himself adoptable. If a family wanted a son who could play basketball, then Victor loved basketball. This might seem innocuous; after all, even biological kids shapeshift to please their parents to some extent, but most children's safety and homes don't depend on making oneself likable. "I didn't have an identity until I became an adult," Victor says. "When you want a family, you do everything you can to get one."

And it's not always as innocent as pretending to like basketball. In one home a biological child loved biting Victor's toenails while he was sleeping. He laughed it off and said it was okay because he desperately wanted a home, but it wasn't okay. Later, when a different family adopted him, they tried to get Victor to stop his habit of biting his fingernails. But behind his behavior was a trauma. If he bit his nails, there was nothing left for anyone else to bite. And so his new mom stopped asking him not to bite his nails.

Not every child in foster care wants to be adopted, though. Some want to be reunified with their biological families. As a potential foster parent, you have to prepare yourself for reunification. At the start of the pandemic, Kevin Gerdes, 35, found himself scrolling through dating apps not because he wanted a relationship but because he wanted to get married, a stepping-stone, or so he initially felt, to having kids. As a gay man, his options for parenthood were either surrogacy or adoption. He didn't feel drawn to having biological children, so he began looking into foster care. Four months later, he completed the training, background check, and home visit required to foster. Within two months, he welcomed in his first foster child, an infant boy. Since then he's fostered several more infants, none of whose case plans currently include adoption. "I had to make peace with the fact that I cannot escape reunification," he says. "It's not easy, you're human, you get attached, but you get through it. If there's ever an opportunity for permanency, I'm ready. I will adopt."

It's been 18 years since foster care happened. It's amazing how trauma still impacts a person years later. Growing up, it didn't matter to me that my mom was on drugs because a grandmother's love makes up for any and everything that's going on in the world.

My grandmother's death was my first experience of a broken heart and death. She died when I was 8 and then foster care happened when I was 10. *The Cheetah Girls* had just come out, and I remember watching it. It was the summer and we were so excited because we were going to the best middle school, and then the storm came that interrupted our lives.

All my siblings, us four girls, went into care that same day. The next day, we were split up. My identical twin and I remained together as did our other two siblings. The following year, my mom lost her rights, but between then she lost us three times. She tried and just couldn't keep it together. Later, my twin and my baby sister were adopted together, and I went to a group home. I was 13. I was just left behind. It was just devastating. They didn't think about the long-term effects. I feel like I was robbed of that connection you hear of twins having. The foster home said I was the issue, but they should've said, "Y'all gotta go together." It still angers me today. Here we are living in two different states because that's how we grew up, separated.

I was on an adoption site in Michigan where people look at you and see if they want to adopt you. This lady called and said she was interested, so I did a visit. The visit went great. I went back to a foster home in the city where my sisters were, but the foster mom wouldn't let me go see my siblings. I packed a bag and my journal because at the time I wrote poetry, and the foster mom said, "If you leave, I'm gonna call the police." So I just skipped that part and went to the police myself. I asked if they knew Officer Brisby, a police officer who came to my school in fifth grade as part of the DARE drug prevention program. They radioed her, and she instructed me to go to her mother's house. I remember begging Officer Brisby to take me in, and she just kept saying, "Brittany, I have rules." And I said, "Okay, I'll follow them." The next day I moved in with the Brisbys. They were my longest foster home. I stayed with them for three years until I graduated high school. My foster dad taught me how to drive. You hear a lot of stories of foster kids that never had a license. He's the reason I have a license. My foster parents went above and beyond; they did more than what they were supposed to.

Now that I'm getting to my 30s, I've been having this desire to have my own kids. I wanted to have my own first to see what it feels like before trying to foster a child, but my husband suggested we adopt. So we may adopt first and then have our own. I want to choose to love another child, somebody who feels like there's no hope for them. I want them to know that they have a forever family because I know what it's like to want to be adopted and not be.

Brittney, 29, Georgia, she/her, author of *A Suitcase and a Dream*, Black, cisgender, married

20

SURROGACY

HOW DO YOU HAVE a child when giving birth will most likely kill you? That was the question on 13-year-old Victoria's mind when her doctor told her she had Marfan syndrome and would die in labor if she ever got pregnant.

As she got older, Victoria learned the truth was a bit more complicated. Marfan syndrome is a genetic condition that affects the body's connective tissue causing heart, blood vessel, eye, bone, and joint abnormalities. Most people inherit Marfan syndrome from a parent with the condition, but 25 percent of people, including Victoria, develop the condition as the result of a new mutation in their DNA.

Pregnancy with Marfan syndrome poses two risks. First, there's the risk of passing the condition down to your children. For Victoria, that risk was a one-in-two chance—a risk she didn't want to take. Then, there was the risk to Victoria. During pregnancy, the aorta, the main artery that carries blood away from your heart, expands. Because people with Marfan syndrome have weaker aortas, pregnancy can rupture the aorta, which is fatal without emergency surgery.

Knowing she didn't want to pass down the condition, Victoria and her boyfriend at the time, Jerrad, decided they would do IVF. The IVF process yielded 27 eggs and an engagement ring. Nineteen of those eggs made it to day five, the day embryos are frozen or transferred. Of those 19 eggs, only seven lacked the Marfan gene.

A few months following her egg retrieval, Victoria learned that her aorta had gotten exponentially worse, likely due to the hormones used during IVF, since that was the only thing that had changed at the time. At 27 years old, she was scheduling open-heart surgery, 10 to 12 years earlier than doctors expected and just two months before her wedding.

Victoria made it through her surgery to dance at her wedding. About a month after the wedding, the newlyweds went to see a high-risk ob-gyn who works with Marfan patients to see if it was safe to do an embryo transfer with the hope that the surgery had strengthened her aorta enough for surgery. Unfortunately, the doctor couldn't guarantee that the artery could handle the stress of pregnancy, and so they decided pregnancy wasn't worth the risk of losing Victoria or jeopardizing her health.

Victoria began researching surrogacy agencies at the start of the pandemic. The couple talked to a few agencies and their fertility clinic and then signed with the one they felt most comfortable with. Money was not a deciding factor because the agencies were all priced similarly. Because of the pandemic, they were told to expect a two-year wait for a surrogate to become available. They paid $15,000 just to get on the waitlist. The full estimated cost, $150,000, left Victoria feeling physically ill.

I had our daughter when I was 35 and my husband was 30. I'm a teacher, and he's an actor, so he's the stay-at-home parent. Our daughter was born in February, so I went back to work around spring break time, and he was home by himself with a four-month-old. He went through a serious postpartum depression. I came home one day, and he was just completely spent and said, "I cannot do this again. I can't." I went through a couple of weeks of feeling really sad that I had to choose between my husband's mental health and having more kids. I didn't really want a large family either. We were thinking about maybe having one more kid, but at the end of the day, his mental health was more important to me.

During that time, I was on Facebook in the middle of the night during a midnight feeding and an ad came up for surrogacy. I never had considered anything like that before. We had mild issues getting pregnant, but once we started actively trying, we actually got pregnant pretty fast. I had a few friends and family members who wanted more kids and couldn't or had miscarriages, and I thought surrogacy was a way I could give back. I had grown up pretty scared of pregnancy and delivery, but once I had my daughter, I realized my body is really built for this.

As a surrogate, you get to know a case manager, and they get to know you. They also have portfolios of parents that they look through to say, "Hey, I think this might be a good fit." Then they send my portfolio to the parents and their portfolio to me. We both read through and approve the partnership. I was pretty open to whoever they sent to me.

Legally, there's so much to do. There are contracts, I have lawyers, they have lawyers, and there are full pages in the contract about what a breach of contract entails and what the consequences are for that. For example, there were rules about how and when my husband and I could have intercourse because we don't want the baby to be his instead of theirs, so that would be a breach of contract. Or, if I drink alcohol during my pregnancy, that would be a breach of contract. Any breach of contract means I have to reimburse the parents every penny for everything. So not only my payment, which is considerable, but they buy life insurance and health insurance for me, and they pay for all of the IVF, all of the doctors, the specialists. In the end it's probably close to half a million dollars, and as a teacher, I don't have that kind of money lying around. It is a pretty serious thing to have a breach of contract, so I'm pretty careful about those things.

The number one question that I always get is, "What if you get attached to the baby and can't give it up?"

Okay, well, I would be in the poorhouse. A similar question I get is how can you give up a baby and not be emotionally connected to it. I think that's just a personality thing. I can separate logic from emotion. I teach math, which is very logical, and so that's just my personality. There are a few tricks that I did. I didn't talk to the baby in the uterus as much as I did my own child. I didn't breastfeed after the baby was born. You know, a lot of those things that are really emotional connectors are things I drew the line at. When the time came, I had my husband there to hold my hand and then the parent was right there behind him. I could see her face and the tears in her eyes when the baby came out. That's the emotional connection right there. I'm just doing the business end of it.

Heidi, 41, California, she/her, teacher,
white, cisgender, straight, married

There are two types of surrogacy: traditional and gestational. Traditional surrogacy, in which the surrogate is also the egg donor and therefore the biological mother, is very rare today. Most surrogates are gestational surrogates, also known as gestational carriers, meaning they carry an embryo that is not genetically related to them. The first legal surrogacy agreement came in 1976, though surrogacy existed without such formalities for centuries. The surrogate in 1976 used her own eggs and was not compensated for the pregnancy. The first legally compensated surrogacy agreement followed four years later. The surrogate also used her own eggs and was paid $11,500 for her services.

The first gestational surrogacy occurred five years later in 1985.[1] Gestational surrogacy was seen as a favorable alternative to traditional surrogacy because it severed the biological connection between the surrogate and the child. A court case the following year helped cement the switch from traditional to gestational surrogacy. After giving birth, a surrogate who used her own eggs sued for custody of the child she was paid $10,000 to carry. The New Jersey Supreme Court ruled surrogacy illegal and nullified the contract, reinstating parental rights to the surrogate. The biological father was granted custody, but the surrogate got visitation rights.[2]

A few years later in 1990, the court ruled again in a case known as the "Baby M" trial that would further cement the switch to gestational surrogacy. A gestational surrogate with no biological connection to the child she carried sued for custody. The court ruled in favor of the genetic parents, setting a precedent that made gestational surrogacy agreements legally binding.[3]

The effect of the "Baby M" trial lingered, leading to bans on surrogacy in multiple states, a few of which are still in effect today. There are some exceptions, however, if surrogacy is "medically necessary." Unfortunately those exceptions, if granted, only extend to married heterosexual parents, leaving unmarried, single, and queer folks without protections.

Hoping for an exemption can be a risky strategy. A Michigan couple had to adopt their twins born through gestational surrogacy in 2021 after the courts refused to grant prebirth rights. In this case, the surrogate was not the biological parent. The biological mother was a woman who froze embryos with her husband following a breast cancer diagnosis. When the twins were born, both the gestational carrier and her husband, neither of whom were the biological parents nor claiming parental rights, were listed on the birth certificate. In order to adopt their children, the biological parents had to undergo home inspections and an FBI background check—a process not mandated when the mother first gave birth before her breast cancer diagnosis.[4]

Laws vary even in states where surrogacy is legal, making it important to hire a lawyer before working with a gestational carrier, even if they are a family member or friend. If surrogacy is not allowed in your state or does not apply to you, you have the option to go out of state. Which state's laws apply depends on where the surrogate lives, not where you live.

Two months after signing with a surrogacy agency, Jerrad's cousin Jazmine reached out and offered to be the couple's gestational surrogate. Jazmine had overheard the two talking about their journey a year earlier at a family Fourth of July barbecue. As a mother of two, Jazmine couldn't imagine having to make the decisions Victoria and Jerrad had to make. Jazmine spent a year doing research and talking to her family and doctors before offering to be their surrogate. The couple accepted her offer and stayed on the surrogacy waitlist since they had already paid.

Surrogacy is notoriously expensive, which makes willing family and friends an attractive option. If you plan on asking family members or friends to act as your surrogate, you need to give them time to process your request and prepare yourself in the event they say no. If you don't think you can handle the disappointment of them saying no, you need to consider that before you risk jeopardizing your relationship. Even if the person you ask agrees to be your surrogate, you still need to prepare yourself for difficult discussions. Since you're making a baby together, you need to make sure everyone is on the same page.

When discussing surrogacy with Jazmine, both parties came with lists of questions, such as "How did everyone feel about twins and triplets? When would the other feel comfortable or uncomfortable aborting? Were there circumstances in which they would never abort?" And if Jazmine got ill and the safest thing was to abort, what would happen then? These conversations must come before the pregnancy to make sure everything is mutually agreed upon.

There are no federal regulations for surrogacy nor any government agencies that oversee the surrogacy process in the US. Most surrogacy agencies, fertility clinics, and lawyers follow guidelines set by the American Society for Reproductive Medicine when evaluating surrogates. Even if you choose to go outside of surrogacy agencies, you will likely have to pick someone who meets these criteria since it's what fertility clinics follow. Potential gestational carriers should ideally:

- Have psychological evaluation and counseling to make sure they understand what surrogacy entails.

- Be between 21 and 45 years old, although some exceptions can be made for those who are older and in good health.

- Have one full-term healthy pregnancy and delivery. This leads to better outcomes for both you and the gestational carrier as it suggests they can get pregnant and are less likely to experience complications.

- Have had no more than five deliveries or three C-sections.

Gestational carriers will also need to undergo physical screenings to ensure they are in good health and testing to make sure they don't have any sexually transmitted infections or serious diseases.

Using a family member was less expensive for Victoria and Jerrad than going through an agency, but less expensive doesn't mean free. Not even close. Victoria estimates they spent $40,000 in total. The fertility clinic holding their frozen embryos wouldn't see them for any surrogacy-related appointments until they had a legal contract in place. Since you cannot have the same lawyer as your gestational surrogate, Victoria had to hire two different lawyers. She also had to pay for the contract and parentage order, a legal document that declares the genetic parents are the legal parents of the child. Victoria, Jerrad, and Jazmine also had to undergo mental health evaluations and counseling before scheduling the embryo transfer. For the legal fees and the counseling fees alone for both parties, Victoria estimates she spent $8,000.

The bulk of the costs came from the fertility clinic itself. It took three rounds of medications before Jazmine got pregnant. And because Victoria wasn't technically the patient at this point, any clinic costs related to testing, appointments, or procedures couldn't be sent to insurance. Fortunately, Jazmine's insurance covered her obstetrician visits. Victoria and Jerrad also covered miscellaneous costs for Jazmine like gas money, meals, co-pays, and other expenses incurred during pregnancy.

Another thing you'll want to consider when planning your surrogacy journey is whether your workplace includes surrogacy in its parental leave policies. The nonprofit Victoria worked for had paid maternity leave but did not include surrogacy in its parental leave policy. If she wanted to take time off after her daughter's birth, she'd have to take unpaid leave under the Family Medical Leave Act. When she did the math on how much childcare plus the price of commuting to work would cost, it made more financial sense for her to stay home. And so she quit her job.

Surrogacy gets a bad rap as a way out of childbirth for wealthy and famous women, but it's a powerful family-building tool for folks who want biological children and cannot do so naturally, like Bryan and Chris.

Kids were always in the cards for Bryan and Chris. After Bryan, 36, and Chris, 36, got married, they looked at adoption and foster care, but surrogacy is ultimately what stuck with them. Going through a surrogacy agency is notoriously expensive with an average price tag of $150,000.[5] They knew it would be expensive, but it was doable. They had recently sold their house and planned on using the gains they made to pay for a surrogate. Through friends of a friend, they connected with a new surrogacy agency that offered to walk them through what to expect. "To be honest, it was very overwhelming because we had never done it before and seeing a database of thousands of beautiful surrogates and egg donors was like, *How do we narrow this down because we don't obviously have the time to go through every single profile?*"

Bryan and Chris decided not to go with that agency and instead picked an agency that could do more of the legwork. The fee for the agency's services was $40,000, not including donor eggs, IVF, or the surrogate's services. They picked an egg donor and got 22 eggs, which was more than they expected. They used Chris's sperm to fertilize half of the eggs and Bryan's sperm to fertilize the other half. Out of the 22 embryos they created, nine of Chris's and three of Bryan's became genetically normal day-five embryos. They planned to transfer one embryo each; they just needed to find a surrogate—and that's when things started to get messy.

One of the things that surprised Bryan and Chris was how many surrogates were not willing to work with gay couples. "Not every surrogate or every egg donor is willing to work with you if you are gay, which was something that I didn't think would even be an issue," Bryan says. "We didn't run into that personally with someone we were matched with, but we did see that on a lot of the profiles that we were reviewing. We'd get three pages in and see she's not willing to work with a gay couple. Well, okay, that sucks because we've already gone through the first two pages, so that was kind of a shock."

Their first surrogate they picked had to pull out after discovering she had a small heart defect. The second surrogate was a first-time surrogate. She and her husband were done having kids and were hoping to use the money from surrogacy to buy a house. She lived in California, like them, and passed all of her medical tests with flying colors. The contract was drawn up, and then she got pregnant, just not by Bryan and Chris. Bryan was done at that point. They were out $100,000 and didn't even have a surrogate. Between the $40,000 for the agency, the money to do donor egg IVF, and paying legal fees for both them and the surrogate to draw out contracts, a good chunk of their surrogacy fund was already gone. "I said, 'I don't know if I can keep doing this. Maybe the universe is telling us that we're not supposed to have kids,'" Bryan recalls. But Chris told him it wasn't the universe telling them that they weren't supposed to have kids, it was that these were not the people they were supposed to partner with on their journey."

Bryan and Chris took six weeks off from anything surrogacy related before diving back in. Given all of the previous issues, the agency worked quickly to find them a new surrogate. She was a "proven surrogate," meaning she successfully carried for another couple before. That also meant she was more expensive, but Bryan and Chris didn't care. They found their match. From there, everything moved pretty quickly, including the psych evaluations and the medical clearances. Typically this would not be the case, but after all of the roadblocks they faced, the agency helped to move things along quickly. A few weeks later two embryos were transferred into their surrogate, one from Bryan and one from Chris. Both embryos took, and soon Chris and Bryan would be dads to both a son and a daughter. The final price tag: close to $250,000. Far more than what they budgeted for.

"Our surrogate, her husband, and their two kids are going to be family friends of ours moving forward, and we'll definitely want to keep in touch and see them from time to time and keep her updated on how the babies are doing," Bryan says. "Chris likes to say, 'This is a journey for us, and it's a journey for you, but then there's the journey that all three of us are on together,' which I really love. We're all on this journey together."

My grandmothers have 9 children and 12 children, so as a child, I thought, *Oh, I want to have a whole bunch of kids.* My mom, on the other hand, always said, "two hands, two kids," so we were just two in our family.

Pregnancy with my daughter was super easy, so I knew I wanted to have more kids like my grandparents. Then I realized kids are expensive and a lot of work, so I thought, *Two hands, two kids.* But I also get pregnancy fever like a lot of people who have easy pregnancies or just like going through the process do. I kept seeing surrogacy in the news, and then one day, I just thought, *Ooh, I should be a surrogate.* So I got on Google and found my agency.

I love being a surrogate. The first couple I was a surrogate for was dealing with infertility due to some health concerns; the mom just couldn't carry full-term. The second couple was a male couple, so they obviously couldn't carry for themselves. I think it's different having a mom who, in an ideal scenario, would be able to carry for herself. I really, really tried as best as possible to answer questions about how it felt and things that were happening. I would never discuss my vagina with two dads. But the mom of my first surrogacy was interested in mucus plugs or certain levels of contractions. She wanted to know that sort of thing. Whereas with the two dads, it was just like, "How are you feeling?"

It took three embryo transfers for the pregnancy for the dads. We definitely cried. We didn't cry on camera or anything weird, but they told me they cried it out. I was devastated. Even though it's not your kid, it's your body, it's your experience. You want it to work out; you've already got your mind wrapped around helping another family. I know it's not my fault. It's trial and error. But, at the same time, having those two failed transfers gave me a dose of what it feels like to be a mom who is infertile or even two dads who can't conceive. It kind of humbled me a little bit. It was a reality check: you are still not above science when it comes to an embryo transfer and the stats that go into it.

I've kind of opted out of having twins because of concerns about the maternal mortality rate for Black women. I put my safety first in every situation. There was a medication error at one of the fertility clinics, and then I had a white lady at my agency—I don't think they had anybody of color there—get on the phone with me. And she was trying to unpack why I felt so adamant about having someone be accountable for the medicine error. She asked me if there was some sort of trauma there. And I'm like, "Lady, Black women in birthing situations, that is the trauma." It doesn't have to be specific to me, the stats are there, and that wasn't understood. I don't want to have to go through things that I feel like people who work with Black surrogates should know. I want you to already be educated on that.

My advice for working with a surrogate: Don't stress us out. We have lives outside of surrogacy, all of us have kids, most of us have jobs. I'm going to do my best to put the baby's needs first, make sure it's a mutually beneficial relationship. Also, a lot of us like to get updates. I personally do. We just want to know you guys are doing well because you almost become like an extended family in a sense. You share something that was really monumental in both of your lives, so it's always nice to have that as an option.

Princess High, 30, Illinois, she/her, realtor, Black, cisgender, straight, single

PART IV

YOU DON'T

WANT KIDS

21

SAYING
NO TO
PARENTHOOD

GROWING UP, CLAUDETTE NEVER contemplated a path other than motherhood. In her early 20s, she even had "baby fever." The urge to have kids was intense—a boy and a girl, that was the plan. And then, after four years in a toxic relationship, she realized perhaps she didn't want kids at all.

"I had always thought, *Okay, by 27 I'm going to get married, and then by 30, I'll have my first kid,*" Claudette, 33, says. "After I got out of that relationship, I started realizing that that plan is not how life is going right now. I had no sight of love, marriage, kids—nothing even close to that. So I started thinking, *Okay, maybe this isn't gonna happen. What if it doesn't happen?* And the more I thought about it, the more I enjoyed life and my freedom, the more I was like, okay, maybe it's not that bad if I don't have kids. And then more years went by without having them, and I just became really content with not having them at all."

As she grew more comfortable with the idea of a childfree life, she hatched a foolproof plan. She was going to be up front about her child-free desires from the get go, so early on in a relationship she could avoid getting attached to someone who wanted kids. It was all going well until things started getting more serious. "He was kind of on board but as our relationship progressed, he decided he did want to have children," Claudette says. "He didn't even want to talk about it. He was just like, 'You know, this is something you want and having kids is something I want.' And we just parted ways."

There are many reasons why people choose not to have children. For most, it comes down to personal freedom. People want the right to choose what's best for them, and that's difficult to do considering a child's best interests would need to come before yours. Although this rationale gets framed as "selfish," childfree people argue the opposite. They say it would be selfish to bring a child into a world ravaged by climate change or have kids if you have no real desire to parent. Others choose not to have children because of what parenting entails or because they want to focus on the relationships they already have.

The decision not to have kids, for most people, is a process. It's not some random thought that springs up out of nowhere that people then wholeheartedly commit to. This process often starts in childhood and continues throughout adolescence into adulthood. Part of the reason Jerra, 35, doesn't want to have kids comes from having to help raise her siblings when they were young, and she was a teen. "I was kind of forced to be an adult when I wasn't really ready," Jerra says. "I just knew that I didn't want to have that life as an adult, taking care of a baby, being awakened out of my sleep. I know this may sound selfish to some people, but I consider it being self-aware."

For others, watching siblings and friends struggle with the realities of raising kids was enough to make them realize it wasn't for them. Zoë, 35, never felt a pull toward children, a decision further solidified by watching her twin sister parent. "My nephew is 3 now, so I see the reality of being a mother and it's fucking hard," she says. "Some people just inherently feel like their life is not complete unless they have kids, whereas I always came from the perspective that I didn't need that extra thing in my life."

Research suggests there are some gender differences in how people conceptualize being childfree. Professor of social work Carolyn Morell classifies being voluntarily childfree into two experiences. The first group of cisgender women she studied experienced a "wavering no," in which their comfort with being childfree was disrupted. The second group fostered a "radical openness that allows for various possibilities."[1] Women are more likely to factor in concerns about overpopulation and social issues, whereas men are more likely to cite worries about what they would have to give up and how parenthood would affect their lives. Women also tend to factor in conversations with their partner and make a decision with others in mind, whereas men focus internally.[2]

Being childfree has nothing to do with how I was raised or me shunning my femininity. It's something I've thought about for years, and unless I'm 100 percent sure I want a child, I'm not doing it. I like my time and space. I like to sleep in, have a clean home, and focus on myself, my career, school, my partner, and travel when I want. I love babies but the best part is being able to give them back. I'm not willing to sacrifice my mental, emotional, and physical well-being for a child, and I don't want to pass on hereditary conditions I have.

I definitely bring up that I don't want kids fairly early into dating. There's no point in wasting time on someone who wants different things. It's affected past relationships, but in my current one, we're very much on the same page. We're both content being the fun aunts.

People tell me I'll change my mind, that children are the best thing ever and change your life. It's like my time and energy isn't as important. I'm often scheduled on holidays as if I don't have loved ones I want to spend time with.

Kaily, 23, Arizona, she/her, phlebotomist, white, queer, partnered, disabled

Although the common narrative is "you'll change your mind," research shows plenty of childfree adults knew from a young age they didn't want kids. Samantha, 31, has always known parenthood isn't for her. "I've never really had a desire to have kids. I remember when I was younger, everyone saying,

'Oh, you'll change your mind,' but I'm pretty sure I've known I didn't want kids since before I even got my period." Jim, 52, describes feeling similarly. "I've never wanted kids, never. I've had the same thoughts about it since I was 16," he says. "Everyone said I would change my mind. People would ask me 'Why don't you want kids?' and I would ask why they wanted kids and then tell them none of those reasons matter to me. I've heard all of their crap: 'The Bible says . . .' 'Who will carry on the family name?' 'Who will take care of you when you are old?' And on and on."

While some folks leave the door open to children as part of their processing, entertaining the possibility doesn't mean they anticipate changing their mind. This flexibility just speaks to the process-like nature of deciding whether to have kids, that thoughts and feelings can shift with age or circumstance—especially in relationships. Even if the answer always ends up being no, these temperature checks help people feel confident about their decision.

For example, Adan, 40, isn't anti-kids, it's just the realities of raising children that make the whole thing unappealing. As a single gay man, parenting alone "sounds like hell." "I saw my mother raise three kids by herself more or less because my dad wasn't around," Adan says. "I saw what that did to her, the toll that takes on someone to raise three children by themselves. I could never do that." If he met someone who wanted kids, he'd be open to the possibility, but he's also happy continuing to live life childfree. "No matter how much you want something, it has to actually be feasible," he says. "If it's just going to put me in debt, I'd rather be able to take care of myself and take a nice vacation, to be honest."

Today, Claudette still considers herself decidedly childfree, but she approaches dating with a little more leniency than she did in the past. "That situation with my ex started to change my mind. I started thinking, *Okay, why am I trying to control this so much? Am I making the right decision?*" Claudette says. "If I did have a kid, I always pictured it by myself because that was the example I always had. When I met that person I was like, *I might not mind having a kid with this guy.* So now I'm content either way. If I don't have any, I'm definitely fine, and I'm blessed to have had that time where I was like, *No, I'm not going to have kids,* because if it doesn't happen, I know I'll be okay. But I am a little more open to the possibility if I meet the right person."

While that approach feels right for Claudette, it's not going to feel right for everyone. Kristen, 32, for example, prefers to date people who are certain they don't want kids since she knows she doesn't want them. "I don't want to get involved with someone that will resent me for not wanting to have a kid," Kristen says. "I don't want to be in a situation where I'm three years down the road with someone, and they leave me or are angry because they feel like they were misled. I'm in a relationship now, and he doesn't want kids, but I'd be terrified if he turned around and said he wanted kids. I want dogs, not kids."

Honestly, I don't like kids. When others hear this, people always seem to default to the declaration of, "But you were a kid once!" And to this I respond, "Yeah, and I didn't like kids even then." Kids stress me out, and the worst sound to bring out my anxiety is a baby screaming. I just know I don't have a motherly bone in my body, and it would be completely unfair to any theoretical kid I would have. Despite this, people are always insistent that I would be a good mom, which only frustrates me and fuels my desire to never have kids. It's frustrating that people equate having children to achieving fulfillment in life and can't comprehend any other form of happiness. I love being my own person without any obligations to another life form, other than maybe a future cat. Even if I had all the money in the world, all the time in the world, I would still never want a child. I respect and commend anyone who decides to be a parent, because that's a lot of work that I just refuse to do.

I've only ever been in one relationship, my current one, and she is on the fence a bit. We would have to adopt if we ever wanted a kid. I doubt either one of us would be willing to do fertility treatments because of how it would change our bodies. She says it might be nice to be a parent one day, but at the same time really enjoys the freedom of being childless, not to mention the money it saves. It is something that brings me a little anxiety, if we ever have to cross that bridge, because I just don't think it would be possible for me to experience happiness while taking care of a kid.

Margo, 29, North Carolina, she/her, artist, white, cisgender, asexual, partnered

Deciding not to have children can be an emotionally challenging process. As the name implies, most people who are childfree by choice make the conscious decision not to have kids. Though stereotypes suggest people flippantly choose not to have children, those who decide to be childfree are just as thoughtful about their choice, if not more so, than people who decide to have children. While early narratives of childfree folks characterized those without children as deviant and selfish, language shifted in the 1970s to differentiate those who were purposefully childfree from those who wanted children but were childless. The selfish label persisted for those who choose not to have kids while those facing infertility were met with pity. It's worth noting that some people also use childfree by circumstance or childfree after infertility to convey that they choose being childfree over pursuing IVF or adoption.

"I was called selfish once," Corrine, 33, says of her decision not to have kids. Corrine and her partner spent two years trying to decide whether they wanted kids. After much deliberation, they decided they didn't want kids and haven't looked back since. "People ask, 'What will you do with your life?' Though annoying and narrow-minded, I find these comments humorous. I guess I will selfishly hike, climb mountains, travel, work, spend time with friends, volunteer, join book clubs, and do all the things you do in life but probably with a bit more sleep. Selfish me."

Because of the disapproval childfree people face, choosing not to have children often means adopting a stigmatized identity. People view childfree adults as less mature, selfish, cold, and materialistic. However, these descriptions do not accurately reflect childfree adults. They just depict the opposite of society's idealized version of parents. In reality, childfree adults are more likely to have strong connections to their families and their communities.

They're also more likely to provide financial, emotional, and practical support to family members, as well as invest in relationships outside of the typical nuclear family and engage in volunteer opportunities.[3] The support networks of childfree folks tend to be more diverse with stronger links to family, friends, and community.[4]

While it helps to know there's no legitimate basis for the hurtful comments lobbed at childfree folks, barbs sting whether you choose not to have kids or can't for other reasons. Psychotherapist Rebecca Harrington, DSW, LCSW, articulated such feelings after a patient who was a mother of three, replied, "Fuck you" in a therapy session after Harrington shared she was taking a vacation to Italy:

> We acknowledged the mutual jealousy we shared: she of my childfree lifestyle, I of her life with children. Although neither of us wanted to exchange her life for the other's nor to deprive the other of what she had, we were able to transition into a place of mutual understanding in which we recognized that, together, we represented the inherent gains and losses of "the road not taken." She had the children for whom I sometimes yearned; I had the childfree lifestyle she missed and craved. Neither one of us could have both. We acknowledged the regrets each of us had and the impossibility of "having it all."[5]

As Harrington writes, it's often viewed as socially acceptable for parents to antagonize or belittle the lives of childfree folks but not the other way around. "What if we expressed our jealousy of what others have in this same way: 'Fuck you for conceiving so easily. Fuck you for those blissful moments when you're holding your sleeping baby. Fuck you for getting to experience a kind of love and joy we will never personally know.' I think it's safe to say that it would be inappropriate and aggressive if we articulated such feelings in the same offhand, hostile way that people feel comfortable expressing theirs to us," Harrington writes. "People with children seem to land higher up in the social hierarchy than those without them, but it is also considered socially acceptable and normative for people with children to complain about parenthood and having children—sometimes with self-righteousness, sometimes as if they're martyrs."

These types of interactions come up everywhere. Zoë, who founded the We Are Childfree community, says childfree women are often pitted against mothers despite there being no actual competition. "I'm never going to judge any parents for ever having a bad day because to me, as an outsider, it looks fucking difficult," she says. "But no one ever talks critically about mothers when they say motherhood is the role of their lives. There's this thing when people announce they're childfree or talk about it, that we're the ones viewed as a problem, which I can feel intensifying a little bit, especially with the birth rates going down in some countries. Obviously, we are the scapegoat, instead of actually thinking about the realities of why more women are choosing to have fewer children."

Being an early childhood educator has given Marina, 31, a front-row seat to the many challenges parents face. But even though she's well versed in how difficult caring for kids is, time and time again, she's made to feel as though her needs matter less because she doesn't have children. "My friends with children will often use their parent identity to disregard my opinions or needs because I'm not a parent," she says. "For example, when I say, 'I need a vacation,' they immediately answer, 'Yeah, YOU need a vacation,' which sometimes affects the way I feel about sharing with them." And it's not just her friends, it's her workplace too. Every year, Marina goes on vacation. Except this year her regularly scheduled holiday fell around the cusp of maternity leave for four pregnant employees. "My supervisor refused to sign the time off request I submitted four months prior because 'everyone was getting ready to have their babies,'" she says. "It was surreal to hear that be the reason, so my response was naturally dramatic, but I think that was just boiling over from not being equally considered in society just because I am not a mother."

It's for all of these reasons that telling people you don't want kids can feel so nerve-racking. "I made the decision to not have kids when I turned 30, and I waited about two years before sharing because I didn't know how people were going to react," Claudette says. "The few people that I did tell weren't really close to me, but their reactions were always so negative. I feel like as soon as you say you know you don't want to have children, people think you hate kids and that you're like a monster. I definitely had anxiety about it because I felt like I was going to be judged. When I realized, *Okay, I really do enjoy my childfree life and I value my freedom*, I decided to move forward and start telling people. I also wanted to normalize it because I'm sure there are other women who are scared to say anything, so I'm like, I'll just do it, and then hopefully when another woman tells someone it won't be such a shock to them."

I have been married for 18 years. My husband and I grew up in religious households and got married young (19 and 22), so we assumed we would eventually start a family together. However, we were both pursuing rigorous professions—I went into medicine, and he studied advanced biology—so we agreed to postpone starting a family until we were personally and financially ready.

After about 10 years of marriage, we recognized our perspective had shifted. We were very happy together without children and could see ourselves continuing to be happy without them. We saw the problems with climate change driven by population growth, and have fulfilling careers that contribute to making a better world. Plus, I became a pediatrician and witnessed how challenging and unpredictable parenting could be.

We had many conversations and, thankfully, we are on the same page about not having children after all. I love children and feel very fulfilled helping them and their families through my work as a pediatrician. I also love going home to a quiet house and not feeling the weight of parenting responsibilities personally. I never ever want to be pregnant or give birth. As incredible as the process is, I don't desire it at all. I'm so glad my spouse and I ended up on the same page.

Marina, 38, Utah, she/her, pediatrician, Latinx, cisgender, heterosexual, married

22

LIVING A
CHILDFREE LIFE

IN 1974, MARCIA DRUT-DAVIS went on *60 Minutes* with her then-husband to share with the world their intention to live a childfree life. The idea for the segment seemed innocent enough. Marcia and her husband would share their decision to remain childfree with his parents and viewers. It was an opportunity to show that kids didn't make a family, legitimizing the relatively new concept of reproductive choice.

Unsurprisingly in hindsight, Marcia's in-laws did not take the news well. Her former mother-in-law later penned a poem lamenting, "So this is how our story ends? Our children though married, they're really just friends." But the worst was yet to come. Had Marcia known how the 20-minute long segment would air, she likely never would have agreed to it. At the close of the episode, a somber Mike Wallace, whom Marcia never met, left viewers with a message that would change Marcia's life: "Pardon our perversion for airing this on Mother's Day. Good night, everyone."[1] And just like that, Marcia was canceled a good forty-plus years before cancel culture was even a thing.

Shortly after her television debut, Marcia lost her job as a school teacher. Parents didn't want her near their children. How can you teach kids if you hate them? Of course, Marcia didn't hate children; she just didn't want any of her own. "There was picketing," Marcia says. "There was a sign that said,

'Godless bitch keep away from our kids.' I asked the cop, 'Who's coming?' And he said, 'I don't know, some insane woman who says, don't have kids.' I went, 'Oh, that's me!'"

Along with the insults came death threats—on her life and her dog's. People spat and hissed at her, shouting horrible things wherever she went. The outrage didn't just blow over in a week; it followed Marcia for decades, causing her to develop post-traumatic stress disorder. Her entire life changed just because she was bold enough to say she was choosing a childfree life.

Choice is a funny thing. Katherine Franke, a Columbia University law professor and director of the Center for Gender and Sexuality Law, argues that "reproduction has been so taken for granted that only women who are not parents are regarded as having made a choice—a choice that is constructed as non-traditional, nonconventional, and for some, non-natural."[2]

It's hard to estimate how many people are childfree by choice because surveys largely don't differentiate between those who choose not to have children and those who are unable to. In the 2000s, nearly twice as many women ages 40 to 44 were childless than in the 1970s. Today, approximately 15 percent of women between the ages of 40 and 44 don't have children, with estimates suggesting nearly half are childfree by choice.[3]

We don't see many positive examples of adults aging in society, which makes it hard to imagine what a life without kids looks like. With age comes less visibility in society. For older folks with children, becoming a grandparent helps mediate the societal effects of aging. Even though age brings fewer questions about when you're going to have kids, stigma still persists into old age. Both straight and gay childless men report concerns over being seen as "creepy old men" or "sex offenders." Meanwhile, childfree lesbians are afraid of having their identities erased since they don't conform to the heterosexual "grandma" stereotype.[4] Despite the persistence of stigma, childfree adults report just as high, if not higher, levels of happiness, life satisfaction, well-being, and marital adjustment as parents and less depression.[5] Older childless adults also tend to have more financial resources than those who decided to parent. Compared with married parents, childless married couples tend to have slightly more income and about 5 percent more wealth. Compared to unmarried mothers, unmarried childless women have up to 31 percent more income and about 33 percent more wealth. Unmarried childless men don't have significant income differences but have up to a third more wealth than unmarried men with children.[6]

Despite all the strife it initially caused her, to this day Marcia, now 79, does not regret her decision to be childfree. "All those people who would say to me, 'Wait until you're older, you're going to regret this.' Well, one of the joys is I can finally say, 'I have no regrets,'" Marcia says. "But to think, you have a child to take care of you? That's selfish. And yet, childfree people are the ones called 'selfish' for not trying to have a baby. I have friends who have children and grandchildren. I have heard the anguish among many of my friends over grandchildren, who at a certain age, kind of lose interest or have their own lives. It's a passage of time."

Contrary to popular belief, studies of elderly populations show that childlessness is not always associated with loneliness or depression.[7] Some childfree folks fare better than others. For example, people who choose to be childfree report better mental health than those who are childless due to infertility, and childfree women tend to fare better than childfree men. A study of older Americans found that unmarried childless men were more likely to have depression or be lonely, whereas older unmarried childless women did well later in life.[8] Another study of people between the ages of 63 and 93 in New Zealand who identified as childfree found that childfree people generally do not regret their choice and describe their lives as rich and meaningful.[9]

> I've never had the desire for kids. Growing up I played house and played with dolls and often pretended to be a mom, but I knew it was pretend. I took an after-school babysitting class when I was 11 and the day they brought in a baby for us to interact with, I froze. I assumed that when I got older that my feelings would change and I'd have kids because that's just what you do. By the time I was in college, I knew pretty firmly I didn't want kids, but again, figured that might change as I got older. I met someone in my early 20s who ended up becoming my husband, and we just kept living life, putting off kids.

We had discussions about it, and I came to a personal decision that if I hit 35 and still felt the same way, it wasn't going to happen. Here I am in my late 30s, and my husband and I just know it's not for us. We really like to interact with our friends' kids, but we just know we don't want that daily parenting life. It's too much for us. Additionally, we have concerns about the environment and political state of the world, and we'd rather channel our energy into doing what makes us happy and doing what we can to make the world a better place for the kids who are already here. Postpartum depression runs really strong in my family as well, and I just don't think I can put myself through that. I worry about what long-lasting effects my mental state would have on my child.

Having kids is the cycle of life that you're supposed to take part in, and you're seen as strange when you actively step outside of it. I've also been told I don't understand what love is until I'm holding my own baby, seeing it look back at me. I think society doesn't respect the time of childfree people. It's wonderful to see my close girlfriends go through this life-changing journey to motherhood, but it's bittersweet for me too, because I feel like I can't follow them on that journey. I always worry that a friendship won't last past a change to motherhood status, but happily I've been wrong about that sometimes.

Sally, 37, Vermont, she/her, archivist, white, cisgender, heterosexual, married

WHEN THE CHILDFREE LIFE CHOOSES YOU

Unfortunately, we don't always get to choose whether or not we have children. For some people, like Erik and Melissa, life has other plans. Erik went into his relationship with Melissa with a different perception of parenthood.

Erik had a daughter from a previous relationship that died in childhood after facing significant health challenges, shattering the rose-colored glasses through which prospective parents often view parenthood. "I didn't have the whole get pregnant and that's the solution to all your problems," Erik says. "I had hesitations about wanting to do that again. Sometimes things don't work out the way you think they're going to work out."

But being a mother was important to Melissa, and Erik didn't want to deprive her of that, which is why he waited to propose until he knew he was ready to try again. The pair married when Melissa was 34 and Erik was 35 and started trying to get pregnant soon after. They tried for years, including three rounds of IVF and a significant injury caused by a surgical procedure to unblock Erik's seminal vesicle. After four and a half years of trying, they decided to stop pursuing parenthood. "It kind of feels like life is sort of telling you this isn't for you, and you're trying to force it instead of accept it," Melissa says. "Do I want to spend most of my 40s going through this same hell I've been through that ate up so much of my 30s? I don't want to do that anymore."

"I didn't feel like a burden was lifted," Erik says. "I mean, technically there was a burden lifted because we were done doing all that stuff, but to me it felt like, *holy crap, what are we going to do?* You worry about whether your relationship is going to end. It wasn't like, 'Oh yay, we're done.'" It took time for Erik and Melissa to heal; time and therapy. They needed to mourn the life they lost before they could embrace the possibilities of a childfree one. The more they talked about it, the more it helped, and so they began sharing their story and connecting with others through their podcast *Live Childfree with Erik and Melissa.*

"It's a slow process. I would get frustrated because I was still dealing with grief or things weren't moving fast enough or I wasn't living up to this idea of this new and improved childfree Melissa that I had in my mind," Melissa says. "I always describe it as an identity crisis. You feel like part of you dies. That part of me that felt like I was going to be a mother was dying. I had to grieve all the thousands of things I thought were going to be in my future, and, unfortunately, that just takes time."

Whether you are childfree by circumstance or after infertility, part of accepting a childfree life when you previously wanted kids requires looking beyond what you've been taught about parenthood. A small study of cisgender women who were permanently childless after delaying childbearing found they experienced grief similar to those facing infertility, whether they tried to conceive or not, suggesting it's not just people with infertility who struggle when they can't have kids.[10]

"A lot of people just expect this will happen or that'll happen, and then we get to a certain age where things don't happen," Katie Maynard, LICSW, a childfree psychotherapist, says. What it comes down to, she says, is seeing a life for yourself that goes beyond your reproductive function and creating a personal narrative that works for you. Some people might see that as settling, but it's not. "Settling is always a decision made out of fear, and so I think if you can see things like, 'What if I don't find anyone else' as a fear-based decision and break down what you are really afraid of, then that's something you can get through," she says.

While it may not feel like you have a choice, you still get to decide what you do with your life, even if that means not getting the thing you hoped for. "We've heard from a lot of people who said they just wanted someone to say to them, 'It's okay to stop,'" Erik says. "Sometimes it will be a therapist who said it, or they finally came across someone like us who did, but you feel like all the messages you get from everybody in your life and in our culture say that you have to keep going until you get this baby. Life can be great without kids. Just know that you'll survive. Whatever happens, you will be fine. I think a lot of people think that not having kids is the worst thing in the world, but the funny thing is, I already knew that we would survive."

> My spouse and I have been married for nine years. Part of the reason I don't want children is because I love everything about my spouse and the time we spend together, and I don't want to lose that. We have a double income and no children, so we can take vacations together, go to live theater, and take outdoor excursions at the drop of the hat. I don't want to add a child to the mix and rock the amazing boat we currently have. It's not selfish. We don't hate children.

Since we've been married for nine years, we get questioned by family or are frequently told, "It would be nice to have grandchildren," although both of our parents already have grandchildren. I don't think some family members can fathom the idea that we are childfree by choice and assume we have fertility issues. We currently have a 4-year-old niece living with us as a foster child. This was an emergency placement that has lasted two years and not something we sought out. If she comes up for adoption, we have agreed to provide permanency.

While I feel committed to remaining childfree, my husband likes to say he still is not quite there yet and wants to remain on the fence. We have discussed adoption as an option, because I would prefer not to give birth and we don't need more people on this earth.

Megan, 32, Nebraska, she/her, works in public relations, white, cisgender, straight, married

PICKING A LONG-ACTING BIRTH CONTROL

It took seven years for Hanna Brooks Olsen, 31, to find a doctor who would sterilize her. It took Nick, whom you met in chapter 17, one month—and only because there was a scheduling conflict that kept him from being seen sooner.

"There wasn't a point where I realized, *Oh, I don't want children.* What I realized was I wanted a life that children were not part of. It wasn't a choice not to, I just didn't want to think about it. Children just weren't going to be part of my life," Hanna says. "The efforts I had to go through as a young person, especially as an uninsured person in college, just to keep from that being a part of my life were a struggle. I had a really hard time with hormonal birth control, and then I finally found one that worked, but it was really expensive. Every year that went by I had to go out of my way to make sure that my life was exactly as I wanted it."

Hanna first asked for a more permanent option when she was 21. It was clear almost immediately that finding a doctor who would perform the procedure would be a struggle. "There was this sort of moving target where every time I would go in for my annual and say, 'I want to talk about sterilization,' they'd be like, 'No, you're too young,' 'You can't,' 'We can't do it until you're 25,' then 'We can't do it until you're married,' or 'We can't do it until you're 30.'" It was infuriating, but Hanna kept asking. And then, when she was 28, her provider changed to someone younger. He was the sixth doctor she asked and the first to say yes. She had the procedure soon after.

Unintentional pregnancy is often a major stressor for childfree heterosexual adults and because of this, many people seek out long-acting or permanent birth control. Despite how little we hear about sterilization, it's actually the most commonly used contraceptive method. Nearly half of all married couples utilize sterilization, with tubal sterilization performed more frequently than vasectomies.[11] However, more than half of tubal procedures occur in the early postpartum period signifying just how tied to the end of childbearing these procedures are as opposed to being used to prevent pregnancy altogether. Even then, up to 50 percent of those who request tubal sterilization after childbirth are denied due to age, concerns about "regret," and religiously affiliated hospitals.[12]

Tubal sterilization requires an outpatient surgical procedure called a laparoscopy during which several small incisions are made in the belly button and abdomen. While you're under anesthesia, the surgeon either burns the tubes, scarring them to prevent the passage of an egg, uses metal clips to block the tubes, or removes part or all of the tubes. Hanna opted to have both of her tubes removed entirely, which comes with the added benefit of reducing the risk of ovarian cancer.[13]

A vasectomy, which severs the tubes that transport sperm, is even less invasive, typically requiring no more than a trip to the doctor's office. You will be awake for the procedure, but a numbing agent injected into the scrotum will numb any pain you would feel. Once numbed, the procedure is quick, no more than 30 minutes, and the only thing you may feel is some pressure. Vasectomies are 99.7 percent effective. Less than 0.3 percent of those who undergo a vasectomy require a repeat procedure. Complications occur less than 2 percent of the time. Your doctor will likely request you do a semen analysis two to three months following the procedure to confirm sterility. The risk of pregnancy following a negative semen analysis is 1 in 2,000.[14]

What Happens During a Vasectomy

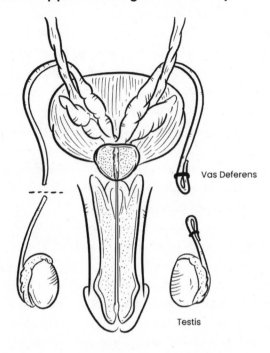

Vas Deferens

Testis

What Happens During Tubal Sterilization

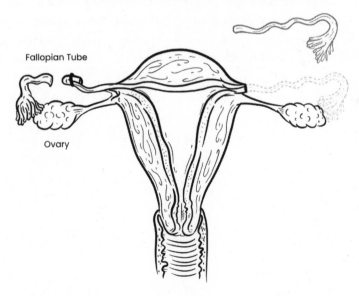

Fallopian Tube

Ovary

Tubal sterilization and vasectomies are considered permanent forms of contraception. If you change your mind and decide you want to have children later, it may still be possible, but it certainly won't be easy. The surgery to reverse a vasectomy has a lower success rate than the vasectomy itself. The most common reasons for vasectomy reversals are divorce and remarriage. In the cases where a vasectomy cannot be undone, doctors can use a minimally invasive surgical procedure to retrieve sperm. IUI or IVF would then need to occur to achieve pregnancy. The type of fertility treatment depends on the amount and quality of sperm retrieved. Tubal procedures are much harder to reverse. If you decide to have children following tubal sterilization, you will need IVF to retrieve eggs from the ovaries and then implant them into the uterus, which does not guarantee a child.

Outside of permanent sterilization, longer-acting options include birth control implants, which go into the arm, and IUDs that sit inside the uterus. For people who don't tolerate hormonal contraceptives well, a copper IUD might be a better option. Given her difficulties with hormonal contraceptives, Hanna opted for a copper IUD until she could have her tubes removed. The IUD insertion process can be painful, so it's important to have a provider you feel comfortable talking about pain control with. Some providers will offer light sedation, prescription pain medication, or muscle relaxers for the procedure. Different brands have different longevities, so it's important to know how long your device lasts and get it replaced in a timely fashion to best prevent pregnancy. The failure rate, or pregnancy rate, following tubal ligation is 0.5 per 100 people within the first year of unprotected sex compared to 0.2 per 100 for hormone-based IUDs, 0.8 per 100 for copper IUDs, 0.05 per 100 for contraceptive implants, and 0.15 per 100 for vasectomies.[15]

What an IUD Looks Like

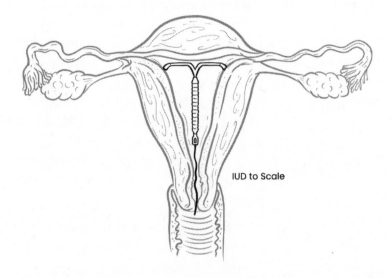

IUD to Scale

For Hanna and many other childfree folks, sterilization is the best option. There are no regrets, just the weight of parenthood off their shoulders. "I think people are so heavily invested in convincing themselves that having kids was exactly how they wanted their life to be," Hanna says. "For people who are undecided, it feels like all these people are so happy. They're talking about it all the time, telling me how great it is to have kids. They must know something I don't know. When you feel sort of conflicted, you wonder if there's some part of you that's missing that you don't understand. But there's this massive ad campaign, and parents are lobbying for you not necessarily to have your own kids, but for you to believe that having kids is the right decision."

I came to the conclusion I didn't want to have children while dating in my 30s. I wavered when I was young. When I was in my 20s, I thought maybe I would like a child or two like everybody else because it's traditional. As I got older, and my friends kept having kids, I realized I didn't want to live like that. It was basically a lifestyle issue. I didn't want to do the things that I saw good parents doing. I don't want to go to some 7-year-old's soccer game and stand on some cold field at seven in the morning with the other dads talking about whatever and watching bad soccer. I just didn't want to do that stuff.

When you're dating women in their 30s, they're looking for a potential father for their children. Day after day, we'd have that discussion. I'd say I don't want to have kids, and they would be pretty pissed about it, or they would try to convince me that kids were a great thing. I didn't want to lead them on. I wanted it to be settled for me so they knew we're not having kids, at least not with my sperm.

I was 42 when I got a vasectomy. It was a little uncomfortable. I was lying on a table and given a shot of some local anesthetic. You can feel something's going on down there, but it didn't hurt. It probably took about 15 minutes. The recovery was the worst part. I was sitting on bags of ice, that kind of thing, for a good day and a half, maybe two days.

Johnnie, 58, California, he/him, comedian,
Black, cisgender, engaged

CONCLUSION

So When Are You Having Kids?

NICOLE, 35, IS EIGHT months pregnant with a planned pregnancy, and she's still not sure having kids was the right decision. Nicole knew she wasn't ready for kids in her 20s. Waiting allowed her to leave corporate America, pursue a career as an entrepreneur, and enroll in a PhD program—things she doesn't think she would have done if she had children earlier. But even though Nicole is happy with the age she decided to have kids and in a comfortable enough financial position to do so, parts of her still question her choice.

"Watching my partner with kids was one of the things that made me realize, *Okay, I really want to do this with this person because he's going to make a great dad.* But where we're at, in terms of climate change and all that, I don't know if we made the right choice," Nicole says. "For me, I could have gone without ever having a kid. I think my ambivalence made it hard for me to argue against it because I didn't have a strong opinion."

While delaying parenthood gives you time to consciously decide whether you're ready to begin a new chapter, that same perk comes with a significant downside: a hyperawareness of what you stand to lose. Decades ago when people had children in lockstep with the end of their schooling, there was no time to cultivate a sense of freedom they'd later miss, whereas today, it's easier to see what you sacrifice by having kids than it is to see what you might gain. So how do people take the plunge and decide to have kids?

One explanation is "fertility contagion." Studies have found a contagious pattern of fertility among siblings, friends, and even coworkers. You've probably noticed something similar; one friend gets pregnant, then another, until suddenly it's as if you can't go a day without seeing a pregnancy announcement on social media. Sociologists Nicoletta Balbo, PhD, and Nicola Barban, PhD, argue that people may wait to have children as a "cost-saving" strategy that decreases the likelihood of feeling left behind. Watching your friends or siblings have kids first also lets you try it before you buy it, letting you see how people similar to you fare under the demands of parenthood. Your risk of having children once your friends start having kids peaks around two years after a friend gives birth and then decreases.[1] The effect of a sibling having kids is even stronger. The influence of a sibling giving birth increases your odds of desiring kids for up to two years following them giving birth. After three years, however, the effect is minimal.[2] When it comes to coworkers, birth rates in offices tend to increase in the year after an employee gives birth, petering out after the second year.[3] For all groups, the effect is strongest in those leaning toward having kids in the first place.

I am the mom of a 3-week-old, so these thoughts are fresh on my mind! My husband and I decided to have kids because we wanted to experience the joys of parenthood. We both have amazing parents and grew up in loving, supportive households. We look forward to watching our son grow and playing a part in showing him the world and learning alongside him. To us, having kids felt like a "peak human experience" that we didn't want to miss out on.

We are very early on in our journey, and it's difficult, no doubt. Lack of sleep and breastfeeding top the list of challenges. But I do feel like carrying him for nine months, giving birth to him, and taking care of him for three weeks has opened up my heart in ways I didn't know about before. I feel more connected to humanity as a whole and more aware of my precious short time on earth than I was before. If I could change anything, I may have considered having children earlier. It really wasn't possible in terms of my financial standing, relationship with my partner, or my own emotional maturity and mental health. But I'm watching my parents as 70-year-old grandparents and knowing that I'll be 50 before my son graduates from high school; I wish I would have had more of my younger vibrant years to spend with him.

Ali, 33, Maryland, she/her, white, cisgender, married

Ultimately, what people really want to know is whether kids will make them happy. If I had an agenda to push, I could easily find a study that says having kids makes people happy. I could also, just as easily, cite research that says the opposite. So what gives? Does having kids make you happier, or not? The answer is, of course, complex. But before we dive into the research, it's worth exploring why it's so difficult to determine whether or not parenthood brings happiness. Think of happiness like intellect. Remember the kids in school who could get an A without studying? Some people have a natural ability to understand, retain, and recall information, whereas other people have to really study to get that A. Happiness works similarly. Some people are just "naturally" happy; the result of an intermingling of factors discussed throughout this book like genes, environment, and societal norms. This creates a sort of chicken or the egg problem that makes it difficult to say whether kids make parents happy or if happy people have kids.

Looking at a sample of 1.8 million Americans, researchers found little difference in subjective well-being between people with and without children. Parents reported more joy as well as more stress, experiences that tend to cancel each other out. Parents who reported higher well-being were also more likely to be married, richer, better educated, more religious, and healthier, all factors that increase well-being irrespective of having kids. When researchers adjusted their analysis to control for these factors, they found parenthood led to a small negative association with life evaluation, with more positive and negative effects on pleasure.

The researchers concluded their study by noting that if people wished to make their lives "as good as possible" and could visualize their lives with and without children in an unbiased way, then those who believe their lives will be enriched by children despite all of the challenges will likely feel satisfied with their choice. Similarly, those who feel their lives are complete without children won't regret forgoing parenthood.[4]

I want to want kids. I struggle with whether fear of possible hardships is something holding me back and whether that's valid since so many other parents seemingly get by. If there are people out there who made the choice to have kids and regret it, I'm certainly not hearing their voices. What I do hear is the constant venting of parents and how hard it is in each season of parenthood. I'm not faulting them for expressing honest emotions; I guess I just don't see them showcase the positives in such an effusive way publicly.

I feel like I'd make a good parent and I'd be committed to doing my best and repairing whenever I blow it, but I don't have clarity on whether I should make that choice or whether it's collectively what my spouse and I want. We have honest discussions about how we feel, yet the ball hasn't moved solidly in one direction or another. I worry I'd expect fulfillment in life to come from my child and parenting, but at the same time I feel like that's the pitfall for anything in life, which is fixable if you realize it. It feels like biological realities will decide for us within a matter of years.

Joel, 36, Alabama, he/him, white, cisgender, married

Instead of looking at children as purveyors of happiness, it might be more useful to see them as agents of change. Parents report having children as "the most positive event" of their lives, and 94 percent of parents say having kids is worth the cost.[5] But kids, especially young ones, do not increase their parents' well-being. Parents of children under the age of 18 tend to report more distress than their childfree-by-choice counterparts as well as decreased marital satisfaction, depression, financial strain, and issues related to work-life balance.[6]

Having kids leads to a boost in satisfaction, but that boost doesn't last throughout one's life span. Studies using data from the UK, Germany, and

Australia found increases in satisfaction among both cisgender men and women during pregnancy and the first year of parenthood that returned to prepregnancy levels within the first two years of their child's life. A similar pattern was found for the birth of a second child; however, the increase in life satisfaction after a second child did not last as long as it did for the first.[7] And when it comes to deciding how many kids to have, those who report a decline in well-being after their first child are less likely to have more kids.[8] The "life meaning" that follows having kids does not increase with additional children.[9]

How you arrive at parenthood matters too. Births following unintended pregnancies tend to be viewed as more stressful and lead to an increase in depressive symptoms and a decrease in happiness.[10] Whereas those who postponed parenthood to later in life were more likely to experience an increase in life satisfaction compared to younger parents.[11]

Our brains also play a role in how we take to parenthood, so as much as you may want to prepare ahead of time, there are some things you just can't plan for. Our brains change when we become parents. Parents produce more oxytocin—a hormone associated with intimacy and trust—and experience more activation in the areas of the brain associated with emotion, attention, vigilance, and reward. While this "parenting network" of the brain was previously thought to only prompt cisgender women to nurture and protect their children, research suggests it turns on for parents regardless of sex. A study looking at cisgender heterosexual couples and same-sex male couples found that it's not your sex that activates the parenting network of the brain but how much time you spend caring for your children.[12] The circuitry is there within all of us and develops the more you care for your kids.

> If we're being honest, both of my children were unplanned, so technically, there was no choice. I was waiting until the perfect time when I was prepared, but now I believe no one is ever fully prepared to start having kids. I had my first at 25, and my second is due at the end of this year at 27.

I always knew I wanted kids. The only thing that changed is I used to think I wanted more kids and wanted to be younger when I had them. Now I know I'm good with just my two, and I'm a little better prepared at this age. I do enjoy being a mom. I get to stay home with my son every day, and we get to play and watch TV or visit my mother, whom he adores. Sometimes all we do is cuddle, and that's honestly worth everything for me. Watching a child grow from a tiny baby that can't hold his head up to a walking, talking toddler is amazing. It's fascinating to see how his mind is developing and what new skills he's learning. Obviously there are things about parenthood that aren't always fun, but I don't think I'd change anything.

I got really lucky finding my husband because he's always been an active part of our marriage. I knew I didn't want to end up in a relationship where I did all or most of the work, and he never makes me feel that way. When he's at work, I'm responsible for all of the parenting, but as soon as he's home, he starts parenting with me.

Tara, 27, Pennsylvania, she/her, stay-at-home mom, white, cisgender, straight, married

Ultimately, a big part of happiness comes down to expectations. If I tell you I'm going to give you $100 and only give you $50, you'd likely feel disappointed. But if I tell you I'm going to give you $25 and then give you $50, you'd be happy. In both scenarios you get $50, making happiness not about the value but the expectation.

When parents experience regret, it's often because their expectations of parenthood don't align with the realities. According to a Gallup survey, 7 percent of American parents wouldn't have children if they had to do it again.[13] However, it's hard to study regret among parents because it's taboo to admit you regret having children. People temper their emotions based on what they think others in their community would feel, which leads to shame, guilt, and embarrassment over deviating from what's perceived as normal. So while parents might regret having children on a personal level, they tend to avoid expressing that because it goes against the cultural norms of how they're supposed to feel.

Some people regret having children altogether, and others regret the circumstances associated with having children. Those who regret having children tend to view their children as difficult, perceive themselves as bad parents, or mourn the lives they had before children. Whereas those who regret circumstances often wish they could change when they had kids, how many kids they have, the sacrifices associated with parenthood, their partner, or society.[14]

At the end of the day, you may never feel 100 percent confident in your decision. After all, time and circumstance can change even the strongest of intentions. The best you can do is decide what feels right in this moment while acknowledging that feelings can change, and perhaps, set aside safeguards in case they do. You know what it's like to be childfree so take time to dwell in parenting spaces. If you're still struggling, take a moment to put pen to paper and work through some of the major questions explored in this book:

- What have I been taught about parenthood and how does that shape my views?

- What are the external factors affecting my decision-making? What can I do to empower myself in light of these factors?

- If I can't commit to a decision now, do I want to preserve my fertility to improve my odds of conceiving a biological child later in life?

- Do I need to have a biological or legal connection to a child to feel fulfilled? Are there other ways to be involved in a child's life like stepparenting, mentorship, or foster care that could feel equally valuable?

- Do I have a realistic expectation of the stressors associated with parenthood?

- Am I open to the prospect of my life changing or am I happy with the way things are?

Deciding whether or not to have children is the first, and perhaps final, parenting decision of your life. We can't predict the future for ourselves or for our children. All we can do is try our best.

ACKNOWLEDGMENTS

THIS BOOK WOULD NOT be possible without all of the people who took the time to share their stories and expertise with me. Thank you for your trust. Telling your stories has truly been the greatest honor of my life.

To my agent, Stacy Testa, thank you for championing this project and for believing in me, especially during the times when I struggled to believe in myself. Your support and the continuous advocacy of the Writer's House team truly made this project possible.

To the Sounds True team, thank you for all of your guidance and work on this project. Diana Ventimiglia, your enthusiasm for this project is what brought me to Sounds True in the first place. Thank you for shepherding it along. Gretel, or should I say "Great"el, Hakanson, you made the editing process an absolute dream and for that I am forever grateful. Jade Lascelles, Lisa Kerans, Huma Ahktar, Meredith Jarrett, Merlin Evans, Grayson Towler, and Jill Rogers, thank you for taking my thoughts and words and turning them into an actual book. And of course thank you to the Sounds True marketing and publicity team, Samantha Sacks, Mike Onorato, and Chloe Prusiewicz, for helping to get this book out into the world.

The year I spent writing this book was not without challenges. My deepest appreciation to who kept me sane this year. Lori, who pulled me out of the depths of my grief, allowing space for this book to form. Caroline Reilly, whose friendship is the greatest gift. Angelica Catalano, my tireless cheerleader and trusted friend. Renèe Fabian, who despite no longer being on my team is still somehow my right hand. And my sister, Taylor Davidson, who graduated from playing nurse to saving actual lives. I am so grateful to have you all in my life.

I would, of course, not be here without my parents Karen Vogt and Michael Davidson, who thankfully decided they wanted to have kids. (Or so they tell me.) I am lucky that my parents and my grandmother Miriam not only sparked but encouraged my lifelong obsession with books.

And to my partner, Zack Whittaker, to whom this book is dedicated, it is your love and support that got me through this process. Thank you for giving me the space and encouragement to pursue my dreams.

NOTES

Introduction

1 Thomas J. Mathews and Brady E. Hamilton, "Mean Age of Mothers Is on the Rise: United States, 2000–2014," *NCHS Data Brief* 232 (2016): 1–8.

2 Quoctrung Bui and Claire Cain Miller, "The Age That Women Have Babies: How a Gap Divides America," *New York Times*, August 4, 2018.

Chapter 1: The Waiting Game

1 Joyce A. Martin et al., *Births: Final Data for 2019*, National Vital Statistics Reports 70, no. 2 (Hyattsville, MD: National Center for Health Statistics, 2021), 1–51.

2 Melanie Hanson, "Average Student Loan Debt," Education Data, July 10, 2021, educationdata.org/student-loan-debt-statistics; "Housing Data," Zillow, 2021, zillow.com/research/data/; Simon Workman and Mathew Brady, "The Cost of Child Care During the Coronavirus Pandemic," Center for American Progress, September 3, 2020, americanprogress.org /article/cost-child-care-coronavirus-pandemic/.

3 Lauren Jade Martin, "Delaying, Debating and Declining Motherhood," *Culture, Health & Sexuality* (2020): 1–16.

4 Andrew J. Cherlin, David C. Ribar, and Suzumi Yasutake, "Nonmarital First Births, Marriage, and Income Inequality," *American Sociological Review* 81, no. 4 (2016): 749–70.

5 Chris Knoester, "Transitions in Young Adulthood and the Relationship Between Parent and Offspring Well-Being," *Social Forces* 81, no. 4 (2003): 1431–58.

6 Martin, "Delaying, Debating," 1–16.

7 Mikko Myrskylä and Rachel Margolis, "Happiness: Before and After the Kids," *Demography* 51, no. 5 (2014): 1843–66.

8   John Mirowsky and Catherine E. Ross, "Depression, Parenthood, and Age at First Birth," *Social Science & Medicine* 54, no. 8 (2002): 1281–98.

9   Christine Overall, *Why Have Children? The Ethical Debate* (Cambridge, MA: MIT Press, 2012).

10   D'Vera Cohn and Gretchen Livingston, "The New Demography of American Motherhood," Pew Research Center, May 6, 2010, pewresearch.org/social-trends/2010/05/06/the-new-demography-of -american-motherhood/.

11   Lawrence B. Finer and Mia R. Zolna, "Declines in Unintended Pregnancy in the United States, 2008–2011," *New England Journal of Medicine* 374, no. 9 (2016): 843–52.

12   Debra Friedman, Michael Hechter, and Satoshi Kanazawa, "A Theory of the Value of Children," *Demography* 31, no. 3 (August 1994): 375–401.

13   Amy L. Byers, Becca R. Levy, Heather G. Allore, Martha L. Bruce, and Stanislav V. Kasl, "When Parents Matter to Their Adult Children: Filial Reliance Associated with Parents' Depressive Symptoms," *The Journals of Gerontology Series B: Psychological Sciences and Social Sciences* 63, no. 1 (2008): 33–40.

14   Mark Lino et al., *Expenditures on Children by Families, 2015*, miscellaneous report no. 1528–2015 (Alexandria, VA: United States Department of Agriculture, Center for Nutrition Policy and Promotion, 2017).

15   Emily A. Greenfield and Nadine F. Marks, "Linked Lives: Adult Children's Problems and Their Parents' Psychological and Relational Well-Being," *Journal of Marriage and Family* 68, no. 2 (May 2006): 442–54.

16   Karen L. Fingerman, Yen-Pi Cheng, Kira Birditt, and Steven Zarit, "Only as Happy as the Least Happy Child: Multiple Grown Children's Problems and Successes and Middle-Aged Parents' Well-Being," *Journals of Gerontology Series B: Psychological Sciences and Social Sciences* 67, no. 2 (2012): 184–93.

17   Joan R. Kahn, Frances Goldscheider, and Javier García-Manglano, "Growing Parental Economic Power in Parent–Adult Child Households: Coresidence and Financial Dependency in the United States, 1960–2010," *Demography* 50, no. 4 (2013): 1449–75.

18 Robert F. Schoeni and Karen E. Ross, *Material Assistance from Families During the Transition to Adulthood* (Chicago: University of Chicago Press, 2008).

19 Julia Moore, "Facets of Agency in Stories of Transforming from Childless by Choice to Mother," *Journal of Marriage and Family* 79, no. 4 (2017): 1144–59.

20 Rachel G. Riskind and Samantha L. Tornello, "Sexual Orientation and Future Parenthood in a 2011–2013 Nationally Representative United States Sample," *Journal of Family Psychology* 31, no. 6 (2017): 792; Geva Shenkman, Henny Bos, and Shir Kogan, "Attachment Avoidance and Parenthood Desires in Gay Men and Lesbians and Their Heterosexual Counterparts," *Journal of Reproductive and Infant Psychology* 37, no. 4 (2019): 344–57.

21 Jorge Gato, Sara Santos, and Anne Marie Fontaine, "To Have or Not to Have Children? That Is the Question: Factors Influencing Parental Decisions among Lesbians and Gay Men," *Sexuality Research and Social Policy* 14, no. 3 (2017): 310–23.

22 Rebecca L. Stotzer, Jody L. Herman, and Amira Hasenbush, "Transgender Parenting: A Review of Existing Research," Williams Institute, October, 2014, williamsinstitute.law.ucla.edu/publications /transgender-parenting/.

23 Samantha L. Tornello and Henny Bos, "Parenting Intentions among Transgender Individuals," *LGBT Health* 4, no. 2 (2017): 115–20.

24 Damien W. Riggs and Clare Bartholomaeus, "Fertility Preservation Decision-Making Amongst Australian Transgender and Non-Binary Adults," *Reproductive Health* 15, no. 1 (2018): 1–10.

25 Lois W. Hoffman and Martin L. Hoffman, *The Value of Children to Parents: Psychological Perspectives on Population* (New York: Basic Books, 1973).

26 Gisela Trommsdorff and Bernhard Nauck, *The Value of Children in Cross-Cultural Perspective: Case Studies from Eight Societies* (Lengerich: Pabst Science, 2005).

27 Sharon K. Houseknecht, "Timing of the Decision to Remain Voluntarily Childless: Evidence for Continuous Socialization," *Psychology of Women Quarterly* 4, no. 1 (1979): 81–96; Monika Mynarska, Anna Matysiak,

Anna Rybińska, Valentina Tocchioni, and Daniele Vignoli, "Diverse Paths into Childlessness over the Life Course," *Advances in Life Course Research* 25 (2015): 35–48; Kristin Park, "Choosing Childlessness: Weber's Typology of Action and Motives of the Voluntarily Childless," *Sociological Inquiry* 75, no. 3 (2005): 372–402.

28 Icek Ajzen and Jane Klobas, "Fertility Intentions: An Approach Based on the Theory of Planned Behavior," *Demographic Research* 29 (2013): 203–32.

29 S. Philip Morgan and Christine A. Bachrach, "Is the Theory of Planned Behaviour an Appropriate Model for Human Fertility?" *Vienna Yearbook of Population Research* 9 (2011): 11–18.

Chapter 2: Where Do Parenting Desires Come From?

1 Richard Dawkins, *The Selfish Gene*, (Oxford, UK: Oxford University Press, 1989).

2 Steven Pinker, "Against Nature," *Discover* (1997), discovermagazine.com /health/against-nature.

3 Robert Sapolsky, "A Gene for Nothing," *Discover* 18, no. 10 (1997): 40–46.

4 S. Philip Morgan and Rosalind Berkowitz King, "Why Have Children in the 21st Century? Biological Predisposition, Social Coercion, Rational Choice," *European Journal of Population* 17, no. 1 (2001): 3–20.

5 Morgan, "Why Have Children?" 3–20.

6 Miri Scharf and Ofra Mayseless, "Buds of Parenting in Emerging Adult Males: What We Learned from Our Parents," *Journal of Adolescent Research* 26, no. 4 (March 14, 2011): 479–505.

7 Kim Bartholomew and Leonard M. Horowitz, "Attachment Styles among Young Adults: A Test of a Four-Category Model," *Journal of Personality and Social Psychology* 61, no. 2 (August 1991): 226.

8 Jonathan Mohr and Skyler Jackson, *Handbook of Attachment: Theory, Research, and Clinical Applications*, 3rd ed. (New York: Guilford Publications, 2016), 484–506.

9 Robyn A. Zakalik and Meifen Wei, "Adult Attachment, Perceived Discrimination Based on Sexual Orientation, and Depression in Gay

Males: Examining the Mediation and Moderation Effects," *Journal of Counseling Psychology* 53, no. 3 (2006): 302.

10   Kristin D. Mickelson, Ronald C. Kessler, and Phillip R. Shaver, "Adult Attachment in a Nationally Representative Sample," *Journal of Personality and Social Psychology* 73, no. 5 (1997): 1092.

11   Eva-Maria Merz, "Fertility Intentions Depend on Intergenerational Relations: A Life Course Perspective," *Family Science* 3, no. 3–4 (2012): 237–45.

12   William S. Rholes, Jeffry A. Simpson, and Barbara S. Blakely, "Adult Attachment Styles and Mothers' Relationships with Their Young Children," *Personal Relationships* 2, no. 1 (1995): 35–54.

13   W. S. Rholes et al., "Adult Attachment Styles, the Desire to Have Children, and Working Models of Parenthood," *Journal of Personality* 65 (1997): 357–85.

14   Geva Shenkman, Henny Bos, and Shir Kogan, "Attachment Avoidance and Parenthood Desires in Gay Men and Lesbians and Their Heterosexual Counterparts," *Journal of Reproductive and Infant Psychology* 37, no. 4 (2019): 344–57.

15   Tina Lavender et al., "Nature Makes You Blind to the Risks: An Exploration of Women's Views Surrounding Decisions on the Timing of Childbearing in Contemporary Society," *Sexual & Reproductive Healthcare* 6, no. 3 (2015): 157–63.

16   Rosanna Hertz, *Single by Chance, Mothers by Choice: How Women Are Choosing Parenthood Without Marriage and Creating the New American Family* (New York: Oxford University Press, 2006).

17   Clare Bartholomaeus and Damien W. Riggs, "Daughters and Their Mothers: The Reproduction of Pronatalist Discourses Across Generations," *Women's Studies International Forum* 62 (2017): 1–7.

18   Angela R. Baerwald, Gregg P. Adams, and Roger A. Pierson, "Ovarian Antral Folliculogenesis During the Human Menstrual Cycle: A Review," *Human Reproduction Update* 18, no. 1 (2012): 73–91.

19   Richard A. Settersten Jr. and Barbara Ray, "What's Going On with Young People Today? The Long and Twisting Path to Adulthood," *The Future of Children* (2010): 19–41.

20   Julia Moore and Patricia Geist-Martin, "Mediated Representations of Voluntary Childlessness, 1900–2012," *The Essential Handbook of Women's Sexuality* (Santa Barbara: Praeger, 2016), 233–51.

21   Marie Van Vorst, *The Woman Who Toils: Being the Experiences of Two Ladies as Factory Girls* (New York: Doubleday, Page & Company, 1905).

22   Settersten and Ray, "What's Going On?," 19–41.

23   Arland Thornton and Linda Young-DeMarco, "Four Decades of Trends in Attitudes Toward Family Issues in the United States: The 1960s Through the 1990s," *Journal of Marriage and Family* 63, no. 4 (2001): 1009–37.

24   Robert H. Frank, *Falling Behind: How Rising Inequality Harms the Middle Class* (Berkeley: University of California Press, 2013).

25   Judith Blake, *Coercive Pronatalism and American Population Policy* (Berkeley: International Population and Urban Research, University of California, 1973).

26   Jessica Semega et al., "Income and Poverty in the United States: 2019," United States Census Bureau, September 15, 2020, census.gov/library /publications/2020/demo/p60-270.html.

27   A. W. Geiger, Gretchen Livingston, and Kristen Bialik, "6 Facts about U.S. Moms," Pew Research Center, May 8, 2019, pewresearch.org/fact-tank /2019/05/08/facts-about-u-s-mothers/.

28   Decennial Censuses, 1890 to 1940 and Current Population Survey, Annual Social and Economic Supplements, 1947 to 2020, United States Census Bureau, census.gov/history/www/genealogy/decennial_census_records/.

29   Andrew J. Cherlin, "American Marriage in the Early Twenty-First Century," *The Future of Children* (2005): 33–55.

30   Decennial Censuses, 1890 to 1940.

31   Elizabeth Wildsmith, Jennifer Manlove, and Elizabeth Cook, "Dramatic Increase in the Proportion of Births Outside of Marriage in the United States from 1990 to 2016," Child Trends, 2018, childtrends.org /publications/dramatic-increase-in-percentage-of-births-outside-marriage -among-whites-hispanics-and-women-with-higher-education-levels.

Chapter 3: Managing External Expectations

1   Lisa Kiang, Terese Glatz, and Christy M. Buchanan, "Acculturation Conflict, Cultural Parenting Self-Efficacy, and Perceived Parenting Competence in Asian American and Latino/a Families," *Family Process* 56, no. 4 (2017): 943–61.

2   Jennifer Hickes Lundquist, Michelle J. Budig, and Anna Curtis, "Race and Childlessness in America, 1988–2002," *Journal of Marriage and Family* 71, no. 3 (2009): 741–55.

3   David B. Seifer, Linda M. Frazier, and David A. Grainger, "Disparity in Assisted Reproductive Technologies Outcomes in Black Women Compared with White Women," *Fertility and Sterility* 90, no. 5 (2008): 1701–10.

4   Rosario Ceballo, Erin T. Graham, and Jamie Hart, "Silent and Infertile: An Intersectional Analysis of the Experiences of Socioeconomically Diverse African American Women with Infertility," *Psychology of Women Quarterly* 39, no. 4 (2015): 497–511.

5   Fady I. Sharara and Howard D. McClamrock, "Differences in In Vitro Fertilization (IVF) Outcome Between White and Black Women in an Inner-City, University-Based IVF Program," *Fertility and Sterility* 73, no. 6 (2000): 1170–73.

6   Dawn Marie Dow, *Mothering While Black: Boundaries and Burdens of Middle-Class Parenthood* (Oakland: University of California Press, 2019).

7   Sinikka Elliott and Megan Reid, "Low-Income Black Mothers Parenting Adolescents in the Mass Incarceration Era: The Long Reach of Criminalization," *American Sociological Review* 84, no. 2 (2019): 197–219.

8   "Racial Disproportionality and Disparity in Child Welfare," Child Welfare Information Gateway, 2016, childwelfare.gov/pubs/issue-briefs/racial -disproportionality.

9   Conrad Hackett et al., "The Future Size of Religiously Affiliated and Unaffiliated Populations," *Demographic Research* 32 (2015): 829–42.

10   Sarah R. Hayford and S. Philip Morgan, "Religiosity and Fertility in the United States: The Role of Fertility Intentions," *Social Forces* 86, no. 3 (2008): 1163–88.

11 Maryam Dilmaghani, "Religiosity, Secularity and Fertility in Canada," *European Journal of Population* 35, no. 2 (2019): 403–28.

Chapter 4: Moving from Desire to Intention

1 Michael Wagner, Johannes Huinink, and Aart C. Liefbroer, "Running Out of Time? Understanding the Consequences of the Biological Clock for the Dynamics of Fertility Intentions and Union Formation," *Demographic Research* 40 (2019): 1–26.

2 Wagner, "Running Out of Time?" 1–26.

Chapter 5: The Demands and Rewards of Parenthood

1 Sharon Hays, *The Cultural Contradictions of Motherhood* (New Haven, CT: Yale University Press, 1996).

2 Kei Nomaguchi and Melissa A. Milkie, "Parenthood and Well-Being: A Decade in Review," *Journal of Marriage and Family* 82, no. 1 (2020): 198–223.

3 Julia Moore and Jenna Abetz, "'Uh Oh. Cue the [New] Mommy Wars': The Ideology of Combative Mothering in Popular U.S. Newspaper Articles about Attachment Parenting," *Southern Communication Journal* 81, no. 1 (2016): 54.

4 Nomaguchi and Milkie, "Parenthood and Well-Being," 198–223.

5 Angie Henderson, Sandra Harmon, and Harmony Newman, "The Price Mothers Pay, Even When They Are Not Buying It: Mental Health Consequences of Idealized Motherhood," *Sex Roles* 74, no. 11–12 (2016): 512–526.

6 Gretchen Livingston and Kim Parker, "8 Facts about American Dads," Pew Research Center, June 12, 2019, pewresearch.org/fact-tank/2019/06/12/fathers-day-facts/.

7 "Parenting in America," Pew Research Center, December 17, 2015, pewresearch.org/social-trends/2015/12/17/parenting-in-america/.

8 Meghan A. Lee, Sarah J. Schoppe-Sullivan, and Claire M. Kamp Dush, "Parenting Perfectionism and Parental Adjustment," *Personality and Individual Differences* 52, no. 3 (2012): 454–57.

9   Nomaguchi and Milkie, "Parenthood and Well-Being," 201.

10   James T. Fawcett, "The Value of Children and the Transition to Parenthood," *Marriage & Family Review* 12, no. 3–4 (1988): 11–34.

11   Daniel Kahneman et al., "A Survey Method for Characterizing Daily Life Experience: The Day Reconstruction Method," *Science* 306, no. 5702 (2004): 1776–80.

12   Kei Nomaguchi and Wendi Johnson, "Parenting Stress among Low-Income and Working-Class Fathers: The Role of Employment," *Journal of Family Issues* 37, no. 11 (2016): 1535–57.

13   Kei Nomaguchi, "Parenthood and Psychological Well-Being: Clarifying the Role of Child Age and Parent-Child Relationship Quality," *Social Science Research* 41, no. 2 (2012): 489–98.

14   Suniya S. Luthar and Lucia Ciciolla, "What It Feels Like to Be a Mother: Variations by Children's Developmental Stages," *Developmental Psychology* 52, no. 1 (2016): 143.

15   Ann Meier et al., "Mothers' and Fathers' Well-Being in Parenting Across the Arch of Child Development," *Journal of Marriage and Family* 80, no. 4 (2018): 992–1004.

16   Debra Umberson, Tetyana Pudrovska, and Corinne Reczek, "Parenthood, Childlessness, and Well-Being: A Life Course Perspective," *Journal of Marriage and Family* 72, no. 3 (2010): 612–29.

17   Ranae J. Evenson and Robin W. Simon, "Clarifying the Relationship Between Parenthood and Depression," *Journal of Health and Social Behavior* 46, no. 4 (2005): 341–58.

18   Nomaguchi and Milkie, "Parenthood and Well-Being," 198–223.

Chapter 6: Family Planning and Relationships

1   E. Kurdi, "Many Couples Need Just One Conversation to Decide Not to Have Children" (paper, Annual Meeting of the British Sociological Association in Leeds, April 25, 2014).

2   Maria Iacovou and Lara Patrício Tavares, "Yearning, Learning, and Conceding: Reasons Men and Women Change Their Childbearing

Intentions," *Population and Development Review* 37, no. 1 (2011): 89–123.

3   Wesley Durham and Dawn O. Braithwaite, "Communication Privacy Management Within the Family Planning Trajectories of Voluntarily Child-Free Couples," *Journal of Family Communication* 9, no. 1 (2009): 43–65.

4   Abbie E. Goldberg, Jordan B. Downing, and April M. Moyer, "Why Parenthood, and Why Now? Gay Men's Motivations for Pursuing Parenthood," *Family Relations* 61, no. 1 (2012): 157–74.

5   Debra Umberson, Tetyana Pudrovska, and Corinne Reczek, "Parenthood, Childlessness, and Well-Being: A Life Course Perspective," *Journal of Marriage and Family* 72, no. 3 (2010): 612–29.

6   Judith Stacey, "Gay Parenthood and the Decline of Paternity as We Knew It," *Sexualities* 9, no. 1 (2006): 27–55.

7   Nancy J. Mezey, *New Choices, New Families: How Lesbians Decide about Motherhood* (Baltimore, MD: John Hopkins University Press, 2008).

8   Kathleen Gerson, *No Man's Land: Men's Changing Commitments to Family and Work* (New York: Basic Books, 2003).

9   Elizabeth Ty Wilde, Lily Batchelder, and David T. Ellwood, "The Mommy Track Divides: The Impact of Childbearing on Wages of Women of Differing Skill Levels" (working paper 16582, National Bureau of Economic Research, December 2010), nber.org/papers/w16582.

10 Jeffry A. Simpson et al., "Adult Attachment, the Transition to Parenthood, and Depressive Symptoms," *Journal of Personality and Social Psychology* 84, no. 6 (2003): 1172.

11 Leann E. Smith and Kimberly S. Howard, "Continuity of Paternal Social Support and Depressive Symptoms among New Mothers," *Journal of Family Psychology* 22, no. 5 (2008): 763.

12 Kim Parker and Wendy Wang, "Modern Parenthood," Pew Research Center, 2013, pewresearch.org/social-trends/2013/03/14/modern -parenthood-roles-of-moms-and-dads-converge-as-they-balance-work -and-family/.

13　Kim Parker and Juliana Menasce Horowitz, "Parenting in America: Outlook, Worries, Aspirations Are Strongly Linked to Financial Situation," Pew Research Center, 2015, pewresearch.org/social-trends/2015/12/17 /parenting-in-america/.

14　Melissa A. Milkie, Kei Nomaguchi, and Scott Schieman, "Time Deficits with Children: The Link to Parents' Mental and Physical Health," *Society and Mental Health* 9, no. 3 (2019): 277–95.

15　Kei Nomaguchi and Melissa A. Milkie, "Parenthood and Well-Being: A Decade in Review," *Journal of Marriage and Family* 82, no. 1 (2020): 198–223.

16　Carolyn Pape Cowan and Philip A. Cowan, "Who Does What When Partners Become Parents: Implications for Men, Women, and Marriage," *Marriage & Family Review* 12, no. 3–4 (1988): 105–31.

17　Samantha L. Tornello, "Division of Labor among Transgender and Gender Non-Binary Parents: Association with Individual, Couple, and Children's Behavioral Outcomes," *Frontiers in Psychology* 11 (2020): 15.

Chapter 7: Kids, in This Climate?

1　Walt Hickey and Eliza Relman, "More Than a Third of Millennials Share Rep. Alexandria Ocasio-Cortez's Worry about Having Kids While the Threat of Climate Change Looms," Business Insider, 2019, businessinsider.com/millennials-americans-worry-about-kids-children -climate-change-poll-2019-3; Claire Cain Miller, "Americans Are Having Fewer Babies. They Told Us Why," *New York Times,* July 5, 2018, nytimes.com/2018/07/05/upshot/americans-are-having-fewer-babies -they-told-us-why.html.

2　Frank W. Notestein, "Zero Population Growth," *Population Index* (1970): 444–52.

3　Rebecca Lindsey, "Climate Change: Atmospheric Carbon Dioxide," Climate.gov, August 14, 2020, climate.gov/news-features/understanding -climate/climate-change-atmospheric-carbon-dioxide.

4　K. Krygsman et al., *Let's Talk Communities & Climate: Communication Guidance for City and Community Leaders,* 2016, ecoamerica.org/wp -content/uploads/2017/03/ea-lets-talk-communities-and-climate-web.pdf.

5   N. Fann et al., "Air Quality Impacts," chap. 3 in *The Impacts of Climate Change on Human Health in the United States: A Scientific Assessment* (Washington, DC: U.S. Global Change Research Program, 2016), 69–98.

6   S. Doney et al., "Oceans and Marine Resources," chap. 24 in *Climate Change Impacts in the United States: The Third National Climate Assessment*, eds. J. M. Melillo, T. C. Richmond, and G. W. Yohe (Washington, DC: U.S. Global Change Research Program, 2014), 557–78, nca2014.globalchange.gov/report/regions/oceans.

7   Adam S. Parris et al., *Global Sea Level Rise Scenarios for the United States National Climate Assessment*, NOAA.gov, 2012, scenarios.globalchange .gov/sites/default/files/NOAA_SLR_r3_0.pdf.

8   J. Trtanj et al., "Climate Impacts on Water-Related Illness," chap. 6 in *The Impacts of Climate Change on Human Health in the United States: A Scientific Assessment* (Washington, DC: U.S. Global Change Research Program, 2016), health2016.globalchange.gov/low/ClimateHealth2016 _FullReport_small.pdf; Katarzyna Alderman, Lyle R. Turner, and Shilu Tong, "Floods and Human Health: A Systematic Review," *Environment International* 47 (2012): 37–47.

9   C. B. Beard et al., "Vector-Borne Diseases," in *The Impacts of Climate Change on Human Health in the United States: A Scientific Assessment* (Washington, DC: U.S. Global Change Research Program, 2016), 129–56.

10   L. Ziska, et al., "Food Safety, Nutrition, and Distribution," chap. 7 in *The Impacts of Climate Change on Human Health in the United States: A Scientific Assessment* (Washington, DC: U.S. Global Change Research Program, 2016), 189–216.

11   Daniel Martinez Garcia and Mary C. Sheehan, "Extreme Weather-Driven Disasters and Children's Health," *International Journal of Health Services* 46, no. 1 (2016): 79–105.

12   Frederica P. Perera, "Multiple Threats to Child Health from Fossil Fuel Combustion: Impacts of Air Pollution and Climate Change," *Environmental Health Perspectives* 125, no. 2 (2017): 141–48.

13   W. James Gauderman et al., "Association of Improved Air Quality with Lung Development in Children," *New England Journal of Medicine* 372 (2015): 905–13.

14   Ronald C. Kessler et al., "Trends in Mental Illness and Suicidality after Hurricane Katrina," *Molecular Psychiatry* 13, no. 4 (2008): 374–84.

15   Susan Clayton Whitmore-Williams et al., *Mental Health and Our Changing Climate: Impacts, Implications, and Guidance*, American Psychological Association, March 2017, apa.org/news/press/releases/2017/03/mental-health-climate.pdf.

16   Trevor Houser et al., *Economic Risks of Climate Change: An American Prospectus* (New York: Columbia University Press, 2015).

17   K. Gordon, "The Economic Risks of Climate Change in the United States" (Risky Business Project and Rhodium Group, 2014), Risky Business, riskybusiness.org/report/national/.

18   Whitmore-Williams, *Mental Health*.

19   Matthew Ranson, "Crime, Weather, and Climate Change," *Journal of Environmental Economics and Management* 67, no. 3 (2014): 274–302.

20   Whitmore-Williams, *Mental Health*.

21   Seth Wynes and Kimberly A. Nicholas, "The Climate Mitigation Gap: Education and Government Recommendations Miss the Most Effective Individual Actions," *Environmental Research Letters* 12, no. 7 (2017): 074024, iopscience.iop.org/article/10.1088/1748-9326/aa7541.

22   Brian C. O'Neill et al., "Global Demographic Trends and Future Carbon Emissions," *Proceedings of the National Academy of Sciences* 107, no. 41 (2010): 17521–26.

23   Tim Gore, "Confronting Carbon Inequality: Putting Climate Justice at the Heart of the COVID-19 Recovery," Oxfam, September 21, 2020, oxfamilibrary.openrepository.com/handle/10546/621052.

24   Bastien Girod et al., "Climate Policy Through Changing Consumption Choices: Options and Obstacles for Reducing Greenhouse Gas Emissions," *Global Environmental Change* 25 (2014): 5–15.

25   Wynes and Nicholas, "Climate Mitigation Gap."

26   "Total Fertility Rate—the World Factbook," Central Intelligence Agency, 2021, cia.gov/the-world-factbook/field/total-fertility-rate/.

27   "CO2 Emissions (Metric Tons per Capita)," World Bank, 2018, data.worldbank.org/indicator/EN.ATM.CO2E.PC.

28   Whitmore-Williams, *Mental Health*.

29   Maria Ojala and Hans Bengtsson, "Young People's Coping Strategies Concerning Climate Change: Relations to Perceived Communication with Parents and Friends and Proenvironmental Behavior," *Environment and Behavior* 51, no. 8 (2019): 907–35.

30   Ann V. Sanson, Susie E. L. Burke, and Judith Van Hoorn, "Climate Change: Implications for Parents and Parenting," *Parenting* 18, no. 3 (2018): 200–17.

31   Elizabeth Cripps, "Do Parents Have a Special Duty to Mitigate Climate Change?" *Politics, Philosophy & Economics* 16, no. 3 (2017): 3.

Chapter 8: Getting Your Finances in Order

1   Mark Lino et al., *Expenditures on Children by Families, 2015*, miscellaneous report no. 1528–2015 (Alexandria, VA: United States Department of Agriculture, Center for Nutrition Policy and Promotion, 2017).

2   Robert F. Schoeni and Karen E. Ross, *Material Assistance from Families During the Transition to Adulthood* (Chicago: University of Chicago Press, 2008).

3   Patrick Hanzel, Hannah Horvath, and Jeanine Skowronski, "Parents and Money," Policygenius, 2019, policygenius.com/personal-finance/news/parents-and-money-survey/.

4   Centers for Disease Control and Prevention, "About Natality, 2016–2020 Expanded," CDC Wonder, 2020, wonder.cdc.gov/natality-expanded-current.html.

5   Office of the Surgeon General, "Breastfeeding: Surgeon General's Call to Action Fact Sheet," U.S. Department of Health & Human Services, 2019, hhs.gov/surgeongeneral/reports-and-publications/breastfeeding/factsheet/index.html.

6   S. Bacchus et al., "The Cost of Baby-Led vs. Parent-Led Approaches to Introducing Complementary Foods in New Zealand," *European Journal of Clinical Nutrition* 74, no. 10 (2020): 1474–77.

7   "Is Paid Leave Available to Mothers and Fathers of Infants?" World Policy Analysis Center, 2019, worldpolicycenter.org/policies/is-paid-leave-available-for-both-parents-of-infants.

8   Hiroshi Ono and Kristen Schultz Lee, "Welfare States and the Redistribution of Happiness," *Social Forces* 92, no. 2 (2013): 789–814.

9   Administration for Children and Families, "Child Care and Development Fund (CCDF) Program," *Federal Register* 81, no. 190 (September 30, 2016), federalregister.gov/documents/2016/09/30/2016-22986/child-care-and-development-fund-ccdf-program.

10 Simon Workman and Mathew Brady, "The Cost of Child Care During the Coronavirus Pandemic," Center for American Progress, 2020, americanprogress.org/article/cost-child-care-coronavirus-pandemic/.

11 Michael Madowitz, Alex Rowell, and Katie Hamm, "Calculating the Hidden Cost of Interrupting a Career for Child Care," Center for American Progress, 2016, americanprogress.org/article/calculating-the-hidden-cost-of-interrupting-a-career-for-child-care/.

12 Kei Nomaguchi and Marshal Neal Fettro, "Childrearing Stages and Work-Family Conflict: The Role of Job Demands and Resources," *Journal of Marriage and Family* 81, no. 2 (2019): 289–307.

13 Abbie E. Goldberg and JuliAnna Z. Smith, "Work Conditions and Mental Health in Lesbian and Gay Dual-Earner Parents," *Family Relations* 62, no. 5 (2013): 727–40.

14 Richard J. Petts and Chris Knoester, "Paternity Leave and Parental Relationships: Variations by Gender and Mothers' Work Statuses," *Journal of Marriage and Family* 81, no. 2 (2019): 468–86.

Chapter 9: Is Passing On Your Genes Really the Best Thing?

1   William A. Horton, Judith G. Hall, and Jacqueline T. Hecht, "Achondroplasia," *The Lancet* 370, no. 9582 (2007): 162–72.

2   David Benatar, *Better Never to Have Been: The Harm of Coming into Existence* (Oxford, UK: Clarendon Press, 2006), 6.

3   Michael D. Kessler et al., "De Novo Mutations Across 1,465 Diverse Genomes Reveal Mutational Insights and Reductions in the Amish Founder Population," *Proceedings of the National Academy of Sciences* 117, no. 5 (2020): 2560–69.

4   Myrna M. Weissman et al., "A 30-Year Study of 3 Generations at High Risk and Low Risk for Depression," *JAMA Psychiatry* 73, no. 9 (2016): 970–77.

5   Holly Peay and Jehannine Claire Austin, *How to Talk to Families about Genetics and Psychiatric Illness* (New York: W. W. Norton, 2019).

Chapter 10: You're Concerned You Might Not Be a Good Parent

1   Danielle M. Seay et al., "Intergenerational Transmission of Maladaptive Parenting Strategies in Families of Adolescent Mothers: Effects from Grandmothers to Young Children," *Journal of Abnormal Child Psychology* 44, no. 6 (2016): 1097–109.

2   Samuel P. Putnam, Ann V. Sanson, and Mary K. Rothbart, "Child Temperament and Parenting," in *Handbook of Parenting: Children and Parenting*, ed. M. H. Bornstein (Mahwah, NJ: Lawrence Erlbaum Associates Publishers, 2002).

3   Eleanor E. Maccoby, Margaret E. Snow, and Carol N. Jacklin, "Children's Dispositions and Mother-Child Interaction at 12 and 18 Months: A Short-Term Longitudinal Study," *Developmental Psychology* 20, no. 3 (1984): 459.

4   Seay et al., "Intergenerational Transmission," 1097–109.

5   Jessica Pereira et al., "Parenting Stress Mediates Between Maternal Maltreatment History and Maternal Sensitivity in a Community Sample," *Child Abuse & Neglect* 36, no. 5 (2012): 433–37.

6   Jason D. Jones, Jude Cassidy, and Phillip R. Shaver, "Parents' Self-Reported Attachment Styles: A Review of Links with Parenting Behaviors, Emotions, and Cognitions," *Personality and Social Psychology Review* 19, no. 1 (2015): 44–76.

7   Jones et al., "Parents' Self-Reported Attachment Styles," 44–76.

8   Ron Roberts, "The Effects of Child Sexual Abuse in Later Family Life: Mental Health, Parenting, and Adjustment of Offspring," *Child Abuse & Neglect* 28, no. 5 (2004): 525–45.

9   Vincent J. Felitti et al., "Relationship of Childhood Abuse and Household Dysfunction to Many of the Leading Causes of Death in Adults: The Adverse Childhood Experiences (ACE) Study," *American Journal of Preventive Medicine* 14, no. 4 (1998): 245–58.

10   Sharon Borja et al., "Adverse Childhood Experiences to Adult Adversity Trends among Parents: Socioeconomic, Health, and Developmental Implications," *Children and Youth Services Review* 100 (2019): 258–66.

11   Joan Kaufman and Edward Zigler, "Do Abused Children Become Abusive Parents?" *American Journal of Orthopsychiatry* 57, no. 2 (1987): 186–92; Cathy Spatz Widom, Sally J. Czaja, and Kimberly A. DuMont, "Intergenerational Transmission of Child Abuse and Neglect: Real or Detection Bias?" *Science* 347, no. 6229 (2015): 1480–85.

12   Brittany C. L. Lange, Laura S. Callinan, and Megan V. Smith, "Adverse Childhood Experiences and Their Relation to Parenting Stress and Parenting Practices," *Community Mental Health Journal* 55, no. 4 (2019): 651–62.

13   Adam Schickedanz et al., "Parents' Adverse Childhood Experiences and Their Children's Behavioral Health Problems," *Pediatrics* 142, no. 2 (2018).

14   *Preventing Adverse Childhood Experiences (ACEs): Leveraging the Best Available Evidence*, CDC, 2021, cdc.gov/violenceprevention/pdf /preventingACES.pdf.

15   Diana Baumrind, "Effects of Authoritative Parental Control on Child Behavior," *Child Development* (1966): 887–907.

16   E. E. Maccoby, "Socialization in the Context of the Family: Parent-Child Interaction," *Handbook of Child Psychology* 4 (1983): 1–101.

17   Leigh A. Leslie and Emily T. Cook, "Maternal Trauma and Adolescent Depression: Is Parenting Style a Moderator?" *Psychology* 6 (2015): 681–688, dx.doi.org/10.4236/psych.2015.66066.

18   Laurence Steinberg, "We Know Some Things: Parent–Adolescent Relationships in Retrospect and Prospect," *Journal of Research on Adolescence* 11, no. 1 (2001): 1–19.

19   Ariel Knafo and Robert Plomin, "Prosocial Behavior from Early to Middle Childhood: Genetic and Environmental Influences on Stability and Change," *Developmental Psychology* 42, no. 5 (2006): 771.

20   John M. Gottman, Lynn Fainsilber Katz, and Carole Hooven, "Parental Meta-Emotion Philosophy and the Emotional Life of Families: Theoretical Models and Preliminary Data," *Journal of Family Psychology* 10, no. 3 (1996): 243.

Chapter 11: You're Afraid of Pregnancy or Childbirth

1   Alex F. Peahl et al., "Rates of New Persistent Opioid Use After Vaginal or Cesarean Birth among US Women," *JAMA Network Open* 2, no. 7 (2019): 1–14.

2   S. Philip Morgan and Christine A. Bachrach, "Is the Theory of Planned Behaviour an Appropriate Model for Human Fertility?" *Vienna Yearbook of Population Research* 9 (2011): 11–18.

3   Institute of Medicine (US) and National Research Council (US) Committee to Reexamine IOM Pregnancy Weight Guidelines, "Weight Gain During Pregnancy: Reexamining the Guidelines," eds. Kathleen M. Rasmussen and Ann L. Yaktine (Washington, DC: National Academies Press, 2009).

4   Charlotte Sollid, Loa Clausen, and Rikke Damkjær Maimburg, "The First 20 Weeks of Pregnancy Is a High-Risk Period for Eating Disorder Relapse," *International Journal of Eating Disorders* 54, no. 12 (2021): 2132–42.

5   American College of Obstetricians and Gynecologists, "Obesity in Pregnancy: ACOG Practice Bulletin, Number 230," *Obstetrics and Gynecology* 137, no. 6 (2021): e128–44.

6   "Hair Loss in New Moms," American Academy of Dermatology Association, 2010, aad.org/public/diseases/hair-loss/insider/new-moms.

7   "Pregnancy and Oral Health," U.S. Centers for Disease Control and Prevention, 2019, cdc.gov/oralhealth/publications/features/pregnancy -and-oral-health.html; Margreet Meems et al., "Prevalence, Course and

Determinants of Carpal Tunnel Syndrome Symptoms During Pregnancy: A Prospective Study," *BJOG* 122, no. 8 (2015): 1112–18.

8   Michal Dubovicky et al., "Risks of Using SSRI/SNRI Antidepressants During Pregnancy and Lactation," *Interdisciplinary Toxicology* 10, no. 1 (2017): 30.

9   Elizabeth Werner et al., "Preventing Postpartum Depression: Review and Recommendations," *Archives of Women's Mental Health* 18, no. 1 (2015): 41–60.

10 Manjeet Singh Bhatia and Anurag Jhanjee, "Tokophobia: A Dread of Pregnancy," *Industrial Psychiatry Journal* 21, no. 2 (2012): 158.

11 Eelco Olde et al., "Posttraumatic Stress Following Childbirth: A Review," *Clinical Psychology Review* 26, no. 1 (2006): 1–16.

12 Meghan A. Bohren et al., "Continuous Support for Women During Childbirth," *Cochrane Database of Systematic Reviews* 7 (2017).

13 American College of Obstetricians and Gynecologists, "Health Care for Transgender and Gender Diverse Individuals: ACOG Committee Opinion, Number 823," *Obstetrics & Gynecology* 137, no. 3 (2021): e75.

14 Alexis D. Light et al., "Transgender Men Who Experienced Pregnancy After Female-to-Male Gender Transitioning," *Obstetrics & Gynecology* 124, no. 6 (2014): 1120–27.

15 Trevor MacDonald et al., "Transmasculine Individuals' Experiences with Lactation, Chestfeeding, and Gender Identity: A Qualitative Study," *BMC Pregnancy and Childbirth* 16, no. 1 (2016): 1–17.

16 Donna L. Hoyert, "Maternal Mortality Rates in the United States, 2020," NCHS Health E-Stats, 2022, stacks.cdc.gov/view/cdc/113967.

17 Elizabeth A. Howell, "Reducing Disparities in Severe Maternal Morbidity and Mortality," *Clinical Obstetrics and Gynecology* 61, no. 2 (2018): 387.

18 Marian F. MacDorman and T. J. Mathews, "Understanding Racial and Ethnic Disparities in US Infant Mortality Rates," CDC, 2011, stacks.cdc.gov/view/cdc/12375.

19 Jamila Taylor et al., "Eliminating Racial Disparities in Maternal and Infant Mortality: A Comprehensive Policy Blueprint," *Center for American Progress* 1, no. 1 (2019): 1–93.

Chapter 12: Fertility 101

1   Kirstin MacDougall, Yewoubdar Beyene, and Robert D. Nachtigall, "Age Shock: Misperceptions of the Impact of Age on Fertility Before and After IVF in Women Who Conceived After Age 40," *Human Reproduction* 28, no. 2 (2013): 350–56.

2   Joyce A. Martin et al., "Births: Final Data for 2019," *National Vital Statistics Reports* 70, no. 2 (2021): 1–51.

3   Marinus J. C. Eijkemans et al., "Too Old to Have Children? Lessons from Natural Fertility Populations," *Human Reproduction* 29, no. 6 (2014): 1304–12.

4   J. Habbema et al., "Realizing a Desired Family Size: When Should Couples Start?" *Human Reproduction* 30, no. 9 (2015): 2215–21.

5   Y. Sajjad, "Development of the Genital Ducts and External Genitalia in the Early Human Embryo," *Journal of Obstetrics and Gynaecology Research* 36, no. 5 (2010): 929–37.

6   Danielle Wilson and Bruno Bordoni, "Embryology, Mullerian Ducts (Paramesonephric Ducts)," StatPearls, 2021, statpearls.com /ArticleLibrary/viewarticle/25337.

7   Divya Renu, B. Ganesh Rao, and Namitha K. Ranganath, "Persistent Mullerian Duct Syndrome," *The Indian Journal of Radiology & Imaging* 20, no. 1 (2010): 72.

8   Melanie Blackless et al., "How Sexually Dimorphic Are We? Review and Synthesis," *American Journal of Human Biology* 12, no. 2 (2000): 151–66.

9   M. J. Faddy et al., "Accelerated Disappearance of Ovarian Follicles in Mid-Life: Implications for Forecasting Menopause," *Human Reproduction* 7, no. 10 (1992): 1342–46.

10 Pawel Wilkosz, et. al, "Female Reproductive Decline Is Determined by Remaining Ovarian Reserve and Age," *PLOS One* 9, no. 10 (2014): e108343.

11 Malcolm J. Faddy and Roger G. Gosden, "Physiology: A Mathematical Model of Follicle Dynamics in the Human Ovary," *Human Reproduction* 10, no. 4 (1995): 770–75.

12 Gregory F. Erickson, "Follicle Growth and Development," GLOWM, 2009, glowm.com/section-view/item/288.

13 Misao Fukuda et al., "Right-Sided Ovulation Favours Pregnancy More Than Left-Sided Ovulation," *Human Reproduction* 15, no. 9 (2000): 1921–26.

14 Ana Direito et al., "Relationships Between the Luteinizing Hormone Surge and Other Characteristics of the Menstrual Cycle in Normally Ovulating Women," *Fertility and Sterility* 99, no. 1 (2013): 279–85.

15 Nathan R. Brott and Jacqueline K. Le, "Mittelschmerz," StatPearls, 2021, ncbi.nlm.nih.gov/books/NBK549822/.

16 Shelbie D. Kirkendoll and Dhouha Bacha, "Histology, Corpus Albicans," StatPearls, 2021, statpearls.com/ArticleLibrary/viewarticle/36376.

17 Larry Johnson, Charles S. Petty, and William B. Neaves, "Further Quantification of Human Spermatogenesis: Germ Cell Loss During Postprophase of Meiosis and Its Relationship to Daily Sperm Production," *Biology of Reproduction* 29, no. 1 (1983): 207–15.

18 Adolf-Friedrich Holstein, Wolfgang Schulze, and Michail Davidoff, "Understanding Spermatogenesis Is a Prerequisite for Treatment," *Reproductive Biology and Endocrinology* 1, no. 1 (2003): 1–16.

19 R. P. Amann, "The Cycle of the Seminiferous Epithelium in Humans: A Need to Revisit?" *Journal of Andrology* 29, no. 5 (2008): 469–87.

20 Amann, "Cycle of the Seminiferous Epithelium," 469–87.

21 Lauralee Sherwood, *Human Physiology: From Cells to Systems*, 9th ed. (Pacific Grove, CA: Brooks Cole, 2015).

22 Susan S. Suarez and A. A. Pacey, "Sperm Transport in the Female Reproductive Tract," *Human Reproduction Update* 12, no. 1 (2006): 23–37.

23 Diane S. Settlage, Masanobu Motoshima, and Donald R. Tredway, "Sperm Transport from the External Cervical Os to the Fallopian Tubes in Women: A Time and Quantitation Study," *Fertility and Sterility* 24, no. 9 (1973): 655–61.

24 Molina Puga et al., "Molecular Basis of Human Sperm Capacitation," *Frontiers in Cell and Developmental Biology* 6 (2018): 72.

25   Harvey M. Florman and Rafael A. Fissore, "Fertilization in Mammals," in *Knobil and Neill's Physiology of Reproduction,* vol. 1 (Cambridge, MA: Academic Press, 2015), 149–96.

26   Rebecca Oliver and Hajira Basit, "Embryology, Fertilization," StatPearls, 2021, pubmed.ncbi.nlm.nih.gov/31194343/.

27   Samantha Pfeifer et al., "Optimizing Natural Fertility: A Committee Opinion," *Fertility and Sterility* 107, no. 1 (2017): 52–58.

28   David B. Dunson et al., "Day-Specific Probabilities of Clinical Pregnancy Based on Two Studies with Imperfect Measures of Ovulation," *Human Reproduction* 14, no. 7 (1999): 1835–39.

29   Pfeifer et al., "Optimizing Natural Fertility."

30   Horacio B. Croxatto, "Physiology of Gamete and Embryo Transport Through the Fallopian Tube," *Reproductive Biomedicine Online* 4, no. 2 (2002): 160–69.

31   R. Robin Baker and Mark A. Bellis, "Human Sperm Competition: Ejaculate Manipulation by Females and a Function for the Female Orgasm," *Animal Behaviour* 46, no. 5 (1993): 887–909.

32   Allen J. Wilcox, Donna Day Baird, and Clarice R. Weinberg, "Time of Implantation of the Conceptus and Loss of Pregnancy," *New England Journal of Medicine* 340, no. 23 (1999): 1796–99.

33   David B. Dunson, Donna D. Baird, and Bernardo Colombo, "Increased Infertility with Age in Men and Women," *Obstetrics & Gynecology* 103, no. 1 (2004): 51–56.

34   Kenneth J. Rothman et al., "Volitional Determinants and Age-Related Decline in Fecundability: A General Population Prospective Cohort Study in Denmark," *Fertility and Sterility* 99, no. 7 (2013): 1958–64.

35   Rothman et al., "Volitional Determinants."

Chapter 13: Getting Your Fertility Assessed

1   Korula George and Mohan S. Kamath, "Fertility and Age," *Journal of Human Reproductive Sciences* 3, no. 3 (2010): 121.

2   "Infertility Workup for the Women's Health Specialist," *Obstetrics & Gynecology* 133, no. 6 (2019): e377–84.

3   Aleksandra Kruszyńska and Jadwiga Słowińska-Srzednicka, "Anti-Müllerian Hormone (AMH) as a Good Predictor of Time of Menopause," *Menopause Review* 16, no. 2 (2017): 47.

4   Omar Shebl et al., "Age-Related Distribution of Basal Serum AMH Level in Women of Reproductive Age and a Presumably Healthy Cohort," *Fertility and Sterility* 95, no. 2 (2011): 832–34.

5   Anne Z. Steiner et al., "Association Between Biomarkers of Ovarian Reserve and Infertility among Older Women of Reproductive Age," *JAMA* 318, no. 14 (2017): 1375.

6   M. Y. Thum, E. Kalu, and H. Abdalla, "Elevated Basal FSH and Embryo Quality: Lessons from Extended Culture Embryos," *Journal of Assisted Reproduction and Genetics* 26, no. 6 (2009): 313–18.

7   A. Cobo et al., "Elective and Onco-Fertility Preservation: Factors Related to IVF Outcomes," *Human Reproduction* 33, no. 12 (2018): 2222–31.

8   Peter N. Schlegel et al., "Diagnosis and Treatment of Infertility in Men: AUA/ASRM Guideline Part 1," *The Journal of Urology* 205, no. 1 (2021): 36–43.

9   "Testosterone Use and Male Infertility," ReproductiveFacts.org, 2015, reproductivefacts.org/news-and-publications/patient-fact-sheets-and -booklets/documents/fact-sheets-and-info-booklets/testosterone-use-and -male-infertility/.

10   Jeanne H. O'Brien et al., "Erectile Dysfunction and Andropause Symptoms in Infertile Men," *The Journal of Urology* 174, no. 5 (2005): 1932–34.

11   Trevor G. Cooper et al., "World Health Organization Reference Values for Human Semen Characteristics," *Human Reproduction Update* 16, no. 3 (2010): 231–45.

12   L. Farrell, L. Brennan, and M. Lanham, "Knowledge, Attitudes, and Perceptions of Infertility: A National Survey," *Fertility and Sterility* 110, no. 4 (2018): e6.

13   Alexandra Farrow et al., "Prolonged Use of Oral Contraception Before a Planned Pregnancy Is Associated with a Decreased Risk of Delayed Conception," *Human Reproduction* 17, no. 10 (2002): 2754–61; Hani K. Atrash and Carol J. Rowland Hogue, "The Effect of Pregnancy Termination on Future Reproduction," *Baillière's Clinical Obstetrics and Gynaecology* 4, no. 2 (1990): 391–405; Andrea Sansone et al., "Smoke, Alcohol and Drug Addiction and Male Fertility," *Reproductive Biology and Endocrinology* 16, no. 1 (2018): 1–11.

14   Anjani Chandra, Casey E. Copen, and Elizabeth H. Stephen, *Infertility and Impaired Fecundity in the United States, 1982–2010: Data from the National Survey of Family Growth*, National Health Statistics Reports no. 67 (Hyattsville, MD: National Center for Health Statistics, 2013).

15   Ashok Agarwal et al., "A Unique View on Male Infertility Around the Globe," *Reproductive Biology and Endocrinology* 13, no. 1 (2015): 1–9.

16   Alison Taylor, "ABC of Subfertility: Extent of the Problem," *BMJ* 327, no. 7412 (2003): 434.

17   José Bellver et al., "Blastocyst Formation Is Similar in Obese and Normal Weight Women: A Morphokinetic Study," *Human Reproduction* 36, no. 12 (2021): 3062–73.

18   Alaina Jose-Miller et al., "Infertility," *American Family Physician* 75, no. 6 (2007): 849–56.

19   Marcello Cocuzza, Conrado Alvarenga, and Rodrigo Pagani, "The Epidemiology and Etiology of Azoospermia," *Clinics* 68 (2013): 15–26.

20   Practice Committee of the American Society for Reproductive Medicine, "Report on Varicocele and Infertility: A Committee Opinion," *Fertility and Sterility* 102, no. 6 (2014): 1556–60.

21   "Pregnancy Problems? Boost the Chance of Having a Baby," NIH News in Health, July 2015, newsinhealth.nih.gov/2015/07/pregnancy -problems.

22   Katrin van der Ven et al., "Cystic Fibrosis Mutation Screening in Healthy Men with Reduced Sperm Quality," *Human Reproduction* 11, no. 3 (1996): 513–17.

23 Darius A. Paduch et al., "New Concepts in Klinefelter Syndrome," *Current Opinion in Urology* 18, no. 6 (2008): 621–27.

24 Eric Chung and Gerald B. Brock, "Cryptorchidism and Its Impact on Male Fertility: A State of Art Review of Current Literature," *Canadian Urological Association Journal* 5, no. 3 (2011): 210.

25 "Quick Facts about Infertility," ReproductiveFacts.org, American Society for Reproductive Medicine, 2017, reproductivefacts.org/faqs/quick-facts-about-infertility/.

26 Helena Teede et al., "Polycystic Ovary Syndrome: Perceptions and Attitudes of Women and Primary Health Care Physicians on Features of PCOS and Renaming the Syndrome," *The Journal of Clinical Endocrinology & Metabolism* 99, no. 1 (2014): E107–11.

27 Helena J. Teede et al., "Assessment and Management of Polycystic Ovary Syndrome: Summary of an Evidence-Based Guideline," *The Medical Journal of Australia* 195, no. 6 (2011): S65.

28 Roshan Nikbakht et al., "Evaluation of Oocyte Quality in Polycystic Ovary Syndrome Patients Undergoing ART Cycles," *Fertility Research and Practice* 7, no. 1 (2021): 1–6.

29 Practice Committee of the American Society for Reproductive Medicine, "Endometriosis and Infertility: A Committee Opinion," *Fertility and Sterility* 98, no. 3 (2012): 591–98.

30 Cordula Schippert et al., "Reproductive Capacity and Recurrence of Disease After Surgery for Moderate and Severe Endometriosis: A Retrospective Single Center Analysis," *BMC Women's Health* 20, no. 1 (2020): 1–11.

31 Fatemeh Mostaejeran, Zeinab Hamoush, and Safoura Rouholamin, "Evaluation of Antimullerian Hormone Levels Before and After Laparoscopic Management of Endometriosis," *Advanced Biomedical Research* 4 (2015).

32 "Fibroids and Fertility," ReproductiveFacts.org, American Society for Reproductive Medicine, 2015, reproductivefacts.org/news-and-publications/patient-fact-sheets-and-booklets/documents/fact-sheets-and-info-booklets/fibroids-and-fertility/.

33   R. Abir et al., "Turner's Syndrome and Fertility: Current Status and Possible Putative Prospects," *Human Reproduction Update* 7, no. 6 (2001): 603–10.

Chapter 14: Fertility Preservation

1   A. Cobo et al., "Elective and Onco-Fertility Preservation: Factors Related to IVF Outcomes," *Human Reproduction* 33, no. 12 (2018): 2222–31.

2   Anne Z. Steiner and Anne Marie Z. Jukic, "Impact of Female Age and Nulligravidity on Fecundity in an Older Reproductive Age Cohort," *Fertility and Sterility* 105, no. 6 (2016): 1584–88.

3   Zeynep Gurtin, "More and More Women Are Freezing Their Eggs—but Only 21% of Those Who Use Them Have Become Mothers," The Conversation, 2019, theconversation.com/more-and-more-women-are -freezing-their-eggs-but-only-21-of-those-who-use-them-have-become -mothers-117028.

4   Brie Alport et al., "Does the Ovarian Stimulation Phase Length Predict In Vitro Fertilization Outcomes?" *International Journal of Fertility & Sterility* 5, no. 3 (2011): 134.

5   "Ovarian Hyperstimulation Syndrome (OHSS)," ReproductiveFacts.org, American Society for Reproductive Medicine, 2014, reproductivefacts .org/news-and-publications/patient-fact-sheets-and-booklets/documents /fact-sheets-and-info-booklets/ovarian-hyperstimulation-syndrome-ohss/; Klaus Fiedler and Diego Ezcurra, "Predicting and Preventing Ovarian Hyperstimulation Syndrome (OHSS): The Need for Individualized Not Standardized Treatment," *Reproductive Biology and Endocrinology* 10, no. 1 (2012): 1–10.

6   Ali Abbara et al., "Follicle Size on Day of Trigger Most Likely to Yield a Mature Oocyte," *Frontiers in Endocrinology* 9 (2018): 193.

7   Mitchell P. Rosen et al., "A Quantitative Assessment of Follicle Size on Oocyte Developmental Competence," *Fertility and Sterility* 90, no. 3 (2008): 684–90.

8   Suneeta Mittal et al., "Serum Estradiol as a Predictor of Success of In Vitro Fertilization," *The Journal of Obstetrics and Gynecology of India* 64, no. 2 (2014): 124–29.

9   S. Ouhilal, H. Lachgar, and N. Mahutte, "What Is the Optimal Number of Eggs at Oocyte Retrieval?" *Fertility and Sterility* 100, no. 3 (2013): S262.

10   Sesh Kamal Sunkara et al., "Association Between the Number of Eggs and Live Birth in IVF Treatment: An Analysis of 400 135 Treatment Cycles," *Human Reproduction* 26, no. 7 (2011): 1768–74.

11   Ana Cobo et al., "Six Years' Experience in Ovum Donation Using Vitrified Oocytes: Report of Cumulative Outcomes, Impact of Storage Time, and Development of a Predictive Model for Oocyte Survival Rate," *Fertility and Sterility* 104, no. 6 (2015): 1426–34.

12   Lisa Campo-Engelstein, "For the Sake of Consistency and Fairness: Why Insurance Companies Should Cover Fertility Preservation Treatment for Iatrogenic Infertility," *Oncofertility* (2010): 381–88.

13   "IVF Refund and Package Programs," FertilityIQ, fertilityiq.com/topics/cost/ivf-refund-and-package-programs.

14   "Medicare Prescription Drug, Improvement, and Modernization Act of 2003," 108th Congress Public Law 173, Congress.gov, 2003, congress.gov/bill/108th-congress/house-bill/1.

15   S. Silber et al., "Use of a Novel Minimal Stimulation In Vitro Fertilization ('Mini-IVF') Protocol for Low Ovarian Reserve and for Older Women," *Fertility and Sterility* 100, no. 3 (2013): S18.

16   Yash S. Khandwala et al., "Association of Paternal Age with Perinatal Outcomes Between 2007 and 2016 in the United States: Population Based Cohort Study," *BMJ* 363 (2018).

17   Peter N. Schlegel et al., "Diagnosis and Treatment of Infertility in Men: AUA/ASRM Guideline Part 1," *The Journal of Urology* 205, no. 1 (2021): 36–43.

18   Paul De Sutter, "Gender Reassignment and Assisted Reproduction: Present and Future Reproductive Options for Transsexual People," *Human Reproduction* 16, no. 4 (2001): 612–14.

19   P. De Sutter et al., "The Desire to Have Children and the Preservation of Fertility in Transsexual Women: A Survey," *International Journal of Transgenderism* 6, no. 3 (2002); Katrien Wierckx et al., "Reproductive Wish in Transsexual Men," *Human Reproduction* 27, no. 2 (2012): 483–87.

20   Diane Chen et al., "Fertility Preservation for Transgender Adolescents," *Journal of Adolescent Health* 61, no. 1 (2017): 120–23.

21   Leena Nahata et al., "Low Fertility Preservation Utilization among Transgender Youth," *Journal of Adolescent Health* 61, no. 1 (2017): 40–44.

22   I. Yaish et al., "Functional Ovarian Reserve in Transgender Men Receiving Testosterone Therapy: Evidence for Preserved Anti-Müllerian Hormone and Antral Follicle Count Under Prolonged Treatment," *Human Reproduction* 36, no. 10 (2021): 2753–60.

23   Iris G. Insogna, Elizabeth Ginsburg, and Serene Srouji, "Fertility Preservation for Adolescent Transgender Male Patients: A Case Series," *Journal of Adolescent Health* 66, no. 6 (2020): 750–53.

24   Emily P. Barnard et al., "Fertility Preservation Outcomes in Adolescent and Young Adult Feminizing Transgender Patients," *Pediatrics* 144, no. 3 (2019).

25   American College of Obstetricians and Gynecologists, "Health Care for Transgender and Gender Diverse Individuals: ACOG Committee Opinion, Number 823," *Obstetrics & Gynecology* 137 (2021): e75.

Chapter 15: Fertility Treatments

1   "FAQs about Infertility," ReproductiveFacts.org, American Society for Reproductive Medicine, 2017, reproductivefacts.org/faqs/frequently -asked-questions-about-infertility/.

2   Richard S. Legro et al., "Letrozole Versus Clomiphene for Infertility in the Polycystic Ovary Syndrome," *New England Journal of Medicine* 371 (2014): 119–29.

3   "IUI Success Rates," CNY Fertility, September 15, 2021, cnyfertility.com /iui-success-rates/.

4   I. Ferrara, R. Balet, and J. G. Grudzinskas, "Intrauterine Donor Insemination in Single Women and Lesbian Couples: A Comparative Study of Pregnancy Rates," *Human Reproduction* 15, no. 3 (2000): 621–25.

5   "IUI Success Rates."

6   "IUI or 'Artificial Insemination,'" FertilityIQ, fertilityiq.com/iui-or-artificial -insemination.

7 Ethics Committee of the American Society for Reproductive Medicine, "Oocyte or Embryo Donation to Women of Advanced Age: A Committee Opinion," *Fertility and Sterility* 100, no. 2 (2013): 337–40.

8 Maryam Eftekhar et al., "Comparison of Conventional IVF Versus ICSI in Non-Male Factor, Normoresponder Patients," *Iranian Journal of Reproductive Medicine* 10, no. 2 (2012): 131.

9 "State Laws Related to Insurance Coverage for Infertility Treatment," National Conference of State Legislatures, 2014, ncsl.org/research/health /insurance-coverage-for-infertility-laws.aspx; "What Does ICSI Cost?" FertilityIQ, fertilityiq.com/topics/icsi/what-does-icsi-cost.

10 Aaron M. Bernie, Ranjith Ramasamy, and Peter N. Schlegel, "Predictive Factors of Successful Microdissection Testicular Sperm Extraction," *Basic and Clinical Andrology* 23, no. 1 (2013): 1–7.

11 Jinliang Zhu et al., "Does IVF Cleavage Stage Embryo Quality Affect Pregnancy Complications and Neonatal Outcomes in Singleton Gestations After Double Embryo Transfers?" *Journal of Assisted Reproduction and Genetics* 31, no. 12 (2014): 1635–41.

12 Centers for Disease Control and Prevention, American Society for Reproductive Medicine, Society for Assisted Reproductive Technology, *2016 Assisted Reproductive Technology National Summary Report* (Atlanta, GA: U.S. Department of Health and Human Services, 2018).

13 Céline Bouillon et al., "Obstetric and Perinatal Outcomes of Singletons After Single Blastocyst Transfer: Is There Any Difference According to Blastocyst Morphology?" *Reproductive Biomedicine Online* 35, no. 2 (2017): 197–207.

14 Centers for Disease Control and Prevention, *2016 Assisted Reproductive Technology Report*.

15 Centers for Disease Control and Prevention, American Society for Reproductive Medicine, Society for Assisted Reproductive Technology, *2010 Assisted Reproductive Technology: Fertility Clinic Success Rates Report* (Atlanta, GA: U.S. Department of Health and Human Services, 2012).

16 "Growing Embryos to Cleavage or Blastocyst Stage," FertilityIQ, fertilityiq .com/ivf-in-vitro-fertilization/cleavage-vs-blastocyst-embryos-day3-day5.

17   Manuel Viotti et al., "Using Outcome Data from One Thousand Mosaic Embryo Transfers to Formulate an Embryo Ranking System for Clinical Use," *Fertility and Sterility* 115, no. 5 (2021): 1212–24.

18   "Women with Three Normal Embryos Have 95 Percent Chance of Pregnancy, RMA Research Shows," RMA Network, 2021, rmanetwork .com/blog/women-with-three-normal-embryos-have-95-chance-of -pregnancy-rma-research-shows/.

19   Junhao Yan et al., "Live Birth with or Without Preimplantation Genetic Testing for Aneuploidy," *New England Journal of Medicine* 385, no. 22 (2021): 2047–58; Santiago Munné et al., "Preimplantation Genetic Testing for Aneuploidy Versus Morphology as Selection Criteria for Single Frozen-Thawed Embryo Transfer in Good-Prognosis Patients: A Multicenter Randomized Clinical Trial," *Fertility and Sterility* 112, no. 6 (2019): 1071–79.

20   V. A. Flores, D. A. Kelk, and P. H. Kodaman, "Trilaminar Endometrial Pattern Correlates with Higher Clinical Pregnancy Rates in Frozen Embryo Transfer Cycles," *Fertility and Sterility* 108, no. 3 (2017): e358; Jason D. Kofinas et al., "Serum Progesterone Levels Greater Than 20 ng/ dL on Day of Embryo Transfer Are Associated with Lower Live Birth and Higher Pregnancy Loss Rates," *Journal of Assisted Reproduction and Genetics* 32, no. 9 (2015): 1395–99.

21   S. Mackens et al., "To Trigger or Not to Trigger Ovulation in a Natural Cycle for Frozen Embryo Transfer: A Randomized Controlled Trial," *Human Reproduction* 35, no. 5 (2020): 1073–81.

22   *Freezing Embryos*, Fertility Associates, fertilityassociates.co.nz/media/1075 /fertility-facts-freezing-embryos.pdf.

23   Centers for Disease Control and Prevention, *2016 Assisted Reproductive Technology Report*.

24   American Society for Reproductive Medicine, "Progesterone Supplementation During In Vitro Fertilization (IVF) Cycles," ReproductiveFacts.org, reproductivefacts.org/news-and-publications /patient-fact-sheets-and-booklets/documents/fact-sheets-and-info -booklets/progesterone-supplementation-during-in-vitro-fertilization

-ivf-cycles/; Arri Coomarasamy et al., "Micronized Vaginal Progesterone to Prevent Miscarriage: A Critical Evaluation of Randomized Evidence," *American Journal of Obstetrics and Gynecology* 223, no. 2 (2020): 167–76.

25 N. King et al., "Serum hCG Values Are as Predictive of Live Birth After Single Embryo Transfer as Early Pregnancy Ultrasound," *Fertility and Sterility* 108, no. 3 (2017): e345–46.

Chapter 16: Managing the Grief of Infertility

1 Carla Dugas and Valori H. Slane, "Miscarriage," StatPearls, 2021, ncbi.nlm.nih.gov/books/NBK532992/.

2 Practice Committee of the American Society for Reproductive Medicine, "Evaluation and Treatment of Recurrent Pregnancy Loss: A Committee Opinion," *Fertility and Sterility* 98, no. 5 (2012): 1103–11.

3 Lesley Regan, Peter R. Braude, and Paula L. Trembath, "Influence of Past Reproductive Performance on Risk of Spontaneous Abortion," *BMJ* 299, no. 6698 (1989): 541–45.

4 Tristan D. McBain and Patricia Reeves, "Women's Experience of Infertility and Disenfranchised Grief," *The Family Journal* 27, no. 2 (2019): 156–66.

5 Marni Rosner, "Recovery from Traumatic Loss: A Study of Women Living Without Children After Infertility" (DSW diss., University of Pennsylvania, 2012), 20, repository.upenn.edu/edissertations_sp2/20/.

6 Allyson Bradow, "Primary and Secondary Infertility and Post Traumatic Stress Disorder: Experiential Differences Between Type of Infertility and Symptom Characteristics" (PsyD diss., Spalding University, 2012).

7 "The Psychological Impact of Infertility and Its Treatment: Medical Interventions May Exacerbate Anxiety, Depression, and Stress," *Harvard Mental Health Letter* 25, no. 11 (2009): 1–3.

8 Marilyn S. Paul et al., "Posttraumatic Growth and Social Support in Individuals with Infertility," *Human Reproduction* 25, no. 1 (2010): 133–41; Yongju Yu et al., "Resilience and Social Support Promote Posttraumatic Growth of Women with Infertility: The Mediating Role of Positive Coping," *Psychiatry Research* 215, no. 2 (2014): 401–05.

9   Alice D. Domar et al., "Impact of Group Psychological Interventions on Pregnancy Rates in Infertile Women," *Fertility and Sterility* 73, no. 4 (2000): 805–11.

10   Hélène Gaitzsch et al., "The Effect of Mind-Body Interventions on Psychological and Pregnancy Outcomes in Infertile Women: A Systematic Review," *Archives of Women's Mental Health* (2020): 1–13.

11   "The Psychological Impact of Infertility," 1–3.

12   Jane R. W. Fisher and Karin Hammarberg, "Psychological and Social Aspects of Infertility in Men: An Overview of the Evidence and Implications for Psychologically Informed Clinical Care and Future Research," *Asian Journal of Andrology* 14, no. 1 (2012): 121.

13   Staci Jill Rosenthal, "Birthing into Death: Stories of Jewish Pregnancy from the Holocaust" (PhD diss., Boston University, 2016), proquest.com /openview/40fe487e590961757c82a2d483e02cfc/1?pq-origsite=gscholar &cbl=18750.

Chapter 17: Alternative Paths to Parenthood

1   Abbie E. Goldberg, Jordan B. Downing, and Hannah B. Richardson, "The Transition from Infertility to Adoption: Perceptions of Lesbian and Heterosexual Couples," *Journal of Social and Personal Relationships* 26, no. 6–7 (2009): 938–63.

2   Carlos Figueroa, "Fulton v. City of Philadelphia: The Third Circuit's Bittersweet Advancement of LGBTQ+ Rights," *Tulane Journal of Law & Sexuality* 29 (2020): 51.

3   Kei Nomaguchi and Melissa A. Milkie, "Parenthood and Well-Being: A Decade in Review," *Journal of Marriage and Family* 82, no. 1 (2020): 198–223.

4   Ranae J. Evenson and Robin W. Simon, "Clarifying the Relationship Between Parenthood and Depression," *Journal of Health and Social Behavior* 46, no. 4 (2005): 341–58.

5   Nomaguchi and Milkie, "Parenthood and Well-Being," 198–223.

Chapter 18: Using an Egg, Sperm, or Embryo Donor

1   Samantha Fields, "The Cost of Building a Family Using Donor Sperm," Marketplace, 2019, marketplace.org/2019/10/24/the-cost-of-building-a -family-using-donor-sperm/.

2   "Donor Eggs," American Pregnancy Association, 2017, americanpregnancy .org/getting-pregnant/donor-eggs/.

3   Willem Ombelet and Johan Van Robays, "Artificial Insemination History: Hurdles and Milestones," *Facts, Views & Vision in ObGyn* 7, no. 2 (2015): 137.

4   Ombelet and Van Robays, "Artificial Insemination History," 137.

5   Peter Lutjen et al., "The Establishment and Maintenance of Pregnancy Using In Vitro Fertilization and Embryo Donation in a Patient with Primary Ovarian Failure," *Nature* 307, no. 5947 (1984): 174–75.

6   Mark V. Sauer, "Revisiting the Early Days of Oocyte and Embryo Donation: Relevance to Contemporary Clinical Practice," *Fertility and Sterility* 110, no. 6 (2018): 981–87.

7   Maria Bustillo et al., "Delivery of a Healthy Infant Following Nonsurgical Ovum Transfer," *JAMA* 251, no. 7 (1984): 889–89.

8   Centers for Disease Control and Prevention, *2018 Assisted Reproductive Technology: National Summary Report* (Atlanta, GA: U.S. Department of Health and Human Services, 2020).

9   "Meet the First Snowflake Baby," Embryo Adoption Awareness Center, 2015, embryoadoption.org/2015/12/meet-the-first-snowflake-baby/.

10 Centers for Disease Control and Prevention, *2018 Assisted Reproductive Technology Report*.

11 H. N. Sallam and N. H. Sallam, "Religious Aspects of Assisted Reproduction," *Facts, Views & Vision in ObGyn* 8, no. 1 (2016): 33.

12 Ombelet and Van Robays, "Artificial Insemination History," 137.

13 J. Brotherton, "Artificial Insemination with Fresh Donor Semen," *Archives of Andrology* 25, no. 2 (1990): 178.

14 Audrey Koh, Gabriël van Beusekom, Nanette K. Gartrell, and Henny Bos, "Adult Offspring of Lesbian Parents: How Do They Relate to Their Sperm Donors?," *Fertility and Sterility* 114, no. 4 (2020): 879–887.

Chapter 19: Adoption and Foster Care

1 Ellen Herman, "The Adoption History Project," University of Oregon, 2012, pages.uoregon.edu/adoption/about.html.

2 Amanda L. Baden et al., "Delaying Adoption Disclosure: A Survey of Late Discovery Adoptees," *Journal of Family Issues* 40, no. 9 (2019): 1154–80.

3 Tik Root, "The Baby Brokers: Inside America's Murky Private-Adoption Industry," *Time*, 2021, time.com/6051811/private-adoption-america/.

4 Gretchen Sisson, "'Choosing Life': Birth Mothers on Abortion and Reproductive Choice," *Women's Health Issues* 25, no. 4 (2015): 349–54.

5 Children's Bureau, "Trends in Foster Care & Adoption: FY 2011–2020," Administration for Children & Families, U.S. Department of Health & Human Services, 2021, acf.hhs.gov/cb/report/trends-foster-care -adoption.

6 Child Welfare Information Gateway, "Planning for Adoption: Knowing the Costs and Resources," Administration for Children & Families, U.S. Department of Health & Human Services, 2016, childwelfare.gov/pubs /s-cost/.

7 Child Welfare Information Gateway, "Exploring the Pathways to Adoption," Administration for Children & Families, U.S. Department of Health & Human Services, 2021, childwelfare.gov/pubs/f-adoptoption/.

8 Matthew Desmond, *Evicted: Poverty and Profit in the American City* (New York: Crown Publishers, 2016).

9 Child Welfare Information Gateway, "Exploring the Pathways to Adoption."

Chapter 20: Surrogacy

1 Bonnie Johnson, "And Baby Make Four: For the First Time a Surrogate Bears a Child Genetically Not Her Own," *People*, May 4, 1987.

2 "Noel Keane, Father of Surrogate Parenting, Dead at 58," Associated Press, January 27, 1997, apnews.com/article /f0661ef8bad583affab55d130af6fa95.

3 Eric A. Gordon, "The Aftermath of Johnson v. Calvert: Surrogacy Law Reflects a More Liberal View of Reproductive Technology," *St. Thomas Law Review* 6 (1993): 191.

4 Maria Cramer, "Couple Forced to Adopt Their Own Children After a Surrogate Pregnancy," *New York Times*, January 31, 2021, nytimes.com /2021/01/31/us/michigan-surrogacy-law.html.

5 Susannah Snider, "The Cost of Using a Surrogate—And How to Pay for It," *U.S. News & World Report*, November 24, 2020, money.usnews.com /money/personal-finance/family-finance/articles/how-much-surrogacy -costs-and-how-to-pay-for-it.

Chapter 21: Saying No to Parenthood

1 Carolyn Morell, "Saying No: Women's Experiences with Reproductive Refusal," *Feminism & Psychology* 10, no. 3 (2000): 313–22.

2 Amy Blackstone and Mahala Dyer Stewart, "'There's More Thinking to Decide': How the Childfree Decide Not to Parent," *The Family Journal* 24, no. 3 (2016): 296–303.

3 Robin A. Hadley, "Ageing Without Children, Gender and Social Justice," in *Ageing, Diversity and Equality: Social Justice Perspectives*, ed. Sue Westwood (Abingdon: Routledge, 2018), 66–81; Marco Albertini and Martin Kohli, "Childlessness and Intergenerational Transfers in Later Life," in *Childlessness in Europe: Contexts, Causes, and Consequences*, eds. Michaela Kreyenfeld and Dirk Konietzka (New York: Springer Cham, 2017), 351–68.

4 Amy Blackstone and Mahala Dyer Stewart, "Choosing to Be Childfree: Research on the Decision Not to Parent," *Sociology Compass* 6, no. 9 (2012): 718–27.

5 Rebecca Harrington, "Childfree by Choice," *Studies in Gender and Sexuality* 20, no. 1 (2019): 29.

Chapter 22: Living a Childfree Life

1 Marcia Drut-Davis, *Confessions of a Childfree Woman: A Life Spent Swimming Against the Mainstream* (self-pub., 2013).

2   Katherine M. Franke, "Theorizing Yes: An Essay on Feminism, Law, and Desire," *Columbia Law Review* 101 (2001): 181.

3   Joyce C. Abma and Gladys M. Martinez, "Childlessness among Older Women in the United States: Trends and Profiles," *Journal of Marriage and Family* 68, no. 4 (2006): 1045–56.

4   Robin A. Hadley, "Ageing Without Children, Gender and Social Justice," in *Ageing, Diversity and Equality: Social Justice Perspectives*, ed. Sue Westwood (Abingdon: Routledge, 2018), 66–81.

5   Julia Moore, "Performative and Subversive Negotiations of Face in Parent-Child Communication about Childbearing Choice Across Generations," *Journal of Family Communication* 18, no. 2 (2018): 124–37; Debra Umberson, Tetyana Pudrovska, and Corinne Reczek, "Parenthood, Childlessness, and Well-Being: A Life Course Perspective," *Journal of Marriage and Family* 72, no. 3 (2010): 612–29.

6   Robert D. Plotnick, "Childlessness and the Economic Well-Being of Older Americans," *Journals of Gerontology Series B: Psychological Sciences and Social Sciences* 64, no. 6 (2009): 767–76.

7   Zhenmei Zhang and Mark D. Hayward, "Childlessness and the Psychological Well-Being of Older Persons," *The Journals of Gerontology Series B: Psychological Sciences and Social Sciences* 56, no. 5 (2001): S311–20.

8   Umberson et al., "Parenthood, Childlessness, and Well-Being," 612–29.

9   Ruth E. S. Allen and Janine L. Wiles, "How Older People Position Their Late-Life Childlessness: A Qualitative Study," *Journal of Marriage and Family* 75, no. 1 (2013): 206–20.

10   Emily Koert and Judith C. Daniluk, "When Time Runs Out: Reconciling Permanent Childlessness After Delayed Childbearing," *Journal of Reproductive and Infant Psychology* 35, no. 4 (2017): 342–52.

11   Jo Jones, William D. Mosher, and Kimberly Daniels, "Current Contraceptive Use in the United States, 2006–2010, and Change in Patterns of Use Since 1995," *National Health Statistic Reports* 60 (2012): 1–25.

12   American College of Obstetricians and Gynecologists, "ACOG Practice Bulletin No. 208: Benefits and Risks of Sterilization," *Obstetrics and Gynecology* 133, no. 3 (2019): e194–e207.

13　Sharon Sung and Aaron Abramovitz, "Tubal Ligation," StatPearls, 2021, ncbi.nlm.nih.gov/books/NBK549873/.

14　Gavin Stormont and Christopher M. Deibert, "Vasectomy," StatPearls, 2021, ncbi.nlm.nih.gov/books/NBK549904/.

15　Markus J. Steiner et al., "Communicating Contraceptive Effectiveness: A Randomized Controlled Trial to Inform a World Health Organization Family Planning Handbook," *American Journal of Obstetrics and Gynecology* 195, no. 1 (2006): 85–91.

Conclusion

1　Nicoletta Balbo and Nicola Barban, "Does Fertility Behavior Spread among Friends?" *American Sociological Review* 79, no. 3 (2014): 412–31.

2　Torkild Hovde Lyngstad and Alexia Prskawetz, "Do Siblings' Fertility Decisions Influence Each Other?" *Demography* 47, no. 4 (2010): 923–34.

3　Sebastian Pink, Thomas Leopold, and Henriette Engelhardt, "Fertility and Social Interaction at the Workplace: Does Childbearing Spread among Colleagues?" *Advances in Life Course Research* 21 (2014): 113–22.

4　Angus Deaton and Arthur A. Stone, "Evaluative and Hedonic Wellbeing among Those With and Without Children at Home," *Proceedings of the National Academy of Sciences* 111, no. 4 (2014): 1328–33.

5　Dorthe Berntsen, David C. Rubin, and Ilene C. Siegler, "Two Versions of Life: Emotionally Negative and Positive Life Events Have Different Roles in the Organization of Life Story and Identity," *Emotion* 11, no. 5 (2011): 1190–1201; Gladys M. Martinez et al., "Fertility, Contraception, and Fatherhood: Data on Men and Women from Cycle 6 (2002) of the 2002 National Survey of Family Growth," *Vital Health Statistics* 23, no. 26 (2006): 1–142.

6　Thomas Hansen, "Parenthood and Happiness: A Review of Folk Theories Versus Empirical Evidence," *Social Indicators Research* 108, no. 1 (2012): 29–64; Matthias Pollmann-Schult, "Parenthood and Life Satisfaction: Why Don't Children Make People Happy?" *Journal of Marriage and Family* 76, no. 2 (2014): 319–36.

7   Kei Nomaguchi and Melissa A. Milkie, "Parenthood and Well-Being: A Decade in Review," *Journal of Marriage and Family* 82, no. 1 (2020): 198–223.

8   Rachel Margolis and Mikko Myrskylä, "Parental Well-Being Surrounding First Birth as a Determinant of Further Parity Progression," *Demography* 52, no. 4 (2015): 1147–66.

9   Kei M. Nomaguchi and Susan L. Brown, "Parental Strains and Rewards among Mothers: The Role of Education," *Journal of Marriage and Family* 73, no. 3 (2011): 621–36.

10 Megan L. Kavanaugh et al., "Parents' Experience of Unintended Childbearing: A Qualitative Study of Factors That Mitigate or Exacerbate Effects," *Social Science & Medicine* 174 (2017): 133–41; Jessica Houston Su, "Pregnancy Intentions and Parents' Psychological Well-Being," *Journal of Marriage and Family* 74, no. 5 (2012): 1182–96.

11 Mikko Myrskylä and Rachel Margolis, "Happiness: Before and After the Kids," *Demography* 51, no. 5 (2014): 1843–66.

12 Eyal Abraham et al., "Father's Brain Is Sensitive to Childcare Experiences," *Proceedings of the National Academy of Sciences* 111, no. 27 (2014): 9792–97.

13 Frank Newport and Joy Wilke, "Desire for Children Still Norm in U.S.," Gallup News, 2013, news.gallup.com/poll/164618/desire-children-norm .aspx.

14 Julia Moore and Jenna S. Abetz, "What Do Parents Regret about Having Children? Communicating Regrets Online," *Journal of Family Issues* 40, no. 3 (2019): 390–412.

INDEX

ABOUT THE AUTHOR

JORDAN DAVIDSON is an award-winning health journalist and the editorial director of Health. Her work has appeared in *Parents*, BuzzFeed, CBS Interactive, *Men's Health*, *Teen Vogue*, Everyday Health, Verywell Family, Scary Mommy, Upworthy, *Prevention*, *Bitch*, Bustle, and Rewire News. Her advocacy in the reproductive space has appeared on *NBC Nightly News with Lester Holt* and in the documentary *Below the Belt*. While writing this book, she also worked as part of the Citizen Endo research team at Columbia University Irving Medical Center on reproductive health-related projects. She lives just outside of New York City with her partner and their two cats.

ABOUT SOUNDS TRUE

SOUNDS TRUE is a multimedia publisher whose mission is to inspire and support personal transformation and spiritual awakening. Founded in 1985 and located in Boulder, Colorado, we work with many of the leading spiritual teachers, thinkers, healers, and visionary artists of our time. We strive with every title to preserve the essential "living wisdom" of the author or artist. It is our goal to create products that not only provide information to a reader or listener but also embody the quality of a wisdom transmission.

For those seeking genuine transformation, Sounds True is your trusted partner. At SoundsTrue.com you will find a wealth of free resources to support your journey, including exclusive weekly audio interviews, free downloads, interactive learning tools, and other special savings on all our titles.

To learn more, please visit SoundsTrue.com/freegifts or call us toll-free at 800.333.9185.

sounds true
WAKING UP THE WORLD